The Mummy on Screen

The Mummy on Screen

Orientalism and Monstrosity in Horror Cinema

Basil Glynn

BLOOMSBURY ACADEMIC
LONDON • NEW YORK • OXFORD • NEW DELHI • SYDNEY

BLOOMSBURY ACADEMIC
Bloomsbury Publishing Plc
50 Bedford Square, London, WC1B 3DP, UK
1385 Broadway, New York, NY 10018, USA
29 Earlsfort Terrace, Dublin 2, Ireland

BLOOMSBURY, BLOOMSBURY ACADEMIC and the Diana logo are trademarks
of Bloomsbury Publishing Plc

First published in Great Britain 2020
This paperback edition published in 2021

Copyright © Basil Glynn, 2020

Basil Glynn has asserted his right under the Copyright, Designs and Patents Act, 1988,
to be identified as Author of this work.

For legal purposes the Acknowledgements on p. xi constitute an extension
of this copyright page.

Cover design by Charlotte Daniels
Cover image: Boris Karloff as The Mummy (1932) (© Courtesy of Everett Collection /
Mary Evans Picture Library)

All rights reserved. No part of this publication may be reproduced or transmitted
in any form or by any means, electronic or mechanical, including photocopying,
recording, or any information storage or retrieval system, without prior permission
in writing from the publishers.

Bloomsbury Publishing Plc does not have any control over, or responsibility for, any
third-party websites referred to or in this book. All internet addresses given in this book were
correct at the time of going to press. The author and publisher regret any inconvenience
caused if addresses have changed or sites have ceased to exist, but can accept no
responsibility for any such changes.

A catalogue record for this book is available from the British Library.

A catalog record for this book is available from the Library of Congress.

ISBN: HB: 978-1-7883-1408-4
PB: 978-1-3501-9483-0
ePDF: 978-1-3501-2937-5
eBook: 978-1-3501-2938-2

Series: International Library of the Moving Image

Typeset by Deanta Global Publishing Services, Chennai, India

To find out more about our authors and books visit www.bloomsbury.com
and sign up for our newsletters

For Vincent, Kathleen and Vincent

Contents

List of figures ix
Acknowledgements xi
Author's notes xii

Introduction: Death is only the beginning – Unravelling the Mummy on Screen 1

Part 1 The Mummy in the West and in Western cinema 23

1 The creature's features: Moulding the Mummy and the Mummy movie 25
   The Oriental Mummy as Western projection 25
   The Mummy genre: *Inter*est and *Disinter*est 28

2 The Mutating Mummy: From ancient artefact to modern attraction 32
   Mummy medicine: An Egyptian prescription 34
   The Mummy as memento: A collectable corpse 34
   The Mummy as public attraction: Exhumed, examined and exhibited 36

Part 2 The Mummy in literature, on stage and on the silent screen 39

3 On the page and stage: The Mummy movie's literary and theatrical influences 41
   The Mummy's tome: A body of literature 41
   The rediscovery of ancient Egypt: A pharaoh to remember 42
   The Mummy's literary life: Electrifying tales! 43
   Romance and the Mummy: Amorous archaeologists and comely corpses 46
   Literature's monstrous Mummies: Dread, despair and Doyle 47
   The empire strikes back: Stoker's *Au Revoir* to the voyeur archaeologist 50
   Playing dead: The Mummy in the theatre 52

4 Preserved on film: The silent Mummy of early cinema 60
   Egypt and the cinema: Monoliths, mesmerism and Mummies 61
   The 'Mummy Complex' and the preservative nature of film 63

The first on-screen Mummies: Short-lived moments of horror in the trick film	63
Winding people up: Pretend Mummies and Mummy mix-ups in silent comedies	64
Mummy dearest: The Mummy as romantic character	69
Tomb raiders: Egypt and early horror	78
Teutonic terrors: The first Mummy horror movies	80
Grave danger: Tutmania, the curse and the death of the silent Mummy	84

Part 3 Universal studios and the Mummy of the 1930s and 1940s 95

5 *The Mummy* (1932): Overcoming the silent treatment 97

The Mummy: Art horror or production line horror?	99
The delicate horror of *The Mummy*: A shudder not a shriek!	102
A dichotomized damsel: A 1920s/1930s Eastern/Western woman	106
A real lady-killer: *The Mummy* as Gothic romance	111
The Mummy and the Nubian: Yellow peril and black brute	114

6 The 1940s Mummy film: A decade of decay? 119

The Mummy returns: The 1940s Mummy as cadaverous copy	121
More than the sum of its parts: Innovation and the 1940s Mummy	122
The Mummy's Hand (1940): Reinventing the Mummy	124
The Mummy's Tomb (1942): A memorably murderous Mummy	126
Lon Chaney Jr.: Cursing the Mummy!	128
The Mummy in America: Fear and roaming in New England	131
The Mummy's Ghost (1944): Escaping bandaged bondage	133
The Mummy's Curse (1944): The female Mummy returns	135
The demise and rise of the Mummy: To buffoon and back again	137

Part 4 Hammer Film Productions and beyond: The Mummy of the 1950s–present 141

7 Hammer's resurrection of the Mummy: Sex and digs and wrap and roll 143

Show me the Mummy: Realism with restraint in *The Mummy*	147
Culture clash: The Mummy's case and the aftermath of Suez	152

8 Wrapping up the Mummy: The last sixty years 158

Bibliography	163
Index	183

Figures

0.1	Lobby card for *The Mummy's Tomb* (1942)	12
3.1	*Frankenstein* (1931), *The Bride of Frankenstein* (1935) and *The Curse of Frankenstein* (1957)	44
3.2	Boris Karloff as Imhotep in *The Mummy* (1932): Reminiscent of Sosra the Mummy	50
4.1	*The Egyptian Mummy* (1914)	66
4.2	*The Mummy and the Cowpunchers* (1912). *Kalem Kalender* 15 November 1912. p. 13	68
4.3	*Den Levande Mumien* (1917)	69
4.4	*Mercy, the Mummy Mumbled* (1918)	69
4.5	*The Mummy* (Thanhouser, 1911): Love despite an age difference. *The Moving Picture World*, 4 March 1911. Vol. 8. No. 9. p. 454	73
4.6	*The Perils of Pauline* (1914): A mummy promotes Pauline's Perils. *The Motion Picture News*, 28 March 1914. Vol. 9. No. 12. p.37	75
4.7	A professor finds a potion in *If I Were Young Again* (1914). *Motography* 14 November 1914. Vol. 12. No. 20. p. 659	76
4.8	A revived Egyptian princess puffs a cigar in *The Dust of Egypt* (1915). *Motion Picture Magazine*, May 1915. Vol 9. No. 4. p. 63	77
4.9	*The Vengeance of Egypt* (1912). *Moving Picture News*, 12 October 1912. Vol. 6. p. 9	79
4.10	*Die Tophar Mumie* (1920). Pressbook cover	82
4.11	Film fortune-tellers: Advertisement for *King Tut-ankh-amen's Eighth Wife* (1923). *Exhibitor's Trade Review* 21 April 1923. p. 7	91
5.1	Dracula's grand entrance in *Dracula* (1931): A stare on the stairs	102
5.2	Helen as Western heroine and as oriental beauty in *The Mummy* (1932)	105
5.3	Helen (re)turns to the past in *The Mummy* (1932)	108
5.4	The disapproving male gaze ignored by besotted gazers in *The Mummy* (1932)	109
5.5	Looking for a ghoul friend?: The Mummy entrances Helen and the audience in *The Mummy* (1932)	110
5.6	The modern heroine gives herself over to her inner Cleopatra in *The Mummy* (1932)	111
5.7	The Nubian dominates the poster and the heroine in *The Mummy* (1932)	115

6.1	Kharis in *The Mummy's Tomb* (1942): Minus the Mummy's hand	127
6.2	The masked killer stalks small-town America decades before the slasher movie in *The Mummy's Tomb* (1942)	132
7.1	Poster for Hammer's *The Mummy* (1959): A hole lot of trouble	148

Acknowledgements

Many gifted scholars have shared their time and ideas with me while writing this book. Among them I would like to especially thank Eithne Quinn, Paul Grainge, Julian Stringer, Mark Jancovich and Judie Newman. I am indebted to the University of Nottingham for funding much of my research and also Middlesex University for being supportive while completing the manuscript. I am also very grateful to my Media Department colleagues, particularly Paul Kerr, Deborah Klika, Tom McGorrian and Paul Cobley, who have always been perfectly happy to talk about ancient corpses over sandwiches. The anonymous peer reviewers of this manuscript who gave their time and graciously offered advice and encouragement I thank too, for they remind me that even at a time when research and ideas are not always prioritized in many higher education institutions, countless scholars who review manuscripts for books and journals nevertheless steadfastly value them, even when they know they will remain nameless. I also want to express my gratitude to Madeleine Hamey-Thomas and Rebecca Barden for their help as editors and for their support throughout the period of writing this book, particularly in 2017 when I had to take a break from it after both my mother Kathleen and brother Vincent passed away and again in 2018 when my father, also called Vincent, had a stroke from which he eventually passed away. Sadly, none of them will ever get to read this book, which is now unreservedly dedicated to them.

I would also like to acknowledge the input of my brother Stephen, a fellow film fanatic, for his advice and for lending me a book or two, although inexplicably in spite of our conversations he still prefers pop music films to horror films. Clearly my brother Vincent, who lived for music, was a greater influence upon him than I.

Last, but by no means least, I would like to thank my wife Jeongmee (another wonderful scholar whose help with this book has been immeasurable) and my children, Austin and Mia, for sticking with me every step of the way despite my disquieting preoccupations with the Hill of the Seven Jackals, the Valley of the Kings, New England swamps and the bandaged residents of these parts. I'm pretty sure they're sick to death of Mummy movies (although they've never actually confessed it), but they have nevertheless unwaveringly supported and encouraged and, yes, sometimes made fun of me, helping me to get through everything and finally finish the book. It exists through their efforts as much as mine.

And, of course, I cannot forget Imhotep, Kharis, Tera and the rest.

Author's notes

The director is provided in brackets for all films and programmes mentioned, followed by the country and year of release (d.u. is used when the director is unknown). In following this convention, I recognize it is far from ideal in regard to television in which the writers, producers or showrunners have often been in greater control of single episodes or series and that many different directors often contribute to different episodes. Occasionally, I have given a director as unknown when a director is provided on the IMDB. I have done this when I have been unable to corroborate this information from any other sources to which I have had access. This is not to say that IMDB is wrong in these instances, just that I have been unable to prove it is right.

For all films before 1930 I have additionally included information regarding who produced the films in parenthesis because many of the production companies mentioned no longer exist; their inclusion helps to better clarify the rapidity of Mummy film production across companies and countries in cinema's early years and helps distinguish between films which often had the same or similar title (there being two films called *The Mummy* in 1911, for example). I have been far more 'encyclopaedic' in terms of the number of films discussed in Chapter 4 because the silent Mummy film has hitherto been something of a lost era of film production. Although, I have no doubt, much still waits to be uncovered, I have attempted to reconstruct the silent age of the Mummy as comprehensively as possible through searching a range of journals from the silent era. Sometimes the plot descriptions cited may appear a little 'old-fashioned' because they are taken from written materials often over 100 years old.

Original language film titles are provided where possible. If a foreign language film has been released under an English title or its title has an existent English translation I have included it; otherwise I have provided only the original title. On a couple of occasions I have only been able to find an English language title rather than the original title.

I have capitalized the Mummy throughout, primarily to distinguish it as a character in literature and film, like the Monster from *Frankenstein*, and to differentiate it from its inanimate equivalent found in museums.

Introduction: Death is only the beginning – Unravelling the Mummy on Screen

The Mummy has stalked, sauntered, lurched and limped its way through the movies, largely unappreciated by critics, academics and cultural commentators, for well over a century. Numerous overviews of the history of the horror film have accused the Mummy of crushing the life out of the vibrant horror genre as readily as the monster does its own victims. Jonathan Lake Crane describes the Mummy as horror's 'least charismatic monster' (1994: 73) and Jeremy Dyson dismisses Mummy films as 'dross' (1997: 125). David Parkinson suggests that Mummy films form 'arguably, horror cinema's least successful sub-genre' (2000: 18), a view echoed by Kim Newman who calls it the 'least rewarding' (1986: 294) and 'most despised of all sub-genres' (1988: 31). Nor do such assessments belong to just the modern era of film criticism. As early as 1944, by which time the Mummy had already managed to notch up over fifty screen appearances, the *New York World Telegram* proclaimed on the release of *The Mummy's Ghost* (Reginald LeBorg, USA) that 'the Mummy always has been the least impressive of movie monsters' (cited in Weaver 1999: 166). Upon the release of the second Mummy film of that year, *The Mummy's Curse*, John McManus of New York's *PM* felt its very existence was tantamount to being a wartime scandal. Because the big studios have first priority on available film, he complained, 'there is a shortage of film available for independents, educational films, etc. This is how one big studio expends its film ration' (cited in Mank 1999b: 332). It was a film, in other words, not good enough to justify the film stock used to make it, a seventy-year-old assessment that stands till today as a pretty fair reflection of the critical status of the Mummy movie and its 'whole rotting bandages sub-genre' (McKay 2007: 242).

Yet such overwhelmingly negative appraisals are difficult to tally with the fact that the Mummy has remained a constant box-office draw since the very earliest years of cinema, featuring in major blockbusters, one-off hits and highly profitable film series. In the 1940s, for instance, out of all of Universal Studios' monsters, it was only the Mummy that carried its own series, in contrast to Dracula, Frankenstein's Monster and the Wolf Man who were all pitted against each other in multiple monster horror pot-boilers such as *Frankenstein Meets the Wolf Man* (Roy William Neill, USA, 1943) and *House of Dracula* (Erle C. Kenton, USA, 1945).[1] Kim R. Holston and Tom Winchester's indifferent appraisal of Universal's 1940s Mummy series as one which 'never garnered much critical acclaim, although it did well enough at the box office' (1997: 342) begs an obvious question: Why have critics and academics found the Mummy so forgettable as a monster while the cinema-going public have found it so appealing? The Mummy 'in terms of movie fame', as Gene Wright points out, 'ranks with the Frankenstein Monster, Dracula and the Wolf Man' (1987: 202), yet, despite this, for so many critics, the Mummy is an unfortunate monstrous misstep in the history of horror movies. R. H. W. Dillard offers one such critical appraisal as to why the Mummy fails:

> He is inflexibly the same, film after film, because he has but one story and that a simple one. All of the myths of the horror films are very limited, perhaps because they are myths, but the Mummy's identity is so restricting that the limitations are as binding as the decayed wrappings of his brittle flesh itself. (1967: 76)

This is a common critical conception of the Mummy, conceived as a static, unchanging, bandaged, 'mindless, foot-dragging corpse' (Pulliam 2015: 195) that features in repetitive, formulaic films. However, rather than being emblematic of binding limitations, the diversity of Mummies, Mummy films and Mummy narratives that have featured in the cinema demonstrate the precise opposite: the Mummy has offered a miscellany of monstrous possibilities. There have been a staggering variety of Mummies that have appeared on screen and, while they have mostly come from Egypt, many others have originated elsewhere, with Incan,[2] Aztec,[3] Roman,[4] Celtic,[5] Caribbean[6] and Chinese[7] Mummies all having risen from the dead to stalk the living at one time or another. As well as emerging from a variety of different countries, Mummies have featured in films from countries all around the world including Brazil,[8] Denmark,[9] Egypt,[10] France,[11] Germany,[12] Hungary,[13] Italy,[14] Japan,[15] Mexico,[16] Spain,[17] and Sweden.[18] There have been girl Mummies,[19] boy Mummies,[20] teen Mummies,[21] octogenarian Mummies,[22] puppet Mummies,[23] robot Mummies,[24] atomic Mummies,[25] teleporting Mummies,[26] transforming Mummies,[27] giant Mummies,[28] miniature Mummies,[29] dog Mummies,[30] hamster Mummies,[31] monkey Mummies,[32] karate Mummies,[33] kung fu Mummies,[34] extra-terrestrial Mummies,[35] indestructible Mummies[36] and cannibalistic Mummies.[37] There have been Mummies with blacked-out eyes,[38] Mummies with glowing eyes,[39] Mummies with flashing eyes[40] and Mummies with eyes that shoot laser beams.[41] The Mummy of Elvis Presley appeared in one film,[42] while Elvis battled a Mummy in another.[43] In addition to pursuing vengeance, lost loves or terrified victims, Mummies have sung songs,[44] taken manicures,[45] babysat,[46] burgled,[47] played basketball,[48] played Russian roulette,[49] played with a yo-yo,[50] gone motorcycling,[51] fishing,[52] ice skating,[53] flying,[54] sailing,[55] nightclubbing,[56] dived deep underwater[57] and gone into deep space.[58] As well as films, television shows[59] and cartoons,[60] they have appeared in books,[61] comics,[62] theatrical productions,[63] video games,[64] pop videos[65] and also in song.[66] The Mummy, as Donald F. Glut noted, is a figure that can be encountered almost anywhere:

> [It has] leered at us from rings, bubble bath dispensers, glo-heads, and Nestlés' 'Spook Group' flavours ... bendable figures, swizzle sticks, spoons and horrorscope viewers ... glow pictures, toy figures, iron-ons, stick-on stamps,

buttons, photo printsets, paint-by-number sets, candy, wallets, pencil sharpeners and wall plaques … model kits, masks, calendars, greeting cards, trading cards, posters and play money. (1978: 412)

In spite of the fact that the Mummy is a figure liable to pop up anywhere in popular culture and has featured in literally hundreds of films to date and been reimagined by visionary and highly regarded directors such as Georges Méliès, Ernst Lubitsch, Karl Freund, Terence Fisher and Mike Newell, it remains a figure disliked and neglected, even today when so many horror genres and figures have been reappraised.

Such oversight was explicable for a long time given that the whole genre of cinematic horror was long considered, as Robin Wood asserts, 'the most disreputable of Hollywood genres' (1984: 173). It was not until 1967 that the first significant English language works on the horror film appeared with the publication of two ground-breaking books: Ivan Butler's *The Horror Film* and Carlos Clarens's *An Illustrated History of the Horror Film*. Despite arriving late on the scene as a subject of cinematic study, however, lost time has been made up with horror today being one of the most popular cinema subjects for critical analysis, so much so that 'even the slasher film can attract something close to a "progressive" reading' (Gelder 2000: 311). Critical reappraisal has taken place for a great many monsters and horror narratives, with numerous academic studies conducted on the vampire, Frankenstein's Monster, werewolf, zombie, serial killer and alien invader. However, the Mummy has not been re-evaluated or critically rescued in the same manner, to the extent that it is even specifically de-selected for critical study on occasion. In the 2014 collection *Screening the Undead*, for instance, the Mummy is emphatically excluded because it 'doesn't seem to have sustained either popular or critical attention', being 'confined to mostly repetitive studio cycles' (Hunt et al. 2014: 2).

Because of the repeated assumption that the Mummy is a repetitious monster, it is unsurprising that the Mummy has tended to feature less than other monsters in discussions of horror. In David J. Skal's wide-ranging *The Monster Show: A Cultural History of Horror*, for instance, the Mummy barely features, with only the plot of *The Mummy* (Karl Freund, USA, 1932) noted in one paragraph. Similarly, the Mummy warrants only a paragraph in Clarens's *An Illustrated History of the Horror Film* (1967: 73) whereas in Ivan Butler's *The Horror Film* it fails to get even that.

The majority of film or horror-focused books and articles that offer detailed analysis of the Mummy in the cinema have tended not to focus on the Mummy film per se. For example, the Mummy has featured in discussions of the works of specific directors such as Karl Freund,[67] Reginald LeBorg[68] and Terence Fisher[69] to illustrate tendencies in the oeuvres of these directors, or in relation to the screen careers of stars who have appeared in Mummy films.[70] The Mummy has also been discussed in books on particular studios such as Universal[71] and Hammer,[72] British horror cinema[73] and particular eras of horror production.[74] Pieces devoted to the cinematic Mummy itself have primarily appeared in works dedicated to monsters in fan magazines like *Famous Monsters of Filmland* and *Castle of Frankenstein*,[75] books and articles about film monsters,[76] reprinted film scripts,[77] books examining lost scenes,[78] classic horror make-up[79] and encyclopaedias on monsters and horror films.[80] The existence of so many fan-focused studies demonstrates the obvious fascination the Mummy holds for horror aficionados, if not for critics.[81] Outside of film and horror studies, far greater interest has been taken in the Mummy as an influential presence in broader popular culture, featuring in works exploring its contributions to areas such as literature, Egyptology, religion, music, art and museums.[82] Within film studies, though, it remains the critical poor relation of horror's mainstays, downgraded as derivative both as a concept and subgenre.

Such a reputation for derivativeness is perhaps partly due to the tendency for major Mummy movies to follow hot on the heels of financially popular screen versions of Dracula and Frankenstein. Universal's *The Mummy* (1932) came after *Dracula* (Tod Browning, USA, 1931) and *Frankenstein* (James Whale, USA, 1931), Hammer's *The Mummy* (Terence Fisher, UK, 1959) after *The Curse of Frankenstein* (Terence Fisher, UK, 1957) and *Dracula* (Terence Fisher, UK, 1958) and Universal's *The Mummy* (Stephen Sommers, USA, 1999) after *Bram Stoker's Dracula* (Francis Ford Coppola, USA, 1992) and *Mary Shelley's Frankenstein* (Kenneth Branagh, UK/USA, 1994). Seemingly little more than a follow-up in Universal and Hammer's efforts to build on the success of previous hits, this pattern of arriving in third place after versions of Dracula and Frankenstein within different horror cycles has probably contributed to establishing the Mummy's 'third-rate' status as a monster. The Mummy's standing among critics has also not been helped by the fact that 'horror' directors have seldom been associated with Mummy films. Unlike celebrated directors such as James Whale with *Frankenstein* and Tod Browning with *Dracula*, it was Karl Freund, a figure better known for his cinematography than his direction, who gave us *The Mummy* in 1932. Further, it was a string of 'B' movie directors who brought us the Mummy in the 1940s. Christy Cabanne, Harold Young, Reginald LeBorg and Leslie Goodwins are not names that instantly spring to mind and none has any real connection with the horror genre or any cult status today – rather than being *auteurs* they are today remembered as 'second-rate craftsmen' (Clarens 1967: 101), when they are remembered at all. At Hammer Film Productions the trend was briefly broken when Terence Fisher directed *The Mummy* in 1959 (although he was still very early in his career as a horror specialist director when he made this film, and did not direct any of Hammer's subsequent Mummy films). The 1980s and 1990s again saw Mummy movies directed by non-horror directors like Mike Newell (*The Awakening*, UK, 1980), Russell Mulcahy (*Tale of the Mummy* a.k.a. *Talos the Mummy*, UK/USA, 1998) and Stephen Sommers (*The Mummy*, 1999), respectively best known beforehand for *The Man in the Iron Mask* (UK/USA, 1977), *Highlander* (UK/USA, 1986) and *The Jungle Book* (USA, 1994). In 2017 *The Mummy* (USA) was directed by Alex Kurtzman, best known previously as a producer of *Star Trek* (J. J. Abrams, USA, 2009), and the failure of this film has been largely attributed to him, as well as the part played by Tom Cruise in making major changes to the film (Setoodeh and Lang 2017).

Tom Cruise is a star not especially renowned for horror films and neither is his co-star, Sofia Boutella, who played the Mummy itself. The Mummy's reputation has long suffered from a lack of association with horror stars because, in contrast to many other major movie monsters, no actor or actress has become truly synonymous with the figure. Iconic horror monsters, from supernatural ones to serial killers, are frequently indebted to the stars that play them, such as Robert Englund as Freddy Kruger from the *Nightmare on Elm Street* series, Doug Bradley as Pinhead from the *Hellraiser* films or John Kramer as the Jigsaw Killer from the *Saw* series. While some big name horror stars have played the Mummy, including Boris Karloff, Lon Chaney Jr. and Christopher Lee, they all became definitively associated with different monsters. Boris Karloff will forever be remembered as Frankenstein's Monster, Lon Chaney Jr. as the Wolf Man while Christopher Lee, like Bela Lugosi before him, became an archetypal Dracula. Boris Karloff repeated his role as Frankenstein's Monster, as did Lee with Dracula, but neither repeated their roles as the Mummy, further encouraging identification with their other portrayals. Nor did Tom Tyler, the first actor to portray Kharis the Mummy in Universal's 1940s paradigm-shifting reimagining of the Mummy in *The Mummy's Hand* (Christy Cabanne, USA, 1940), reappear in the role. He went on instead to repeat performances as Captain Marvel in the twelve-part Republic Pictures serial *Adventures of Captain Marvel* (John English, William Witney, USA, 1941). It was only Lon Chaney Jr., from all of these stars, who played the Mummy more than once. However, unlike his career-defining turn as Lawrence Talbot/the Wolf Man, which he made his own, two actors before him had already established the Mummy at Universal. Unlike his Wolf Man role, Chaney Jr. had little regard for the Mummy, maintaining that movie audiences who spent their money to see Mummy films were 'nuts' (cited in Mank 1999b: 326).

Aside from directors and stars, another means through which the reputation of a monster is often established is through the 'definitive' film that launched it, which creates for all time an indelible image. For Dracula, Tod Browning's 1931 film introduced to cinema audiences the Lugosi persona replete with cape, vampiric stare and Eastern European accent that became iconic, while for Frankenstein James Whale's 1931 version established Karloff's flat-headed and bolt-necked Monster as an interpretation popularly remembered to this day. Karl Freund's 1932 version of *The Mummy* is often singled out as the moment when the image of the Mummy was defined for the public. William K. Everson, for instance, identifies this as the Mummy movie's key film and that the 'the mythology of the revitalized Mummy must be credited solely to Universal Pictures' enterprise in striving to find a successful Karloffian follow-up to Frankenstein' (1974: 89).

The Mummy's critical credentials are impeccable for viewing it as the cinematic urtext. It was made during a golden age period when the producer Carl Laemmle Jr. had decided to make films 'of the highest excellence that the resources of Universal City could achieve' (cited in Pendo 1975: 155). It had an iconic star in Karloff and a director in Karl Freund renowned for prior artistic triumphs as cinematographer on some of the most important films of his generation, including *Der Golem, Wie Er in die Welt Kam* (*The Golem, How He Came into the World*, Germany, PAGU, 1920), *Der Letzte Mann* (*The Last Laugh*, *The Last Man*, F. W. Murnau, Germany, UFA, 1924),

Variety (Ewald André Dupont, Germany, UFA, 1925) and *Metropolis* (Fritz Lang, Germany, UFA, 1927). Many have acknowledged it as the seminal 'quintessential mummy film' (Lupton 2015: 286), with Everson singling it out as a creative tour de force, claiming that 'the most impressive of all the monster films is *The Mummy*, directed by Karl Freund in 1932' (1954: 14). Dennis Fischer is another critic who greatly admires its artistry, its 'subtlety and suggestiveness' and its rather 'strange and eerie kind of poetry', believing it to be 'one of the most poetic horror films ever made' (1991: 431). Gerald C. Wood suggests that *The Mummy* has remained critically favoured primarily because of such attractive features: 'Its look was artily European' and suggestive of 'ennobling sources' such as German Expressionism (1988: 212).

However, while the film has retained a strong reputation for quality, the Mummy that featured in it has faded in the public consciousness in comparison to later versions of the Mummy. While subtlety and artistry in horror create memorable films, it would appear that it is plenty of screen-time for a strikingly impressive monster that creates a horror archetype. Like *The Mummy*, *White Zombie* (Victor Halperin, USA, 1932) has today an impressive reputation for its atmosphere and aesthetics, but few remember the zombies that featured in the film as they had little impact on the zombie subgenre. It would be, as Louise Fenton has argued, the far more visible but less critically regarded 'zombie of the 1940s that placed the living dead in the imagination of mass audiences' (2014: 225). As Mark Jancovich points out, a critical focus on important, defining films is often the case when film histories are compiled, but this can prove to be very distorting because 'the very features that have resulted in their classic status might not make them representative at all' (2002: 9). In the case of *The Mummy*, the film is valued precisely because of its uniqueness and artistry, rather than the degree of its indebtedness to or influence on the horror genre or Mummy film. Karloff's subtle interpretation of the role as a berobed, fragile fez-wearing sorcerer is not the Mummy popularly remembered. Instead, as Brian Senn and John Johnson point out:

> When one thinks of the Mummy an image comes to mind of a bandaged monster sent out to do the evil bidding of a sinister high priest. The creature's face is wrinkled and blank as it slowly and inexorably limps toward the intended victim, its single good arm outstretched to strangle the life out of anyone who stands in its way. (1992: 412)

This mute, monstrous, bandaged Mummy emerged from the 1940s Mummy cycle that consisted of four films made between 1940 and 1944 and not from the 1930s original. The Mummy that has implanted itself into the public consciousness belongs not to Karloff but to Tom Tyler and Lon Chaney Jr. Crucially, this has led to a major drawback for the Mummy as a horror archetype because the iconic creature that everybody knows is tied not to the 'classic' critical darling of the Mummy film, but instead to a critically derided series of films.

Timothy Sullivan suggests that *The Mummy's Hand* (1940), the movie that launched the bandaged marauding Mummy, was 'a film that had nothing to do with Freund's masterpiece' (1986: 164), and this position characterizes one of the main problems for the Mummy. The monstrous Mummy that has become iconic is seen by many as an inferior concept to what came before. Roger Luckhurst, for instance, defines him as 'a shuffling dullard' (2012: 17), David Huckvale 'a characterless corpse' (2012: 212) and James Marriott and Kim Newman a 'limping, pot-bellied, not-terribly-fearsome bandaged bully' (2010: 55). David Flint consigns him to being 'little more than an Egyptian zombie' (2009: 41) and Jonathan Rigby 'a cut-priced bandaged' one at that (2017: 197). Peter Hutchings is less scathing in his estimation of the 1940s Mummy but still suggests that 'there is something vaguely disappointing about this version of the Mummy, as if he has not quite delivered the critical goods in the manner of those other Universal monsters which have lent themselves so well to particular forms of interpretation and analysis' (2002).

The 1940s Mummy was reinvented as part of Universal's general strategy in that decade of revamping all of their monsters, most of which have been critically regarded as inferior to their 1930s originals. Universal horror films of the 1940s such as *Son of Dracula* (Robert Siodmak, USA, 1943) and *Frankenstein Meets the Wolf Man* (1943) have long been perceived as the products of a studio cranking out uncreative money-makers designed primarily to keep the studio afloat,[83] 'reducing the gothic-romantic genre of the 1930s to an assembly line for childish shudder pulps' (Newman 2002: 101). As well as being inferior to previous horror output, Universal's horror movies of the 1940s are also unfavourably compared to Val Lewton's contemporaneous RKO-produced low-budget films such as *Cat People* (Jacques Tourneur, USA, 1942) and *I Walked With a Zombie* (Jacques Tourneur, USA, 1943). Whereas RKO's horror films traded in psychological complexity and are critically considered as 'literate, adult and sophisticated' (Marriott and Newman 2010: 54), by comparison the 1940s Mummy film has been critically consigned to being little more than an 'enjoyable lark' (Brunas 1983: 19), cheap and cheerful with 'an arthritic camp charm' (Holston and Winchester 1997: 342) designed primarily to satisfy saucer-eyed children sitting in the front row of the cinema who were mainly 'drawn to the double-billed feature' (Legassic 2014: 310). For instance, Alan G. Barbour, in an affectionate reminiscence, describes his feelings:

> I could take most of the creatures they threw at me on the screen. The Frankenstein Monster, Dracula, the Wolf Man, the Creeper and all the others entertained but hardly frightened me. But when Tom Tyler (as the Mummy in *The Mummy's Hand*) or Lon Chaney, Jr. (as the Mummy in the three remaining films in the series) came at me on the screen with gnarled hand outstretched and the pulse-quickening music of Hans Salter gathering momentum on the soundtrack, that was just too much. (1971: 45)[84]

When not eulogized for starring in a remarkably artistic and idiosyncratic one-off in the 1930s (a dead end for discussing the development of the figure), the Mummy is considered the product of a generic assembly line in the 1940s that churned out an 'abyss of juvenile horror/comedy' (Lupton 2003: 38) suitable only for minors (another dead end).

Further damaging to the Mummy's standing is the fact that it is not comprehended as deriving from folklore like other monsters such as the vampire or werewolf, who have developed all manner of associated legends and traditions, and so is a creature that has not attained the status of myth. While some critics have assumed that 'the idea of walking Mummies' was 'a pure Hollywood fabrication' (Fischer 1991: 429), they are mistaken because even to the ancient Egyptians the Mummy was a body never fully dead. For centuries ever since there have been all manner of superstitious and pseudo-scientific beliefs attributed to Mummies that have contributed to the genesis of the Mummy from a human into a monster, a number of which will be discussed in Chapter 1.

Nor is the cinematic Mummy's literary ancestry acknowledged in the way that it is for other monsters, in spite of the fact that long before the advent of film there existed numerous significant literary works that featured living Mummies. Les Daniels, for instance, incorrectly assumes no literary tradition behind the Mummy when he asserts that *The Mummy* (1932) 'had no direct literary source but was concocted out of nothing in particular' (1977: 144). Such an assumption is understandable, however, because there is no definitive single origin text. Kim Newman identifies this lack of association with a literary classic or unique literary source as the Mummy's major drawback: 'There's no foundation Mummy text of the caliber and completeness of Frankenstein, Dracula or Jekyll and Hyde ... [and] ... because there is no source novel the Mummy movie has always been the poor relation of other great horror stories' (1996: 225). Despite the fact that many celebrated authors including Edgar Allan Poe, Bram Stoker and Arthur Conan Doyle composed Mummy tales, none of these has been identified as source texts against which to grade the genre – to say whether films are good or bad adaptations – a situation not alleviated by the fact that it was not until *Blood from the Mummy's Tomb* (Seth Holt, Michael Carreras, UK) in 1971 that classical literary inspiration was directly acknowledged in a Mummy film's credits. The bandaged Mummy, as a result of not being considered 'classic' in either a literary or cinematic sense, fails to meet a prime critical criterion for the interrogation of a monster: a cultural starting point. The lack of an accepted cinematic 'generic prototype', to adopt Thomas Schatz's term (1981: 264), or source novel or even a folk history makes it difficult to determine where to begin with the Mummy.

Perhaps as a result of its ambiguous origins the Mummy has often been placed in the shadow of other monsters that are considered more archetypal. James B. Twitchell (1985), for instance, identifies the three major carriers of horror as the vampire, the split-personality werewolf and the hulk with no name. Although obvious candidates for these categories would be, in turn, Dracula, the Wolf Man and Frankenstein's Monster, Twitchell uses the terms loosely so that any creature that sucks the life out of a being can be considered a vampire, Dr. Jekyll transforms and would be a split-personality werewolf and the Creature from the Black Lagoon alongside the giant spiders, robots and blobs from American horror/sci-fi would qualify as hulks with no names. Such archetypes have proven a popular tool in horror studies and have led to much categorizing and classification. Stephen King (1993: 65–100) offers an identical grouping to Twitchell with his three tales of the tarot (but suggests the ghost could be added to the list) and so does David J. Skal (1994: 19) (who in turn suggests the freak as an addition). Andrew Tudor (1989: 133–57) sees the mad scientist as a distinct figure in horror while Randy Loren Rasmussen (1998) identifies his six clearly defined character types as heroines, heroes, wise elders, mad scientists, servants and monsters.

As this book will explore, the Mummy rather than being a static repetitious figure is in fact a far more nebulous figure than given credit for and can be seen to occupy various different positions within these distinct camps. Boris Karloff's Ardath Bey in *The Mummy* is closest to the 'vampire' as an undead man and ersatz Dracula, but can also be read as a 'ghost' who will allow nobody to touch him and whose attacks are not physical but paranormal. So too can the lifeforce sucking 'Queen of the Nile' from *The Twilight Zone* (John Brahm, USA, 1964) and Imhotep from *The Mummy* (1999) be loosely considered as vampires. The brutish Mummy of the 1940s can be placed into the category of 'hulk with no name', as can Hammer's 1959 interpretation. In *Blood from the Mummy's Tomb* (1971) a modern woman gets 'taken over' by the spirit of a murderous ancient Egyptian queen and so proves suitable for the split-personality 'werewolf' archetype.

In addition, the Mummy has not just jumped camps from film to film, but often combines archetypal attributes within single films. As Kim R. Holston and Tom Winchester point out in relation to the 1940s Mummy, 'Kharis seemed to borrow in equal measure qualities of two other Universal monsters of the time: the great strength and shambling gait of the Frankenstein monster, and the penchant for operating under moonlight from the Wolf Man' (1997: 342). Jerry Warren's *Face of the Screaming Werewolf* (Mexico/USA, 1964) overtly combined archetypes with its Mummy who transforms into a werewolf during the full moon.

The critical practice of classification and the Mummy's resistance to being categorically placed into distinct categories, while simultaneously fitting into many of them, suggests that the archetypal status of some monsters has more to do with the construction of particular archetypes than any essence of distinctiveness belonging to the monsters themselves. Horror monsters, even at their most archetypal, commonly incorporate shared features, just as the Mummy does. As J. P. Telotte argues, monsters are often 'quite literally hybrids or mixed forms … combinatory figures' (2003: 219). The terms of classification are so loose in Twitchell's attempt, for instance, that a blob, a giant spider and Frankenstein's Monster are categorized as having more in common as hulks with no names than the human-like Frankenstein's Monster, vampire and (pre-transformed) werewolf, who are all placed into separate categories. As well as sharing human form for long periods, the vampire and the werewolf's abilities are also often entwined, with both spreading their conditions through infectious bite and the vampire frequently having the ability to change into a wolf. Many monsters are actually as mutable and difficult to categorize as the Mummy even though, like it, they have to varying degrees a 'fixed' identity in popular culture. Vampires have appeared as an array of creatures in the cinema including deluded white men in *Martin* (George A. Romero, USA, 1977) and *Vampire's Kiss* (Robert Bierman, USA, 1989), afflicted African American men in *Blacula* (William Crain, USA, 1972) and *Ganja & Hess* (Bill Gunn, USA, 1973), space ghosts in *Planet of the Vampires* (Mario Bava, Italy, 1965) and *Lifeforce* (Tobe Hooper, USA, 1985), children in *Salem's Lot* (Tobe Hooper, USA, 1979) and *Låt den Rätte Komma In* (*Let the Right One In*, Tomas Alfredson, Sweden, 2008), mechanical bloodsuckers in *I Bought a Vampire Motorcycle* (Dirk Campbell, UK, 1990) and *Cronos* (Guillermo del Toro, Mexico, 1993) as well as an assortment of animals including bats in *Nightwing* (Arthur Hiller, USA, 1979), dogs in *Dracula's Dog* (Albert Band, USA, 1977) and werecats in *Sleepwalkers* (Mick Garris, USA, 1992).

Noël Carroll (1990), taking a somewhat different approach to archetype architects, argues that monsters in horror films are threatening precisely because they are indistinct, posing a psychological threat to individual identity because they are impure hybrids constructed from combinations of diverse elements, including those created through fission and those by fusion. In the former group are creatures whose contradictory elements are divided within the monster, resulting in the split-personality werewolf and Dr. Jekyll and Mr. Hyde among others. Those monsters created through fusion remain distinct individuals but are constituted of incompatible elements such as insect and human, machine and flesh or living and dead. Into this latter category falls the Mummy, with its living but desiccated flesh, along with vampires and zombies.

Whatever group the Mummy has been placed into, hulk with no name or creature born of fusion, it has forever remained an outsider, a monstrous manqué, an 'Other' among the great monstrous 'Others' of the cinema. Andrew Tudor, for instance, totally ignores the Mummy and lists Frankenstein and Dracula as Universal studios' major 1930s originals (1989: 162). S. S. Prawer similarly utterly overlooks the Mummy when he celebrates how after the coming of sound '*Dracula* (1931), *Frankenstein* (1931), and *White Zombie* (1932) were all made in Carl Laemmle's Universal Studios' (1980: 9–10). The occupation of *White Zombie*, an independent production from the Halperin Brothers, in the 1932 slot exemplifies the tendency for the Mummy to be a figure excluded from the range of inquiry identifying canonical works within horror (in this case even at Universal), forever a monster (un)living in the shadows of monsters perceived as more profoundly meaningful.

As Peter Hutchings points out, the Mummy has not lent itself as well as other Universal monsters such as Dracula and Frankenstein's Monster to 'particular forms of interpretation and analysis' (2002), but rather than this being due to a deficiency in the make-up of the Mummy itself, this could equally suggest it has just not proven a suitable subject for customary 'forms' of study. Cinema's monsters are often critically examined so as to determine what they represent, what is at the heart of their appeal or what is their essence. Monsters often lend themselves to such lines of enquiry because, as Marie Hélene-Huet points out, the word 'monster' is linked to 'the idea of showing or warning' because of its supposed derivation 'from the Latin *monstrare*: to show, to display (*montrer* in French)' (2000: 87). Actors too often have their own understandings of what the monsters they play mean, Lon Chaney Jr. believing that his monsters were 'extreme variations on physical ugliness, mean-spiritedness and ignorance' (Wells 2000: 54). For both those that play them and those that read or view them, therefore, often 'monsters are meaning machines' (Halberstam 1995: 21).

In relation to Bram Stoker's novel *Dracula*, Ken Gelder explains how it reveals:

> Anxieties about Darwinian notions of human evolution, the proliferation of discourses of decay and degeneration ... the impact of psychoanalysis, the advocacy of late imperialist values, the emergence of new technologies, the influence of eugenics, and so on. *Dracula* is ... a vibrant, bustling, 'sensationalist' novel, almost bursting at the seams with issues and themes. (2000: 145)

As this quotation exemplifies, the essence of a monster's narrative can be multifaceted and difficult to determine, qualities very attractive to critics and cultural commentators. Monsters have been discussed at various times as manifestations of AIDS (Guerrero 1990), capitalism (Cormack 1994), our fear of the nonhuman (Thomas 1972) and physical deviancy (Donne 1972). Harry M. Benshoff (1997) has offered a queer reading of them, Charles Derry (1977) a psychological one, Isabel Cristina Pinedo (1997) a gendered one and David Soren (1977) an art historical one. As Noël Carroll elucidates in the case of critical responses to *King Kong* (Ernest B. Schoedsack, Merian C. Cooper, USA, 1933), we have had Kong 'as Christ, Kong as Black, Kong as commodity, Kong as rapist, Kong enraptured by *L'amour fou*, Kong as Third World, Kong as dream, Kong as myth, Kong according to Freud, according to Jung, and even according to Lacan' (1984: 215–16). Where does the Mummy fare in such readings: a monster who Paula Guran argues 'we lack a solid psychological link to' (2007: 376) and who Peter Hutchings defines as 'undeveloped, devoid of desire, metaphor resistant, and with no subtext to call his own' (2002)?

Rather than being devoid of direct or indirect meaning, desire or distinctiveness, it is worth noting that the Mummy is a creature awash with them all, but who is at a disadvantage because its narratives have largely focused on romance over sex, with the latter tending to prove more critically appealing when analysing horror cinema (the former more readily discussed in respect to genres such as comedy and melodrama). Roger Dadoun, for instance, offers a characteristic interpretation of the metaphor resplendent Dracula as sexual aggressor:

> Dracula carries his body like an erect phallus: you only have to think of his usual stiff posture, his long black cape, his sudden appearances like a bolt from the blue. As if to emphasise this phallic value, the camera often marks a pause – while Dracula poses. In a film like *Nosferatu* [*Nosferatu, eine Symphonie des Grauens*, F. W. Murnau, Germany, Prana, 1922], a prototype of the horror film, the human vampire, as it appears to us almost constantly, is nothing other than this erection, a walking phallus or 'phallambulist', as one might say in French. (1989: 54)

As with Dadoun's vampire, the bandaged male Mummy can be similarly defined as phallic and obsessed. Rather than acting on an insatiable lust, however, the Mummy's sexuality is eternally repressed. It stands rigidly bolt upright in its tomb, alone in the dark in a perpetual state of unfulfilled longing and chastity. The permanent erect stiffness of the Mummy is commonly accentuated by him being presented in films as stepping out from upright coffins (Figure 0.1) in which he is standing as opposed to the male vampire who, upon awakening, is frequently presented as sitting up from coffins resting on the ground (psychosexually speaking, not in a permanent state of libidinous fixation or state of constant arousal because he has rested after sating his desires, becoming limp). This convention for the Mummy to be upright in its coffin may come from the common practice of them being so displayed in travelling shows and museums. It may also derive, as Jonathan Rigby suggests, from Imhotep as first presented at the beginning of *The Mummy* (1932) in an 'impish homage to the awakening of Cesare in *Das Cabinet des Dr Caligari* [*The Cabinet of Dr. Caligari*, Robert Wiene, Germany, Decla-Bioscop, 1919]' (2017: 126). Whatever the derivation, the male Mummy of the cinema is a figure who rigidly embodies sexual longing rather than sexual gratification.

Whereas Dracula hedonistically emerges from his tomb and acts on his lust repeatedly, carnally and messily, the frustrated Mummy, enwrapped and restricted, rarely gets to swap fluids or strip off his bandages. He instead commonly witnesses others, usually modern heroes, win the heart of his object of desire. In contrast to the vampire who gives vent to his feelings through both physical and verbal exchange, the Mummy silently and obsessively focuses on one unattainable relationship, its one arm commonly pulled free, as if its release is all that has been achieved in a centuries-long purgatory of frustrated sexual craving. It can, therefore, be seen as a tragic, onanistic figure whose longings will never be satisfied. Unable to consummate, it is a monster forced to adhere to an ideal of romantic rather than physical love. Jasmine Day suggests that when it comes to the Mummy 'celibacy' is the 'salient concept'

Fig. 0.1 Lobby card for *The Mummy's Tomb* (1942).

(2015: 217) while Griselda Pollock (2007) in her reading of the Mummy goes further and identifies the figure with castration. Christopher Lee, who played the Mummy in Hammer's *The Mummy* (1959), carefully contemplated this aspect of the Mummy too and proved sympathetic to the 'impossibility of such a poor old monster having a love life, owing to the bandages and his mouth being sewn up' (1977: 260).

The lack of direct, penetrative sexual menace that the vampire conveys does not necessarily mean, though, that the Mummy's threat is not as transmittable and pernicious as that of the vampire's. This is primarily because of its associated curse. Sir Frank Whemple in *The Mummy* (1932) recognizes the Mummy's infectivity when he bemoans that his son has fallen in love with a woman and been tainted by the association: 'The curse has struck her, now, through her it will strike my son.' It is usually an archaeologist who is the initial carrier of the Mummy's curse, a man who gains forced access into the undefiled sanctified tomb, usually of a woman, in a foreign land. In contrast to male Mummies who tend to remain hideous figures, as Eleanor Dobson (2017) points out, female Mummies are usually beautifully preserved. His breaking of a sacred seal and pulling open of a sarcophagus to expose, gaze at and manhandle the beauty of the past lying within is redolent with imagery of rape and necrophilia. It proves to be a hazardous endeavour, with Jasmine Day suggesting that in the cinema such tombs persistently prove far from defenceless. When men penetrate them, the tombs are 'retaliatory; they are *vaginae dentatae*, mouth-vaginas that try to destroy the penetrating instrument' (2006: 80).

For the crime of invading the tomb and desecrating the body of the female corpse, who had been buried with great care to avoid this very fate, the archaeologist brings back home with him to civilization a curse as punishment that threatens his loved ones at home. This 'retaliation' is perhaps most explicitly visually rendered in *The Awakening* (1980) when, as the obsessed archaeologist attacks the tomb, so too does the supernatural force from the tomb attack his pregnant wife's womb, each swing of the hammer corresponding with her clutching her stomach in agony. More commonly, though, the curse brings with it a physically rendered agent of retribution, the avenging male Mummy, whose dirtiness and mouldering flesh is as representative of contagion as the infectious fangs of the vampire. The Mummy, fixated on the woman in the tomb, becomes intent on redressing the act of desecration (both to the tomb and his own 'pure' romantic obsession).

Once activated, the Mummy's curse can prove highly destructive and transmittable. For instance, Guy Boothby's novel *Pharos the Egyptian* (1899) makes dramatic use of the fact that plague and ancient Egypt have been closely associated since the time of Moses. Boothby narrates how a stolen Mummy results in the spread of a disease that threatens to apocalyptically wipe out the population of Europe. Exactly one hundred years later, a Mummy in *The Mummy* (1999) could still be found threatening to bring about mass destruction, this time by reviving the ten plagues themselves.

In addition to bringing about destruction and the end of life, the living dead commonly offer new forms of life too, tending to be reproductive; the vampire, werewolf and zombie all create more of themselves through their bite, with Frankenstein's Monster and the Mummy being notable exceptions because of their desire for monogamy. In films and TV shows that focus on the love life of Frankenstein's Monster, such as *The Bride of Frankenstein* (James Whale, USA, 1935) and *Penny Dreadful* (John Logan, UK/USA, 2014–16), he yearns to bring to life a single 'bride' that is to be created through stitching together and reviving the recent dead. The Mummy has a similar yearning, but in his case his 'bride' is to be brought back into the world through re-awakening or reincarnating the ancient dead. It is not the fact that the Mummy does not have desire that makes it an unpopular subject for critical enquiry, therefore. Rather it has more to do with the fact that it does not particularly display it. The Mummy in the cinema has been inclined to be an especially inexpressive monster!

Peter Hutchings suggests that the Mummy possesses 'neither the charisma of Dracula, the pathos of Frankenstein's monster, nor the sexualized rage of the Wolfman' (2002). Yet it is the overt lack of such qualities, the ones identified here as making other monsters more interesting, that actually makes the Mummy so distinctive and effective in its own right. It is the Mummy's frightening impenetrability that makes it so monstrous. First, the bandaged Mummy is further removed from us than virtually any other classic monster; it has been undead for far longer than any of them and the culture it is from is more ancient and alien than theirs. Secondly, the Mummy commonly has no voice, nor does it have facial expression, making it virtually impossible to identify with. The 'archetypal' bandaged Mummy is mute, masked, crippled, sullied, relentlessly slow, unstoppable and impossible to reason with. It lacks 'humanity' or personality, which has contributed to its marginalized position critically, but it is the lack of these very traits that has contributed to it being such a long enduring and effective monster in the cinema.

It is therefore fruitless to apply criteria to the Mummy that apply to other classic monsters in a one-size-fits-all approach. Joyce Tyldesley, for example, argues that 'only those Mummies who can successfully shed their bandages and expose their flesh and feelings can fully engage our sympathies in the way that Dracula does' (1999: 100). James B. Twitchell similarly applies criteria utilized to assess other monsters when he contends that the Mummy fails because it is divorced from our ability to understand it:

> The Mummy, who is hopelessly bogged down in a complicated story that involves capturing his reincarnated girl-princess and returning with her to the world of the dead, lumbered his way through about ten films on both sides of the Atlantic without developing a coherent text, let alone a family. What is really under all that gauze and why can't he articulate his desires? He can talk all right, but no one knows what it is he has to say. (1985: 260)

Actually the male, bandaged Mummy does not articulate his desires primarily because, most commonly, he cannot talk. His bandages impede him from doing so and in numerous versions he has had his tongue removed for committing an act of sacrilege in ancient Egypt. Twitchell is also incorrect in regard to the Mummy having no family. He does have one, albeit like any monster with a family, it is a dysfunctional one. He has his dead princess as a lover who may or may not return to life and/or a high-priest as a companion who protects and/or controls him. His desire is so evident that it does not require articulating. He will defend the tomb and destroy all those who stand in the way of his being reunited with its occupant. He has a mute, compulsive single-mindedness of purpose that has served to make him an iconic monster and which has been adopted by other, more modern monsters too, most effectively in the slasher film of the 1970s and 1980s.

Jason Vorhees from the *Friday the* 13th series and Michael Myers from the *Halloween* series, like the bandaged Mummy first popularized in *The Mummy's Hand* (1940), have black empty eyes and masked faces. There is no way in. They have little personality, charisma or pathos and like the Mummy they are relentless and deaf to all pleas of mercy. It is their inaccessibility that makes them so frightening because, as Bruce Kawin astutely suggests, 'what one can talk with, one can generally deal with' (1984: 8). Just like the Mummy of *The Mummy's Tomb* (Harold Young, USA, 1942) and *The Mummy's Ghost* (1944), Jason and Michael carry out their brutal murders in small-town America and have a flashback story that defines their actions in the present.[85] The slew of zombie films that followed *Night of the Living Dead* (George A. Romero, USA, 1968) testifies to the appeal of the charisma and pathos-free monster who cannot be reasoned with or talked to, to the extent that the Mummy has had to subsequently somewhat reinvent itself to distinguish itself from all of these silent and relentless monsters it preceded on screen by decades. The bandaged Mummy has increasingly diversified, effectively transforming in Universal's big budget reimaginings into a warlock in *The Mummy* (1999) and a witch in *The Mummy* (2017), returning the Mummy full circle to the sorcerer that Universal first offered in *The Mummy* (1932).

Studies of impenetrable monsters like Michael Myers and Jason Vorhees, perhaps because they are difficult to identify with and can thus prove 'metaphor resistant', have tended to concentrate upon how audiences respond to them as opposed to what they represent as 'meaning machines'. Questions that have been asked are the following: Do male audience members identify with the monster in misogynistic pleasure in slasher films, or with the female victim in cross-gender identification? Is there female identification with the 'final girl' as an active female hero?[86] Why and to whom monsters appeal can therefore be just as difficult to pin down as what monsters mean.

A number of critics have argued that monsters are engaging because they address issues that are, as Walter Evans states, 'uniquely tailored to the psyches of troubled adolescents' (1975: 354). James B. Twitchell argues that they reflect the complicated rite of passage from onanism to reproductive sexuality, the vampire for example, having 'everything any adolescent could want (money, all-night parties, uncomplicated sex)' (1985: 89). S. S. Prawer similarly points out that there is 'a good deal of analogy between the fate of such monsters and the adolescent experience: an appearance felt to be awkward and ungainly, the sprouting of hair in unaccustomed places, conflicts with father/creators, experiments with bodies in secluded spots.' Yet he also points out that they have an appeal to adults too, drawing attention to Whale's *Frankenstein* that was 'made without thought of a teenage market' (1980: 247). Les Daniels warns against forgetting that 'these presumably frightening figures are regarded with considerable affection by children' as well, Dracula and Frankenstein being used to sell breakfast cereals like *Count Chocula* and *Frankenberry* through making the products 'more attractive to prepubescent palates' (1977: 257). As one can equally argue that monsters appeal to children, to teenagers and to adults, the conclusion to be drawn is that the same monsters speak to different groups in different ways depending upon how they are reworked and reinterpreted by filmmakers, critics and audiences. As a result, finding any reason for their appeal in general, or specific meaning, even to specific groups, is hugely challenging.

If, as has been claimed with other monsters, the Mummy actually speaks of something other than itself, despite its muteness, then the questions arise as to what it has to say and to whom it is speaking? The answer incontestably depends. It depends upon the particular representation of the Mummy being offered in the cinema, or on television, or online, or in a theme park ride[87] or in a video game and its moment of production, its moment of reception and the cultural and social contexts of these moments of encounter. It depends upon the particular knowledge of the viewer and who that viewer is in terms of age, race and gender. It depends upon whether one believes 'readers and viewers are able to "negotiate their own meanings" or whether there are "preferred readings" or "limits to interpretation"' (Barker and Sabin 1995: 214). As Barbara Klinger summarizes 'the text, "in practice", is an intersection at which multiple and extratextual practices of signification circulate' (1984: 44). Some texts gain mainstream recognition, cult appeal, shock effect, camp charm and/or cultural value. Figures in these texts, as Terry Eagleton argues, can transcend 'the originating textual conditions of their production', and become 'public mythologies, co-ordinates of a mighty moral debate' (cited in Bennett and Woollacott 1987: 277).

The Mummy, like any monster, does not have a meaning that is unchangingly rigid. 'Public mythologies' pertaining to the Mummy have existed in popular culture for centuries and transcend its long-held status as a pale reflection of greater monsters. As well as looking at the many qualities the Mummy shares with other monsters such as its homicidal tendencies, unnatural sexual desire, obsessive personality and ability to live beyond the grave, this book will also focus on what makes the Mummy distinct. It will survey the American and British cinema in which it has especially thrived and discuss that which has become particularly apposite to Mummy narratives by also exploring its pre-cinematic history and how this informed its on-screen manifestations. The main period focused upon is 1899–1959, primarily because this is when the majority of tropes were established (and to provide limits to avoid producing an encyclopaedia of Mummy movies rather than an exploration of the Mummy's growth and development in the movies). The Mummy before and after this period is still considered for completeness and to provide an overall picture, but in less detail.

The book consists of four parts that examine the development of the Mummy over the course of its history and that of the cinema, exploring the various and changing perceptions of the Mummy that have informed its depictions on the big screen. First, Chapter 1 contemplates what constitutes a Mummy film and discusses how the Mummy genre has been informed by Western attitudes towards the East. Chapter 2 then chronicles the Mummy's pre-cinema history and the centuries-held view of the Mummy as a lifeless object, one to be used, displayed and even consumed by the West. Chapter 3 traces how this conception of the Mummy as lifeless translated into early-nineteenth-century literature, with writers over the course of the century then developing and transforming the Mummy to such an extent that by its end it had become primarily a romantic figure. Chapter 4 illustrates how this romantic Mummy featured prominently in the early years of cinema in both romances and comedies until being profoundly redefined as tragic and horrific following the discovery of Tutankhamun. Chapter 5 considers this reconceptualized Mummy in *The Mummy* (1932), which although new in some respects remained heavily indebted to pre-existing narratives of romance from silent cinema and Mummy literature. Chapter 6 discusses Universal's 1940s Mummy as a marked departure from *The Mummy* (1932) and explores just how influential and innovative this cycle of four films actually was, despite its reputation for being repetitive, derivative and 'puerile' (Vieira 2003: 97). Chapter 7 focuses on the British studio Hammer Film Productions' *The Mummy* (1959), which refashioned the narratives established in Universal's Mummy movies into a complex tragedy that explored conflicts between cultures, beliefs and races with great sophistication. Finally, Chapter 8 brings the Mummy up to date with a brief summary of the last sixty years of Mummy film production including Hammer's and Universal's consequent Mummy movies. This over half-century of cinema certainly requires more in-depth analysis than given in this final chapter, but there have simply been too many Mummies from too many places in too many forms to be able to examine them all. Brevity has thus proven unavoidable in regard to more recent significant movies in order to accommodate the discussion of the Mummy's origins, evolution and transformation into one of cinema's towering figures of horror within the space afforded between the covers of this book.

Notes

1. The year 1971 marked 'the first time in screen history' that the Mummy fought another classical monster in *Los Monstruos del Terror* (*The Monsters of Terror*, Tulio Demicheli and Hugo Fregonese, Italy/Germany/Spain) (Senn and Johnson 1992: 419).
2. *Las Aventuras de Tadeo Jones* (*Tad, the Lost Explorer*, Enrique Gato, Spain, 2012).
3. *Ancient Evil: Scream of the Mummy* (David DeCoteau, USA, 1999), *American Mummy* (Charles Pinion, USA, 2014).
4. *Curse of the Faceless Man* (Edward L. Cahn, USA, 1958).
5. *The Eternal* (Michael Almereyda, Ireland/USA, 1998).
6. *Vudú Sangriento* (*Voodoo Black Exorcist*, Manuel Caño, Spain, 1973).
7. *The Mummy: Tomb of the Dragon Emperor* (Rob Cohen, USA, 2008).
8. *O Segredo da Múmia* (*The Secret of the Mummy*, Ivan Cardoso, Brazil, 1982).
9. *Mumiens Halsbånd* (*The Mummy's Necklace/The Fatal Necklace*, Robert Dinesen, Denmark, Nordisk, 1916).
10. *Haram Alek* (*Ismail Yassin Meets Frankenstein*, Issa Karama, Egypt, 1953), *Al-Mummia* (*The Night of Counting the Years* a.k.a. *The Mummy*, Shadi Abdel Salam, Egypt, 1969).

11. *Le Miracle du Brahmane* (*The Brahmin's Miracle*, Segundo de Chomón, France, Pathé, 1908), *La Momie du Roi* (*The Mummy of the King Ramses*, Gérard Bourgeois, France, Lux, 1909), *Le Roman de la Momie* (*The Romance of the Mummy*, Albert Capellani, France, Pathé, 1911), *Il Était une Fois le Diable* (*Devil Story*, Bernard Launois, France, 1985), *Les Aventures Extraordinaires d'Adèle Blanc-Sec* (*The Extraordinary Adventures of Adèle Blanc-Sec*, Luc Besson, France, 2010).
12. *Augen der Mumie Ma, Die* (a.k.a. *Die Mumie Ma, The Eyes of the Mummy Ma*, a.k.a. *The Eyes of the Mummy*, Ernst Lubitsch, Germany, PAGU, 1918).
13. *A Múmia Közbeszól* (*The Mummy Interrupts*, Oláh Gábor, Hungary, 1967).
14. *The Mummy Theme Park* (Alvaro Passeri, Italy, 2000).
15. *Yami Ni Hikaru Me* (*Fear of The Mummy*, Masakura Tamura, Japan, 1958).
16. *La Momia Azteca* (*The Aztec Mummy*, Rafael Lopez, Mexico, 1957), *La Maldición de la Momia Azteca* (*The Curse of the Aztec Mummy*, Rafael Portillo, Mexico, 1957), *El Castillo de los Monstruos* (*The Castle of the Monsters*, Julián Soler, Mexico, 1957), *La Momia Contra el Robot Humano* (*The Robot vs. the Aztec Mummy*, Rafael Portillo, Mexico, 1957), *Muertos de Risa* (Adolfo Fernández Bustamante, Mexico, 1957), *La Cabeza Viviente* (*The Living Head*, Chano Urueta, Mexico, 1959), *La Casa del Terror* (*House of Terror*, Gilberto Martínez Solares, Mexico, 1960), *Las Luchadoras Contra la Momia* (*Rock 'n' Roll Wrestling Women vs. the Aztec Mummy/Wrestling Women vs. the Aztec Mummy*, René Cardona, Mexico, 1964), *Santo y Blue Demon vs. los Monstruos* (*Santo and Blue Demon vs. the Monsters*, Gilberto Martínez Solares, Mexico, 1968), *Santo en la Vengenza de la Momia* (*Santo and the Vengeance of the Mummy*, René Cardona, Mexico, 1971), *Las Momias de Guanajuato* (*The Mummies of Guanajuato*, Federico Curiel, Mexico, 1972), *El Robo de las Momias de Guanajuato* (*Robbery of the Mummies of Guanajuato*, Tito Novaro, Mexico, 1972), *Capulina Contra las Momias* (*Capulina Against the Mummies*, Alfredo Zacharlas, Mexico, 1972), *Chabelo y Pepito Contra los Monstruos* (*Chabelo and Pepito vs. the Monsters*, José Estrada, Mexico, 1973), *Capulina Contra los Monstruos* (*Capulina vs. the Monsters*, Miguel Morayta, Mexico, 1974), *Las Momias de San Ángel* (*The Mummies of San Ángel*, Arturo Martínez, Mexico, 1975), *El Castillo de las Momias de Guanajuato* (*The Castle of the Mummies of Guanajuato*, Tito Novaro, Mexico, 1976), *La Mansion de las Siete Momias* (*The Mansion of the Seven Mummies*, Rafael Lanuza, Mexico, 1977).
17. *La Venganza de la Momia* (*The Mummy's Revenge*, Carlos Aured, Spain, 1973), *La Momia Nacional* (*The National Mummy*, José Ramón Larraz, Spain, 1981), *Escarabajos Asesinos* (*Scarab*, Steven-Charles Jaffe, Spain, 1982).
18. *Den Levande Mumien* (*The Living Mummy*, Fritz Magnussen, Sweden, Svenska Biografteatern, 1917).
19. *Buffy the Vampire Slayer: Inca Mummy Girl* (Ellen S. Pressman, USA, 1997).
20. *The Nightmare before Christmas* (Henry Selick, USA, 1993).
21. *Fade to Black* (Vernon Zimmerman, USA, 1980).
22. *Endeavour: Cartouche* (Andy Wilson, UK, 2018).
23. *Mad Monster Party* (Jules Bass, USA, 1967).

24. *Kiss Meets the Phantom of the Park* (Gordon Hessler, USA, 1978), *Doctor Who: Pyramids of Mars* (Paddy Russell, UK, 1975).
25. *Come Rubammo la Bomba Atomica* (*How We Stole the Atomic Bomb,* Lucio Fulci, Italy, 1966).
26. *El Latigo Contra Las Momias Asesinas* (*The Whip vs. The Killer Mummies*, Ángel Rodríguez Vázquez, Mexico, 1980).
27. Tezomoc, the Mummy from *Las Luchadoras Contra la Momia* (1964) can transform into a vampire bat and tarantula.
28. *Ghostbusters: Mummy Dearest* (Ernie Schmidt, USA, 1986).
29. *The Creeps* (Charles Band, USA, 1997).
30. *Plastic Man: Plastic Mummy Meets Disco Mummy* (Rudy Larriva, USA, 1979).
31. *Frankenweenie* (Tim Burton, USA, 2012).
32. *Bunnicula: Mumkey Business* (Jessica Borutski, USA, 2016).
33. *Milton The Monster: Crumby Mummy* (Hal Seeger, USA, 1966).
34. *The Kung Fu Mummy* (Randy Morgan, USA, 2005).
35. *The Phoenix* (Douglas Hickox, USA, 1981), *Time Walker* (Tom Kennedy, USA, 1982), *Petrified* (Charles Band, USA, 2006).
36. *Centurions: The Mummy's Curse* (d.u., USA, 1986).
37. *Dawn of the Mummy* (Frank Agrama, Egypt/Italy/USA, 1981).
38. *The Mummy's Hand* (1940).
39. *Archie's Weird Mysteries: Curse of the Mummy* (Louis Gassin, USA, 1999).
40. *El Latigo Contra Las Momias Asesinas* (1980).
41. *Ultraman: Cry of the Mummy* (Hajime Tsuburaya, Japan, 1966).
42. *Frankenstein Sings* (a.k.a. *Monster Mash: The Movie*, Joel Cohen, Alec Sokolow, USA, 1994).
43. *Bubba-ho-tep* (Don Coscarelli, USA, 2002).
44. *The Magic Mummy* (John Foster, USA, 1933), *Kid Millions* (Roy Del Ruth, Willy Pogany, USA, 1934).
45. *Halloweentown* (Duwayne Dunham, USA, 1998).
46. *The Mummy Nanny* (Luc Vinciguerra, France/Germany, 2000).
47. *Belphégor: Le Fantôme du Louvre* (*Belphegor, Phantom of the Louvre*, Jean-Paul Salomé, France, 2001).
48. *Monster High* (Rudiger Poe, USA, 1989).
49. *Tales from the Crypt Presents: Bordello of Blood* (Gilbert Adler, USA, 1996).
50. *Tom and Jerry Tales: Tomb It May Concern* (Tim Maltby, USA, 2006).
51. *Amazing Stories: Mummy Daddy* (William Dear, USA, 1985).
52. *Mummies Alive!: Dog Bites Mummy* (Seth Kearsley, USA, 1997).
53. *Brady's Beasts: How to Impress a Girl with Your Mummy* (Gilles Deyriès, Canada/France, 2005).
54. *The Robonic Stooges: I Want My Mummy* (d.u., USA, 1977).
55. *The All-New Super Friends Hour: The Mummy of Nazca* (William Hanna, Joseph Barbera, USA, 1977).
56. *A Night of Magic* (Herbert Wynne, UK, 1944).
57. *Voyage to the Bottom of the Sea: The Mummy* (Harry Harris, USA, 1967).

58. *Doctor Who: Mummy on the Orient Express* (Paul Wilmshurst, UK, 2014).
59. An extensive list of the Mummy's appearances on TV can be found in Lupton (2015: 291–6). Some titles that could be added to it include *Topper: Topper's Egyptian Deal* (Leslie Goodwins, USA, 1955), *Alfred Hitchcock Presents: Museum Piece* (Paul Henreid, USA, 1961), *Ellery Queen: The Adventure of the Pharaoh's Curse* (Seymour Robbie, USA, 1975), *Kolchack the Night Stalker: The Demon and the Mummy* (Don McDougall, USA, 1975), *The Halloween That Almost Wasn't* (Bruce Bilson, USA, 1977), *Bigfoot and Wildboy: The Eye of the Mummy* (Leslie H. Martinson, USA, 1979), *She-Wolf of London: The Bog Man of Letchmoor Heath* (Roger Cheveley, UK/USA, 1990), *Tales from the Cryptkeeper: This Wraps It Up* (Laura Shepherd, Canada/USA, 1993), *Poltergeist the Legacy: Doppleganger* (Neil Fearnley, USA, 1996), *Police Academy the Series: Mummy Dearest* (Mark Jean, Canada/USA, 1997), *Early Edition: Mum's the Word* (John Patterson, USA, 1998), *Veritas: The Quest: Mummy Virus* (Vern Gillum, USA, 2003).
60. Early cartoons featuring Mummies included *Mummy o' Mine* a.k.a. *Egyptian Daze* (Bud Fisher, USA, 1926), *Egyptian Melodies* (Wilfred Jackson, USA, 1931), *Betty Boop's Museum* (Dave Fleischer, USA, 1932), *The Magic Mummy* (John Foster, USA, 1933), *Oswald the Lucky Rabbit: Wax Works* (Walter Lantz, Bill Nolan, USA, 1934) and *The Crystal Gazer* (Sid Marcus, USA, 1941). Mummies have made guest appearances in numerous episodes of cartoons starring other characters including *Superman: The Mummy Strikes* (Seymour Kneitel, USA, 1943), *The Flintstones: Alvin Brickrock Presents* (William Hanna, Joseph Barbera, USA, 1962), *The Jetsons: Haunted Halloween* (Ray Patterson, USA, 1962), *The Dick Tracy Show: Mummy's the Word* (Abe Levitow, USA, 1960), *The Adventures of Jonny Quest: The Curse of Anubis* (William Hanna, Joseph Barbera, USA, 1964), *Scooby Doo: Scooby Doo and a Mummy Too* (William Hanna, Joseph Barbera, USA, 1969), *Inch High Private Eye: The Mummy's Curse* (Charles A. Nichols, USA, 1973), *Goober and the Ghost Chasers: Mummy Knows Best* (Charles A. Nichols, USA, 1973), *Count Duckula: No Sax Please We're Egyptian* (Chris Randall, UK, 1987), *The Simpsons: Halloween Special V* (Jim Reardon, USA, 1994), *Batman: The Animated Series: Avatar* (Kevin Altieri, USA, 1994) and *Vampirina: Mummy Mayhem* (Marten Jonmark, USA, 2017). Mummies have starred in their own series too, such as *Mummies Alive!* (Seth Kearsley, Japan/USA, 1997–8), *The Mummy: The Animated Series* (Eddy Houchins, USA, 2001–2) and *Tutenstein* (Rob LaDuca et al., USA, 2003–7).
61. See Chapter 3.
62. Mummies have proven popular subjects for comics since the 1940s, with titles in that decade alone including *The Lost Mummy* in *Master Comics* (no. 2, 1940), *The Mummy Ray* in *Wow Comics* (no. 3, 1941), *The Mummies Awaken* in *Jungle Comics* (no. 29, 1942), *Menace of the Mummy* in *Fight Comics* (no. 22, 1942), *The Sphinx Speaks* in *Detective Comics* (no. 66, 1942), *Donald Duck and the Mummy's Ring* in *Uncle Scrooge and Donald Duck* (no. 1, 1943), *The Case of the Moaning Mummy* in *Star Spangled Comics* (no. 27, 1943), *The Mummy Case and the Wooden Man* in *All-Flash* (no. 19, 1945), *The Vanishing Mummy* in *Wonder Woman* (no. 23, 1947) and *The Riddle of the Chinese Mummy Case* in *Wonder Woman* (no. 37, 1949).
63. See Chapter 3.

64. Early video games featuring Mummies included *Oh Mummy* from Sinclair/Gem and *Invaders of the Mummy's Tomb* from Bandai, both from 1982. The popularity of the *Tomb Raider* series of games has played a part in helping redefine Mummy films along similar adventure narrative lines. Tim Schadia-Hall and Genny Morris, for instance, point out that *The Mummy* (1999) shared 'many similarities' with the *Tomb Raider* game *The Last Revelation*. (2003: 213).
65. Pop videos featuring Mummies include *Everybody (Backstreet's Back)* (Joseph Kahn, USA, 1997) by the Backstreet Boys and *Around the World* (Michel Gondry, France, 1997) by Daft Punk.
66. Records about Mummies include *The Mummy* by Bob McFadden and Dor Brunswick and *March of the Mummies* by The Ululating Mummies. For more see Carter Lupton (2003: 42). For an account of 'Mummy songs' that proved popular sheet music subjects between the turn of the twentieth century and the early 1920s, see Brier (2013: 157–60). For an account of music from operas to film scores inspired by Egypt and Mummies, see chapter 6 of Huckvale (2012: 188–217).
67. See Fischer (1991) and Luft (1963).
68. See Weaver (1988: 129–42).
69. See Dixon (1991), Fisher (1967), Hallenbeck (1994), Hutchings (2001), Jensen (1996: 155–232), Leggett (2002) and Ringel (1975, 1976).
70. See Ashley (1977), Atkins (1997: 112–23), Barbour et al. (1969), Barnes (1994), Beck (1975, 1978), Bojarski (1966), Bojarski and Beale (1974), Bradley (1996), Brosnan (1976), Brunas (1983), Buehrer (1993), Cushing (1988), Del Vecchio and Johnson (1992), Gifford (1973a), Harrington (1978), Jensen (1974), Jacobs (2011), LeBorg (1978), Lee (1977), Lindsay (1975), Miller (1995), Miller (2000), Parish and Pitts (1973), Pitts (1981), Pohle Jr. and Hart (1983), Rigby (2001), Roman (1964), Smith (1996), Underwood (1972), Watz (2001), Weaver (1999), Welsh (1975) and Winans (1977).
71. See Brunas et al. (1990), Dettman and Bedford (1976), Dick (1997), Fitzgerald (1977), Hirschhorn (2000), Mallory (2009), Mank (1986), Pendo (1975), Soister (1998) and Taves (1987).
72. See Brosnan (1978), Dudley (1993), Eyles et al. (1981), Fellner (1967), Harper (1998), Hearn and Barnes (1997), Hunter (1996), Hutchings (1993), Johnson and Del Vecchio (1996), Kinsey (2002), Maxford (1996b), McCarty (2002), McDonald (1992), Pirie (1980) and Sangster (2001).
73. See Boot (1996), Chibnall and Petley (2002), Coubro (1991), Pirie (1973), Rigby (2002) and Smith (2000).
74. See Fox (1976a, b, c, d, e), Senn (1992) and Sevastakis (1993).
75. See, for example, Ackerman (1959), Daugherty (1994), Haydock (1975), Humphreys (1995), Klemensen (1994), Mitchell (1994), Rigby (1994), Glut (1975) and Weaver and Gingold (1999).
76. See, for instance, Aylesworth (1972), Edelson (1973), Everson (1955), Gifford (1969), Glut (1978), Halliwell (1969), Stacy and Syvertsen (1983) and Steiger (1965a, b).
77. See Riley (1989, 2010) and Mank (2000).
78. See Feramisco (2003), which presents script extracts from scenes unfilmed or edited out from 1940s Mummy films.

79. See Sachs and Wall (1999) and Taylor and Roy (1979).
80. See Barron (1999), Davis (1987), Hardy (1993), Hogan (1981), Jones (1999), Lee (1973), Maxford (1996a), Naha (1975), Stanley (1981), Sullivan (1986) and Willis (1997).
81. Although few and far between, there have been some noteworthy academic studies of Mummy movies. Perhaps predictably with a monster called the 'Mummy', psychoanalysis has proven an especially popular method used to analyse it. See, for instance, Kawin (1984), Hutchings (1993), Pollock (2007) and Peirse (2013). Other works on the Mummy include Halliwell (1988: 185–235), which provides plot synopses and details of inconsistencies in plotting, locations and time periods in books and films featuring Mummies. Telotte (2003) discusses *The Mummy* (1932) in relation to science and modernism, Freeman (2009) identifies some of the recurrent themes in Mummy films and Day (2015) examines the Mummy's oft-times human controller.
82. See Brier (2013), Cardin (2015), Huckvale (2012) and Lupton (2003). Cowie and Johnson's (2002) broad history of the Mummy in popular culture offers accounts of some Mummy movies they considered to be good or poor. Day (2006) examines changing public attitudes towards the 'curse of the pharaohs' including surveys and field observations of museum visitors. It also includes insightful analyses of a number of Mummy films.
83. See, for example, Eyles (1978: 44).
84. The 1940s Mummy, due to being originally certified and released with few restrictions placed on viewing age and then reappearing on television in the 1950s, was especially accessible to children (see Day 2006: 95), perhaps helping to account for its association with childishness. For a nostalgic account of audience memories on seeing *The Mummy* (1932) upon its original release, see Kuhn (2002: 66).
85. Marra (2014) explains how *Psycho* (Alfred Hitchcock, USA, 1960) is frequently identified as a precursor to the slasher film, introducing 'horror tropes essential for its formulation' (27). He further argues that Hitchcock's 'slasher' film had notable and overlooked American-made precursors in 'films from the classical Hollywood era, such as *The Leopard Man* (Jacques Tourneur, 1943), *The Lodger* (John Brahm, 1944), *Bluebeard* (Edgar G. Ulmer, 1944), *The Spiral Staircase* (Robert Siodmak, 1945), and *Hangover Square* (John Brahm, 1945)' (28). However, these proto-slasher films were themselves prefigured by the similarly overlooked Mummy of the early 1940s. Further, so too was *Psycho* itself indebted to the Mummy. The writer of *Psycho*, Robert Bloch, was clearly infatuated with the figure, writing several Mummy stories including *The Secret of Sebek* (1937) and *The Eyes of the Mummy* (1938) before the mummified mother of Norman Bates made her climactic shock appearance in *Psycho*. Bloch proceeded thereafter to present yet another Mummy on-screen in the made-for-TV movie *The Cat Creature* (Curtis Harrington, USA, 1973).
86. For discussions of these questions see, for example, Clover (1992) and Cherry (2002, 2009).
87. The *Revenge of the Mummy: The Ride*, inspired by *The Mummy* (1999), is an indoor rollercoaster that opened in 2004 at Universal Studios Florida. An animatronic Imhotep and monitors playing videos starring Brendan Frasier accompany the ride. The attraction is also to be found, with subtle differences, at Universal Studios Hollywood and Universal Studios Singapore.

ました # Part 1 The Mummy in the West and in Western cinema

1 The creature's features: Moulding the Mummy and the Mummy movie

The Oriental Mummy as Western projection

In *The Mummy* (1932) the film's heroine, Helen, gazes out at the pyramids from the terrace of a dancehall in the company of an occult expert, Dr Muller. 'Is there', he asks, 'a view like this in all the world?' 'The real Egypt', she replies, adding 'Are we really in this dreadful modern Cairo?' In the cinema, 'the real Egypt' has routinely been viewed through such a Western perspective, its Muslim present as well as its post-pharaonic history looked past in favour of its half-knowable ancient gods, exotic rulers and grand monuments, being commonly understood, as Douglas Drake describes it, as 'one enormous mausoleum – a vast, sunbaked, sand-choked museum of the past' (1966: 163–4). Boris Karloff's Mummy in disguise, Ardath Bey, in *The Mummy* (1932) and the various Mummy-mastering high-priests who followed thereafter in films like *The Mummy's Hand* (1940) belong to this 'museum of the past'. They may appear to be finely dressed or fez-wearing Arabs, but they are fundamentally timeless Egyptians who still follow the ancient ways. They seem to be proof of Rider Haggard's eponymous hero's contention in *Smith and the Pharaohs* that 'the East may change its masters and its gods, but its customs never change, and if today Allah wore the feathers of Amen one wonders whether the worshippers would find the difference so very great' (1912 repr. Stephens 2001: 157). Mummy films acknowledge little difference between the ancient and the modern, with only scant attention given to the Muslim country that Egypt has been since AD 639. The archaeologists of Mummy films repeatedly see Egypt as incapable of looking after its own interests (and by extension, its treasures), with modern Arabs only suitable for either granting permits for Western experts or forming gangs to dig for tombs.

Such a view of the Westerner as active and dynamic and the Oriental as passive and incapable has a history that long predates the Mummy film. Following the translation into English of the *Alf Layla wa-Layki* (*The Arabian Nights*) in the eighteenth century, the Orient (the term for Europeans conjuring the Middle East rather than the Far East) became associated with Eastern stagnation and decline and was contrasted with the dynamism of the West: the Arab world newly envisaged as exotic and anaemic with 'moonlit seraglios, the baths, the genii, the magic rings and caskets, the mysterious, blushing princesses and imperious sultans' (Mack 1992: xiv). Like India, its intriguing mysticism and luxury, while greatly appealing to the Western imagination, was attributed with having held it back and making it decadent and weak.¹ Egypt was an impressive and alluring 'Other', but with clearly fading glamour. It was in need of rescuing from its incapable inheritors, the contemporary Egyptians: a view that served to ideologically justify its colonization.

Such an authoritarian imperialistic attitude was prevalent throughout the colonial period and took the form of 'a hierarchical view of the world in which the white races' occupied a permanent place on top 'with the colonized ranged in varying degrees of supposed inferiority' (Chowdhry 2000: 251). Edward Said suggests Egypt was situated near the bottom of such colonial racial ranking: 'Egypt was not just another colony: it was the vindication of Western imperialism; it was, until its annexation by England, an almost academic example of Oriental backwardness; it was to become the triumph of English knowledge and power' (1978: 35).

In spite of such 'backwardness', however, the Orient was still a threat in one important respect. The racial distinctions that justified colonialism had a major drawback in the form of mixed-race children being produced from relationships between European men acting as colonial enforcers and local women (Stoler 1989: 634–60). Such children blurred the distinction between races and so in the twentieth century colonial administrators allowed European women to move to colonial territories in order to stem the generation of mixed-race children. While ensuring that their husbands would not procreate with local women, they also prevented their children from being influenced by local customs and ideas thereby ensuring racial segregation.² As a result, women in the colonies became imperial enforcers too, but at a cost because at the same time they, like their husbands, became highly vulnerable themselves. While serving to prevent their spouses succumbing to temptation in dangerous foreign lands, they did, of course, face temptations of their own. Therefore while reducing the risk of miscegenation on the one hand, they increased it on the other.

The heroine of *The Mummy* (1932) finds herself in such a position of vulnerability and temptation while in Egypt, drawn to an Egyptian while involved with a Westerner, torn between desire and an unwillingness to betray her own sense of propriety. Egypt in this film is not just a land of remote and incomprehensible history but also a present-day source of overwhelming and mysterious exoticism and eroticism, making it a perfect site for her to succumb and transgress: such yielding to temptation proving an essential ingredient of classic horror of the 1930s. Time and again in horror films of this decade, as Rhona J. Berenstein explains, 'well-behaved women' transform after falling 'under the spell of hypnotic creatures … [and] … exhibit a remarkable degree of sexual allure. … Girl gets boy at the conclusion, but her best times, the moments that give her free rein to throw all caution to the wind, are spent with the monster' (1996a: 90).

Egypt was the perfect setting for Helen to fall foul of such sexual spells in *The Mummy* (1932) because the Orient personified that which was forbidden in the West; it was a place where there existed indescribable sexual possibilities, but also great peril. In 1924 E. M. Forster's novel *A Passage to India* related how the colonies could prove too much for the fragile psyches of Western women and Sir George

Fletcher MacMunn's account of half-understood Indian history further reveals other ascribed colonial beliefs of the time in his 1931 *The Romance of the Indian Frontiers*. 'Astounding indecency' was understood as commonplace, MacMunn wrote, with 'bestiality recorded: the mingling of humans and animals in intimate embrace' because 'the ancient religions did permit such terrible abominations' (cited in Harrison 1991: 179).

As MacMunn's account discloses, there was a dangerous, almost alien sexual world to be encountered when visiting the colonies. Alongside the maddening heat and unfamiliar traditions, the ancient gods still haunted such lands and the draw of suppressed urges or forbidden temptations could be attributed to their combined overpowering and seductive power. Helen in *The Mummy* (1932) is a woman who succumbs not only to the influence of the Mummy but also to the lure of Egypt itself and its ancient ways that still hold sway. Such self-serving projections onto an alien divinity or a personification of 'India' or 'Egypt' for those things that are felt to be repressed and outside the sphere of reason or civilized behaviour are today also bound up with the concept of 'the Other' that Robin Wood suggests lies at the thematic core of horror. For Wood, 'the Other' comprises all that our culture 'represses or oppresses' (1984: 171), horror narratives releasing and then ritually re-suppressing what society (as defined chiefly by a white, Western, patriarchal, heterosexual, capitalistic, political and ideological mainstream) denounces. If one accepts Wood's thesis, one can see the Mummy film as having a formidable formula, with the Orient serving as an effective site and its chief monster functioning as a potent medium for the release of the suppressed. Both Egypt and the Mummy offer heroines in particular unthought-of opportunities, tempting them with the promise of their 'best times' if they will only 'throw all caution to the wind', violate the accepted boundaries of social and sexual behaviour and give themselves over to losing themselves. That the Mummy genre fails, as Kim Newman contends, because 'a corpse which has been wrapped up for three thousand years lacks erotic possibilities' (1996: 225), overlooks the erotic possibilities afforded the heroine.

The risks and appeal of miscegenation, necrophilia, unfaithfulness and other forms of off-limits desire are sources of constant tension throughout the Mummy film. The Egyptian Mummy displays a consistent desire to break sexual boundaries by yearning for a hot-blooded Western woman or displaying passion for a departed lover whose blood has run cold. Male archaeologists, heroic adventurers and female heroines are all drawn to enigmatic corpses and/or racial 'Others', being variously hypnotized, transformed, romanced, coerced and/or transported away from their humdrum lives, sometimes through time to re-experience an ancient past in which they once lived, sometimes through space to Egypt where the monster stalks or seduces them.

Western fascination with the Orient and its sexual and spiritual associations lies at the heart of the Mummy genre and its central narratives of colonial incursion, monstrous retaliation and romance, mirroring the troubled politics and sexual politics that have accompanied imperial invasion, the imposition of new values and indigenous resistance. The centrality of the concept of reincarnation to the Mummy's story, alien to the ancient Egyptians but familiar through Britain's colonial relationship with India and the Hindu beliefs encountered there,[3] underscores the centrality of the colonial experience to the Mummy genre and how Egypt's actual past was brought into line with the Western imagination, making it another form of 'Western projection' (Said 1978: 95) that bears little relationship with 'the real Egypt' Helen so longs for at the beginning of The Mummy.

The Mummy genre: *Interest* and *Disinterest*

Just as nebulous as the Egypt of the Mummy film is the Mummy film itself. Although the Mummy projected onto the screen has been for the most part both Oriental and monstrous, there have also been occasions when it has been neither, such as in *Mercy, the Mummy Mumbled* (R. G. Phillips, USA, Ebony, 1918) in which it is both African American and a normal living man. A key question that arises when it comes to the Mummy film, therefore, is not only what a Mummy film 'means' but also what it constitutes. How does one define a Mummy film, or genre – or if not qualifying for that term – a subgenre in the cinema? It is a complicated question because, as Rick Altman explains, the notion of genre is a polyvalent concept. Genre acts as a blueprint, 'as a formula that precedes, programmes and patterns industry production', as a structure, 'as the formal framework on which individual films are founded', as a label, 'as the name of a category central to the decisions and communications of distributors and exhibitors', as well as a contract that establishes 'the viewing position required by each genre film of its audience' (2000: 14). One method a number of critics have applied to set about this 'polyvalent concept' has been to discuss genres through utilizing life-cycle terminology. As Altman (2000) points out, critics including Jane Feuer (1993: 88), John George Cawelti (1986: 200), Brian Taves (1993: 22) and Thomas Schatz (1981: 38) have all discussed how they develop and how they become articulate and self-conscious and then tired, predictable and worn-out. Once they have evolved beyond a certain point, they are seen to peter out, or be replaced, or transform into other cycles. Although horror is arguably a perennially popular genre in the cinema, specific monster cycles can be understood to have thrived and then died out, such as in the 1930s (primarily at Universal),[4] the 1940s (again mainly at Universal), the 1950s (with sci-fi aliens taking over at the expense of classic monsters) and the 1960s and 1970s (with the rise and fall of Hammer's reinterpretations of Universal's classic monsters).

Although monsters evidently rise and fall in popularity, to be resurrected anew, the death of the Mummy genre is one that appears to have been actively sought by a number of critics, being pronounced dead on the screen on a number of occasions. Take the 1980s, for example. In 1980 Arnold Madison stated that 'the enthusiasm for making films about mummies may have ended' (1980: 80) and in 1983 Tom Hutchinson and Roy Pickard claimed that 'the era of movies that dealt with ... the Mummy ... seems to have ended. The vaults of our interest appear to have been finally sealed against those ancient dead "born" from the ancient Egyptian need to embalm' (1983: 67). Similarly, Richard Davis claimed in 1987 that 'while the cult of the zombie still attracts film makers and audiences, the subject of Mummies seems to be currently out of favour' (1987: 134). Yet the Mummy was alive and kicking (or most commonly limping) in 1980s cinema, featuring in, among others, *The Awakening* (1980), *Fade to Black* (1980), *La Momia Nacional* (1981), *Dawn of the Mummy* (1981), *O Segredo da Múmia* (1982), *The Tomb* (Fred Olen Ray, USA, 1986), *Transylvania 6-5000* (Rudy De Luca, USA/Yugoslavia, 1985), *The Dungeonmaster* (Charles Band et al., USA, 1985), *Il Était une Fois le Diable* (1985), *The Monster Squad* (Fred Dekker, USA, 1987), *Waxwork* (Anthony Hickox, USA, 1988) and *Monster High* (1989).[5] As well as proving a popular on-screen subject in the 1980s, in the world of literature it proved to be the Mummy's most successful decade ever with Anne Rice's 1989 novel *The Mummy or Ramses the Damned* becoming 'the best selling mummy novel in history' (Cardin 2015: xxxi). Such a tendency to call time on the Mummy in spite of its continued resurrections in the cinema has continued, with Jasmine Day in 2015 proclaiming that 'Mummy films, *per se,* are dead' (222), only one year after Mummies starred in several horror movies including *American Mummy* (2014), *Day of the Mummy* (Johnny Tabor, USA/Venezuela, 2014), *Frankenstein vs. The Mummy* (Damien Leone, USA, 2014) and *The Mummy Resurrected* (Patrick McManus, USA, 2014).

It would seem that the Mummy movie is repeatedly declared extinct by critics such as Hutchinson, Pickard, Davis and Day because there no longer appear to be films around at the time that for them meet certain criteria to constitute the continued existence of a Mummy genre. This question of genre classification (just as with monster archetypes) is complex and one can easily go the other way to Hutchinson, Pickard and Davis and find a great number of films that one could add to a list of 1980s Mummy movies. The pilot movie for the television series *The Phoenix* (1981) and *Time Walker* (1982), for example, featured ancient aliens who awoke like Mummies from ancient tombs. *The Hunger* (Tony Scott, UK/USA, 1983) and *Vamp* (Richard Wenk, USA, 1986) have centuries-old Egyptian vampire queens, *Young Sherlock Holmes and the Pyramid of Fear* (Barry Levinson, UK/USA, 1985) and *Bloodsucking Pharaohs in Pittsburgh* (Dean Tschetter as Alan Smithey, USA, 1988) ancient Egyptian death cults, *Escarabajos Asesinos* (1982) and *Puppet Master* (David Schmoeller, USA, 1989) immortal Egyptian sorcerers and *Mannequin* (Michael Gottlich, USA, 1987) an ancient Egyptian woman awakening in modern times (a popular premise of the Mummy film in the silent era).

For James Naremore, when looking at genre it is the critical context that is crucial when classifying films, with the categorization of a set of films as generic depending upon contemporary and cultural notions of what that genre is (1995–6: 12–28). One can ask whether *The Fifth Element* (Luc Besson, France/USA, 1997) is a Mummy movie with its opening set in an Egyptian tomb and its bandaged heroine brought back to life. One can question the suitability of *Stargate* (Roland Emmerich, USA, 1994) with its immortal Egyptian alien who reawakens from a sarcophagus within a pyramid, or *X-Men Apocalypse* (Bryan Singer, USA, 2016) with its ancient god-like villain who emerges from his pyramid after ruling ancient Egypt with an ambition to make Cairo once more the centre of the Earth? One could argue that any of them could be a Mummy movie, depending upon the profile of the genre one wishes to build – whether they exhibit genre attributes being looked for or not, or as Andrew Tudor argues, the correct factors 'x, y or z' (1986: 6). For most critics, however, they would not be included. As Rick Altman explains, 'most genre critics prefer to deal with films that are clearly and ineluctably tied to the genre in question. No romantic mixed genres, no crossbreeds, no anomalies.' What is sought is 'a corpus that is incontrovertibly generic' (2000: 17). Thus, many of the films proposed as additions would not be readily accepted as Mummy films because they all appear to belong more to other genres: *The Fifth Element* and *Stargate*, for example, to the sci-fi or 'alien invader' film and *X-Men Apocalypse* to the superhero movie. They may contain certain ingredients for a Mummy movie, but these have been used along with many more ingredients that do not tend to feature to create something else. For many critics, it is the application of such recipes to films and the predominance of specific ingredients that places them within specific genres. Cawelti, for example, argues that the essence of genre criticism is the construction of a supertext, 'an abstract of the most significant characteristics or family resemblances among many particular texts, which can accordingly be analyzed, evaluated, and otherwise related to each other by virtue of their connection with the supertext' (1985: 56).

Today, elements of the Mummy's 'supertext' might include a bandaged Mummy from Egypt that returns to life and pursues vengeance on perceived desecraters of tombs and/or reunion with an ancient lover. However, so multifaceted is the monster and so varied have been the Mummies and Mummy narratives of the cinema that it makes the identification of main ingredients or the construction of a 'supertext' difficult to justify, as the factors 'x, y or z' that could be applied to a Mummy movie require a great many more letters of the alphabet. This is because the Mummy itself and the Mummy film are so diverse, changeable, long-lived and worldwide. Bandaged and unbandaged Mummies of various races, genders and ages have been targeted at audiences of different races, genders and ages for well over a century, with so many different narratives in so many languages that it would require a database or hefty encyclopaedia rather than a book to cover their multitude of forms and reimaginings on screen. Although it is Universal and Hammer Film Productions that from the 1930s onwards principally established and popularized the bandaged male Mummy that still remains the dominating image of the Mummy in popular culture (and is why this book focuses on these studio's interpretations of the Mummy so much), this Mummy has begun to feature less and less in the cinema in recent years. Whether this is part of the ebb and flow of the Mummy's story only time will tell. Whatever its form, though, or its story, an essential aspect of the Mummy is that any 'supertext' that has formed has been a very long time in the making because the Mummy, despite its third-rate reputation, is a figure that has fascinated and captured the imagination of more people for a longer period than any other screen monster. The beginnings of this interest in the Mummy will be the subject of Chapter 2.

Notes

1. See Said (1983) for an overview of how Egypt was perceived as a land ripe for plunder and exploitation by the West.
2. For more detailed discussion of the regulation of sexual boundaries in the colonies, see Hyams (1990) and Chaudhuri and Strobels (1992).
3. John J. Johnston argues that the conflation of ancient Egyptian and Hindu religions in the Mummy tale was largely a result of the popularity of H. Rider Haggard's novels, in which reincarnation commonly featured, accompanied by the fact that so many Britons worked or served in India (2013: 7).
4. There were significant contributions to the genre from other studios in the 1930s including Paramount with *Dr. Jekyll and Mr. Hyde* (Rouben Mamoulian, USA, 1932) and *Island of Lost Souls* (Erle C. Kenton, USA, 1933), MGM with *Freaks* (Tod Browning, USA, 1932) and Warner Bros. with *The Mystery of the Wax Museum* (Michael Curtiz, USA, 1933).
5. The Mummy was equally healthy a decade later in the 1990s, appearing in films such as *Tales From the Darkside: The Movie* (John Harrison, USA, 1990), *The Mummy Lives* (Gerry O'Hara, USA, 1993), the ultra-low budget *The Mummy's Dungeon* (G. W. Lawrence, USA, 1993), the short film *Wet and Dry* (John McKay, UK, 1996), *Under Wraps* (Greg Beeman, USA, 1997), *Bram Stoker's Legend of the Mummy* (Jeffrey Obrow, USA, 1997), *Talos the Mummy* (1998), *The All New Adventures of Laurel and Hardy – For Love or Mummy* (Larry Harmon, John Cherry, South Africa/USA, 1998) and *The Mummy* (1999). Other films might be added to the 1990s catalogue such as *Teenage Cat Girls in Heat* (Scott Perry, USA, 1991), which featured a 4000-year-old Egyptian sphinx that transformed cats into attractive women who killed men during sex. *Vampire in Brooklyn* (Wes Craven, USA, 1995) starred Eddie Murphy as a vampire who was the last of a race of ancient Egyptian vampires living in the Bermuda Triangle while *The Eternal* (1998) featured an American couple trapped in an Irish mansion with a 2000-year-old shape-shifting bog Mummy.

2 The Mutating Mummy: From ancient artefact to modern attraction

The Mummy, like many other monsters including the vampire and zombie, is living but also a corpse, the symbolic nature of the living dead being much discussed in relation to the horror film. Colin Odell and Michelle Le Blanc, for example, contend that such monsters fulfil a ritual function in helping us come to terms with death 'by offering a worse alternative to it' (2001: 10). R. H. W. Dillard argues that they serve an instructive function, teaching us to accept 'the natural order of things and to cope with and even prevail over the evil of life' (cited in Telotte 1987: 115).

Writers have employed the concept of a reanimated corpse for centuries to explore anxieties aroused by our mortality and human fragility. Lucretius, in *On the Nature of Things*, for instance, mused in 50 BCE on why becoming a corpse is so difficult to accept when it is so unavoidable:

> For when in life one pictures to oneself
> His body dead by beasts and vultures torn,
> He pities his state, dividing not himself
> Therefrom, removing not the self enough
> From the body flung far away, imagining
> Himself that body, and projecting there
> His own sense, as he stands beside it: hence
> He grieves that he is mortal born, nor marks
> That in true death there is no second self
> Alive and able to sorrow for self destroyed,
> Or stand lamenting that the self lies there
> Mangled or burning. (trans. 1977: 204)

Horror writers and filmmakers in the pursuit of their craft repeatedly imagine the dead body as infused with life, as Lucretius suggested we all imagine it at times, but in horror eternal life tends to come at a price. In the case of the Mummy the creature is the inverse of Jonathan Swift's immortals presented in 1726 in *Gulliver's Travels* (whose bodies survive but whose minds succumb to senility) because its everlasting life is dependent on an eternally dreadful and half-useless body.

The living dead body has become one of horror's main metanarratives and is generally brought into being through two means: by rational science or through irrational curse. Frankenstein's monster is the obvious result of the former, although there are many variations on the theme such as the zombie produced by man-made virus, with Dracula and the werewolf being prominent examples of the latter. The Mummy is in a peculiar position as a monster because it remains alive through a curse but owes its existence to the scientific process of embalming. It is neither one thing nor the other among the living dead, who are already neither one thing nor the other.

The Mummy's problematical status is further complicated by the fact that Mummies actually exist, albeit inertly. Noël Carroll argues that monsters in horror tend to be fictitious, defining a monster as 'any being not believed to exist according to reigning scientific notions' and being 'native to places outside of and/or unknown to the human world' (1990: 35). Unlike the Frankenstein monster, who was a literary creation, or the folklore origins of the vampire and the werewolf, the Mummy of the cinema is inspired by the existence of Mummies that were all once alive (and, according to their ancient beliefs, would still be in a place 'outside of the human world' if left undisturbed). For the ancient Egyptian the dead body was believed to be a body with a soul because the corpse and the person it was were eternally united. It was not an abject reminder of transience that offered a worse alternative to death, but instead represented life beyond death and literal imperishability. Peter Green explains how Egyptians 'were not so much possessed by death as obsessed with life, and determined to prolong it, or a semblance of it, in any way open to them. Hence, *inter alia,* the mummification of corpses: the body must be preserved as nearly as possible as it was before death' (1992: 270).

The sheer scale of Egyptian mummification is astounding, with some estimates suggesting that embalming was carried out for as long as twenty-eight centuries (Andrews 2002) with 'about five hundred million bodies' mummified up to the Roman period, 'more than in any other civilisation in antiquity' (Leca 1980: 149). Unfortunately, the fact that Egyptians viewed death and the corpse so uniquely and contrary to modern belief systems has ensured that their Mummies have not been left undisturbed. Mummies have been dug up and inspected for centuries in order better to understand why they underwent the procedure and how it was done. The ancient Egyptians had wanted their names to be remembered and their corpses concealed, but for so many who they were has been lost in time, while what they wished to remain hidden has been rediscovered and removed, unravelled or destroyed.

The methods of mummification were never recorded in writing because Egypt's embalmers practised their art in ritual secrecy, resulting in a mystique surrounding the practice ever since. The Greek historian Herodotus offers the oldest account we have, from the fifth century BCE, of how the Egyptians mummified each other and, in a focus on graphic detail, he tells how

> the most perfect process is as follows: as much as possible of the brain is extracted through the nostrils with an iron hook, and what the hook cannot reach is rinsed out with drugs; next the flank is laid open with a flint knife and the whole contents of the abdomen removed; the cavity is then thoroughly cleansed and washed out. (trans. 1988: 160–1)

It was not just the bizarre rituals of mummification that stimulated ancient interest, but also the commercial value of the riches buried with Mummies. The ancient

Egyptians, from the moment they died, have been victims of thieves, with sometimes the very embalmers who mummified them stealing amulets and jewellery intended for burial while bandaging the bodies. Their tombs were sites of grave-robbery in ancient times, but later, unexpectedly, the actual Mummies themselves became of commercial value too, with the increased interest in their marketability most probably giving rise to the word used to describe them.

Mummy medicine: An Egyptian prescription

It is likely that the word 'Mummy' comes from the Persian word 'mummia', meaning bitumen, because of the black glossy resin in which some of the embalmed bodies were coated. Mistakenly, it was believed that the Egyptians preserved their dead by soaking them with pitch or bitumen (Andrews 1998: 8) and so Mummies came to be prized as sources of bituminous materials that could be used in the production of medicines.[1] Prescribed by European physicians from around the eleventh century as an excellent panacea, effective against various ailments including vertigo, nausea and paralysis, powdered Mummy was drunk in a mixture of herbs and water or used in ointments. Catherine de Medici firmly believed in it, as did the haemophiliac Francis I of France who preferred his Mummy mixed with rhubarb (Andrews 2002). With such high-level demand, a roaring trade came into existence with large numbers of Mummies being shipped from Alexandria to Europe for medicinal use: the bodies finally reaching European pharmacists as body fragments or as a thick oily substance created as a residue from burning them. In fact, demand became so great that eventually 'unscrupulous merchants were baking up the flesh of dead lepers, beggars, or camels' to meet it (Sugg 2015: 226).[2]

The trade in Mummies for medicine was not halted en masse until the eighteenth century and not as a result of medical enlightenment but because the Turkish rulers of Egypt imposed a heavy tax on the exportation of Mummies. Even so, as recently as the turn of the millennium powdered Mummy could purportedly 'still be bought for forty dollars an ounce from a New York pharmacy catering to the needs of the occult trade' (Andrews 1998: 88). Mummies were therefore at the centre of widespread European commodification and cannibalism for centuries. Whereas today the zombie has become cinema and television's principal monstrous metaphor for rampant human consumerism and consumption (Newitz 2006), the Mummy was a genuine casualty of both of these for centuries.

The Mummy as memento: A collectable corpse

In addition to Mummies, Egypt conjures images of the great pharaohs Cheops and Rameses II, queens Nefertiti and Cleopatra, gods Isis and Osiris, biblical characters Moses and Aaron and many others more imagined than known. It has been since antiquity, as Edward Said describes, 'a place of romance, exotic beings, haunting memories and landscapes' (1978: 1). By the eighteenth century, Egypt had come to represent something more; it had become a focus point for the competing imperial ambitions of Britain and France. As a result Napoleon invaded Egypt in 1798 and, inspired by the glories attached to Alexander for his conquest of the same land, took along with his invasion force an army of over 150 scientists, artists and engineers to thoroughly archive the expedition and enshrine his accomplishments.

However, it proved to be Egypt, rather than Napoleon, whom the scholars immortalized. It was the achievements of her ancient peoples rather than reports of Napoleon's battles that whetted the European imagination and the expedition became directly responsible for the two key events that caused a remarkable explosion of interest in Egypt to occur in the early nineteenth century. The first of these was the publication of two books by the scholars who had accompanied Napoleon, Dominique Vivant Denon's *Travels in Lower and Upper Egypt* in 1802 and the massive *Description of Egypt* from the Institut d'Égypte, published in instalments between 1810 and 1829. As Rosalie David and Rick Archbold explain in regard to the former,

> The book caused a sensation in Europe, helping give birth to two inextricably linked phenomena: Egyptian tourism and Egyptology. ... Two hundred years after the publication of Denon's *Travels*, it is difficult to comprehend the depth of Europe's ignorance about ancient Egypt at the dawn of the Industrial Revolution. (2000: 43)

The second catalyst for the popularity of all things Egyptian and which further helped overcome Europe's ignorance about ancient Egypt was the decipherment of Egyptian hieroglyphics, the inscrutability of which had silenced the ancient civilization for centuries. In 1799 Napoleon's army had discovered the Rosetta Stone (as it has come to be called), which dated from 196 BCE. It contained the same text written in three scripts (Egyptian hieroglyphic, demotic and Greek), enabling Jean-Francois Champollion in 1822 to finally make the breakthrough in unlocking what ancient Egypt had committed to writing. This subsequently allowed scholars to gradually piece together, from inscriptions and papyri, ancient Egyptian history and culture.

These events opened the way for scientific Egyptology (or looting in its formative years, depending on one's perspective) and Egypt would prove a treasure trove and path to fame for men such as Giovanni Belzoni, Auguste Mariette, Gaston Maspero and Howard Carter. By the Victorian era,

> Egyptology was the height of European fashion. The Valley of the Kings was silent no longer; it echoed to the sound of mattock and spade. ... Thomas Cook had sent his first boatload of tourists down the Nile in 1840, and soon Luxor, once a sleepy east bank village standing on the site of ancient Thebes, had developed into a bustling holiday resort. ... All the tourists wanted the same thing; a visit to the west bank necropolis where they could marvel at the colourful tombs and shudder at the pleasingly gruesome Mummies. (Tyldesley 1999: 71–2)

Such popularity, as Jeffrey Richards suggests, partly arose from timing and the fact that Ancient Egypt catered to 'a taste for the exotic which represented an escape from the drabness and conformity of modern industrial society' (2008: 13). Part of this taste for the exotic in the nineteenth century was satisfied by Mummies, who were portable and thus became mementoes that embellished collections of exotica all over Europe, with demand proving so great that 'some enterprising Egyptians established clandestine Mummy factories where they transformed the not-so-long dead into antique looking Mummies for sale to gullible Europeans. Horrific tales of "ancient" Mummies being recognized as recently vanished Europeans were rife' (Tyldesley 1999: 72). As the Mummy's association with the gruesome and macabre was beginning to evolve, shrewd entrepreneurs latched onto growing public interest and found new ways of making money out of Mummies through public performance and paying customers.

The Mummy as public attraction: Exhumed, examined and exhibited

Egyptomania was given a great boost in England when the archaeologist/treasure hunter Giovanni Belzoni recreated the pharaoh's tomb of Seti I in 1821 with great fanfare at the Egyptian Hall in London. Before he opened the tomb to the public, 'he staged a clever invitation-only promotion event. With an audience of eminent doctors looking on, he unwrapped the Mummy of a young man' (David and Archbold 2000: 46). Greatly inspired, the London surgeon Thomas Joseph Pettigrew took it upon himself to offer his own public unrolling of a Mummy on 6 April 1833 at Charing Cross Hospital. Although he published his findings, his methods were far from subtle, with Pettigrew himself recording how 'it was a task of no little difficulty and required considerable force to separate the layers of bandages from the body; levers were absolutely necessary' (cited in Andrews 1998: 13). Following this,

> Mummy Pettigrew, as he came to be called, staged a series of unwrappings – for a while these became known as the 'mummy of the month' – before standing-room-only audiences. His public success launched such a Mummy craze that in mid-Victorian England, a country weekend for members of the English gentry might very well include among its enticements a Mummy unwrapping. (David and Archbold 2000: 47)

In the midst of this 'Mummy craze' Mummies were unwrapped in Britain virtually everywhere including 'medical and military museums, operating theatres, artists' studios, provincial playhouses, pharmacies and drawing rooms' (Moshenska 2014: 453). They were examined by anatomists, '"quack" doctors, magicians, and respectable Egyptologists, phrenologists and psychoanalysts alike' (Hamam 2006: 26). The Egyptologist George Robins Gliddon effectively went 'on tour' throughout the United States stripping Mummies of their bandages in front of large audiences well into the 1850s. Although ostensibly for scholarly advancement, these public unrollings on both sides of the Atlantic marked the first time that Mummies were used for public entertainment purposes. As would be the case in Mummy films, horror and suspense proved centrally important aspects to their appeal. As Burton R. Pollin envisions,

> There must have been a certain grim satisfaction in discovering the state of decomposition in which each would be found – whether a dust-filled skeleton or a shrivelled figurine or a good 'counterfeit presentment', with artificial eyeballs and gilded nails. Moreover, since artistically carved amulets might be found on the body itself, there was even the charm of a buried treasure at the end of the linen swathings, never shorter than thirty yards – a kind of gruesome strip-tease, may one say? (Pollin 1970: 61)

Alongside 'scientific' Mummy unrollings, in America Mummies began also featuring in carnivals, travelling shows and theatres. In Odell's *Annals of the New York Stage* there are mentions of Mummy exhibitions and 'unwrappings' dating from as early as 1823, with the American Museum publicizing the public dissection of a Mummy in 1832 and P. T. Barnum exhibiting a Mummy from Thebes in 1842 (Pollin 1970: 64).

This growing fascination with Egypt and its Mummies was, however, at great cost and the damage done by collectors and traders over the years following Napoleon's expedition became so great that, following calls from Champollion and others, Sa'id Pasha, Wāli of Egypt and Sudan, installed the French Egyptologist Auguste Mariette as Director of Egyptian Antiquities in 1858 to exert some degree of control over the numerous excavations occurring throughout Egypt. This did little to help the treatment of Mummies, however, as it 'legitimised the continued presence in Egypt of foreign scientists and explorers' (Hamam 2007: 33) who continued to view the dead of Egypt as fair game. In 1886, for example, Mariette's successor, Gaston Maspero, took just fifteen minutes to strip Rameses II of his wrappings.

Such treatment of the Egyptian dead was rendered partway defensible because similar practices were being reported as commonplace among the Egyptians themselves. There were tales of guides snapping off arms or legs from Mummies to use as torches for tourists (Andrews 2002), utilizing their bandages to thatch the roofs of their houses and the wood from their coffins to cook with (Stephens 2001: 2). The Egyptologist Wallis Budge, one-time Keeper of the Egyptian Collection at the British Museum, described how upon watching Mummies burning that they 'break with a sound like the cracking of chemical glass tubing, they burn very freely and give out great heat' (Andrews 1998: 8). Mark Twain stated, light-heartedly, that Mummies were used to fuel Egyptian trains, claiming while in Egypt that he had heard an engineer call out, 'Damn these plebeians, they don't burn worth a cent – pass out a king!' (1869: 632).

In the West mummified bodies continued to be objectified apace, to the degree that they were used on a mass scale as industrial material in products such as fish bait (Stephens 2001: 2) and 'Mummy brown' oil paint (Moshenska 2014: 455).

The linen wrappings from the shrouds and bandages from Mummies were, reportedly, exported to paper mills in Maine for pulp (Luckhurst 2012: 83), with animal Mummies faring little better as hundreds of tons of mummified cats were shipped to Liverpool and converted into fertilizer (Andrews 2002). Perceived as medicine, memento, curiosity, exhibition piece, public attraction or industrial product, for centuries the Mummy was not human but instead a commercial artefact.

However, as the world of ancient Egypt began to be slowly revealed through scholarly works and the decipherment of hieroglyphics in the nineteenth century, the figurative coming to life of the ancient Egyptians was responded to through their literal reawakening in the world of fiction. In accordance with prevailing attitudes, though, these tales initially dwelt little upon the Mummies themselves as human. Instead, as Chapter 3 will discuss, they were generally comic and allegorical tales that satirized contemporary fads and fashions, comparing a great but dead culture of the past with the wonders and shortcomings of the present.

Notes

1. Davis suggests that this belief (which he also shares) may be why 'the cinema has always depicted Mummies as having great strength. This idea is possibly based on the embalming method, using bitumen, which renders the body practically indestructible' (1987: 151).
2. See also Sugg (2011).

Part 2 The Mummy in literature, on stage and on the silent screen

3 On the page and stage: The Mummy movie's literary and theatrical influences

The Mummy's tome: A body of literature

There is no single source novel for the Mummy to compare with Bram Stoker's or Mary Shelley's famous books about vampirism and man-made monsters, or Robert Louis Stevenson's book about Dr. Jekyll and Mr. Hyde. This has proven detrimental to the Mummy's critical standing, as greater attention and respect have tended to be bestowed upon well-known creatures that come with literary credentials. For instance, Paul M. Jensen points out that upon its release *Frankenstein* (1932) was probably selected by *The New York Times* as one of the best films of the year, despite being a horror film, only 'because of the story's distinguished background. The connotation of "Literature" evoked by the name of Shelley apparently had power to soothe even a reviewer's savage breast' (Jensen 1974: 25–6).[1]

Like many other monsters, the Mummy owes a great debt for its widespread presence in popular culture to paraliterature, or as S. S. Prawer described it, the often disparaged 'undergrowth of mass publishing' (1980: 86), proving a popular presence in magazines like *Weird Tales* in the 1920s and 1930s and in EC comics in the 1950s. However, it is a figure that has also emerged from a long and distinguished literary tradition of its own and, unlike many other monsters, its more legitimate literary history has seldom been recognized in film or horror studies. One reason for this is most probably because important authors who wrote Mummy tales attained lasting fame with other creations (such as Bram Stoker with Dracula, Sir Arthur Conan Doyle with Sherlock Holmes and Sax Rohmer with Fu Manchu). Another is that the earliest literary incarnations of the Mummy in the early nineteenth century were talkative and affable figures that bore little relation to the monster it would later become. As the rediscovery of ancient Egypt progressively continued throughout the century, the Mummy developed through story after story into a romantic and sympathetic figure until ultimately becoming the frightening creature it has become associated with today. Thus, rather than making a grand entrance like Dracula or Frankenstein's Monster in a full-fledged monstrous form, the Mummy is a figure who was slowly and incrementally transformed in literature, and then cinema, from an ancient friend into an implacable foe.

The rediscovery of ancient Egypt: A pharaoh to remember

In the early nineteenth century, Egypt was a land with a much forgotten history whose legacy was glorious ruins and enigmatic figures, a view illustrated in Percy Bysshe Shelley's poem *Ozymandias* (1817):

> I met a traveller from an antique land
> Who said: Two vast and trunkless legs of stone
> Stand in the desert. Near them, on the sand,
> Half sunk, a shattered visage lies, whose frown,
> And wrinkled lip, and sneer of cold command,
> Tell that its sculptor well those passions read,
> Which yet survive, stamped on these lifeless things,
> The hand that mocked them, and the heart that fed,
> And on the pedestal these words appear:
> 'My name is Ozymandias, King of Kings:
> Look upon my works, ye Mighty, and despair!'
> Nothing beside remains. Round the decay
> Of that colossal wreck, boundless and bare
> The lone and level sands stretch far away.

The tragedy of vanished greatness and the wonders of ancient Egypt half-lost in sand and time was gradually replaced throughout the nineteenth century with the romance of its rediscovery, and accompanying excitement at how the contemporary world could benefit and learn from newfound knowledge. Following the translation of the Rosetta Stone and the publication of Dominique Vivant Denon's *Travels in Lower and Upper Egypt* and other popular accounts, ancient Egypt increasingly fired the imagination, with, for example, the American Egyptologist George Robins Gliddon's exhilaration palpable in his announcement that 'men of knowledge and arts must return to Egypt to learn the origin of Language and writing – of the calendar and solar motion' (1843: 34).

In the first half of the nineteenth century, as the West began unearthing lost wonders, it was simultaneously astounding itself with its own accomplishments, perhaps most notably in the field of electricity with all its potential uses and applications, which generated great excitement about the new age of modernism that could be ushered in. As Harold Beaver explains:

> Electro-chemistry dominated the early nineteenth century. Galvani and Watt, Volta and Ohm, Ampere, Bunsen, Morse its pioneers embedded their very names into the language … a new light was struck by the discovery of electricity, and, in every sense of the word, both playful and serious, both for good and for evil, it may be affirmed to have electrified the whole frame of natural philosophy. (1977: vii)

The rediscovery of Egyptian knowledge through applying Western knowledge, and how the two compared, became the central theme of the early Mummy tale. The prevailing scientific theories of the day suggested that 'the "divine spark" of life might be electrical or quasi-electrical in nature' (Joseph 1971: ix), implying that the actual raising of the dead could be just around the corner. Science was seemingly on the brink of doing what archaeology had figuratively done, and what Egyptian mummification had failed to do: make the dead live again. In literature, the Mummy first awakened in the fictional world as a figure of allegory, serving to comment on the possibilities of what modern archaeology and science could give to the world, from the unique point of view of a figure who had become the prime benefactor of both.

The Mummy's literary life: Electrifying tales!

The earliest record of a supernatural tale involving a Mummy was circa 1588 in Jean Bodin's *Colloquium of the Seven About Secrets of the Sublime* in which Mummies being transported by ship out of Egypt were reported to be causing storms at sea and so ended up being tossed into the sea (Day 2006: 45). In 1699, the Frenchman Louis Penicher in his book *Traité des Embaumements Selon les Anciens et les Modernes* (*Treatise on Embalming According to the Ancient and Modern Ways*) told a very similar tale that recounted the story of how a priest on a ship was haunted by the spirits of Mummies being transported below decks, until the Mummies, as in Bodin's account, were thrown overboard.

However, it would not be for another hundred years, when science ushered in the age of reason, that the Mummy tale would begin to take off. Rather than being phantoms, Mummies were reimagined as literal bodies of knowledge to be learnt from. These Mummies served to educate modern men of science, with Mary Shelley's *Frankenstein* rather than Bodin and Penicher's ghostly Mummies, proving to be the true forebear of the Mummies of early-nineteenth-century Mummy literature. In Mary Shelley's cautionary tale of a man who defies natural law and becomes haunted by his own scientific creation, the possibility of a Mummy actually coming back to life is envisaged for the very first time in the moment when the monster is first seen moving by its creator. Frankenstein exclaims: 'Oh! No mortal could support the horror of that countenance. A Mummy again endued with animation could not be so hideous as that wretch' (Shelley 1818 repr. 1993: 40). So striking, in fact, is this first description of unnatural revivification that ever since the correlation of the rebirth of the Monster with a Mummy reawakening has remained a mainstay of resurrection scenes in movie versions (Figure 3.1).

At the same time as the *Frankenstein* novel was growing in popularity, the twenty-year-old writer Jane Webb[2] penned a 'strange wild novel' (Loudon 1847: xxxi) of her own, similarly dealing with the moral dangers inherent in technological advancement, but with less monstrous consequences of reanimation in her *The Mummy! A Tale of the Twenty-Second Century*.[3] As well as being beholden to Shelley for the concept of a Mummy's reanimation, it also owes a debt to her 1819 short story, *Valerius*, which told of a Roman brought back to life after 1900 years to revisit his much-changed country and her second novel, *The Last Man* (1826), with its vision of a

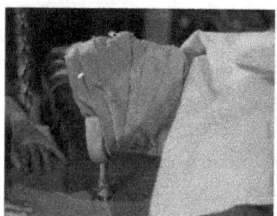

Fig. 3.1 *Frankenstein* (1931), *The Bride of Frankenstein* (1935) and *The Curse of Frankenstein* (1957).

much-changed future.[4] Contemporary events also had their influence on the novel's composition, not least that five years earlier Champollion had deciphered Egyptian writing, laying bare the country's ancient history. Also, just over a decade before Webb's novel, Giovanni Belzoni's exploration of the interior of Cheops' pyramid had been widely reported in the British press. The fact that the sarcophagus was found empty may have suggested to Webb the notion of a Cheops who could get up and walk, especially as it would be Cheops who would become the reawakened Mummy of her novel. Byron had certainly been inspired enough by his unexpected absence to write in *Don Juan* (1821):

> What are the hopes of man?
> Old Egypt's King Cheops erected the first Pyramid
> And largest, thinking it was just the thing
> To keep his memory whole and Mummy hid;
> But somebody or other rummaging,
> Burglariously broke his coffin's lid:
> Let not a monument give you or me hopes,
> Since not a pinch of dust remains of Cheops. (repr. 1973: 100)

Published in three volumes in 1827, Webb's novel was the first book-length Mummy story and 'made a great noise in its day for the daring flights of invention which it exhibited' (*London Literary Journal* 1851, cited in Rauch 1994: xiii). Set in the year 2126, it took an opposing view to Mary Shelley's dystopian future of *The Last Man* by attempting 'to predict the state of improvement to which' England 'might possibly arrive' as a result of scientific advancement (Loudon 1847: xxxiv). In her vision the weather is controlled, London houses are transported on rails to the country for holidays, England and Ireland are connected by tunnel, messages are sent via cannonball, steamboats sail at 60 miles per hour and air travel is speedy and commonplace in giant balloons. Although most of these are yet to be seen, she was predictive in that her women sometimes wear 'trowsers'.

The story itself tells of the exploits of a scholar, Edric, his companion, Dr Entwerfen, and their man-servant, Gregory, who all fly off to Egypt in order to reanimate the Mummy of Cheops with their electrical reanimation machine which contains a 'galvanic battery of fifty surgeon power ... enough to reanimate the dead'

(Loudon 1827: 15). However, once successfully reawakened, Cheops escapes to England where he becomes involved in a power struggle for the throne after being partly responsible for killing its ruler, Queen Claudia. Unexpectedly, he proves to be a benevolent Mummy who, in penance for deeds committed and deeply regretted in the ancient past, commits to actions that bring about the restoration of the country to one of virtue and power.

In stark contrast to Webb's lengthy three-volume novel, the next English language Mummy tale of note was a short story by Edgar Allan Poe entitled *Some Words with a Mummy*, which appeared in the *American Whig Review* in 1845. Similarly satirical, and far more humorous, it features a Mummy called Allamistakeo who, just like Cheops, comments upon the nature of modern progress and is reanimated through an experiment in galvanism.[5] Characteristically for Poe, his Mummy has spent his centuries buried alive after a cataleptic episode, although unusually for his stories relating to premature burial this one features a character who is not at all traumatized by the experience.[6] Instead, he appears simply happy to be alive. The story, if it can be described as such, revolves around a conversation between Allamistakeo and several intellectual figures of the day (including the Egyptologist George Robins Gliddon) regarding the differences between ancient and nineteenth-century knowledge.[7] In spite of the fact that Edward William Lane's popular and influential *An Account of the Manners and Customs of the Modern Egyptians* had recently been published in 1836, Poe makes no attempt to have his Mummy behave like any Egyptian, ancient or modern, as he is quickly transformed in the story into an ersatz Western gentleman:

> It was now observed that the Count (this was the title, it seems, of Allamistakeo) had a slight fit of shivering – no doubt from the cold. The doctor immediately repaired to his wardrobe, and soon returned with a black dress coat, made in Jennings' best manner, a pair of sky-blue plaid pantaloons with straps, a pink gingham *chemise,* a flapped vest of brocade, a white sack overcoat, a walking cane with a hook, a hat with no brim, patent-leather boots, straw-coloured kid gloves, an eye-glass, a pair of whiskers, and a waterfall cravat. (repr. Frayling 1992: 164)

Allamistakeo, a modern remnant of a great past, is dragged out of his current poor condition and effectively given a make-over by the Western academics.

Edward Said argues in *Orientalism* that in the colonial era Egyptians were conceived of as 'useful in the modern world only because the powerful and up-to-date empires' had 'effectively brought them out of the wretchedness of their decline and turned them into rehabilitated residents of productive colonies' (1978: 35). In Poe's story the Mummy is assimilated into the modern world, just as his country had been, at least sartorially. Despite Allamistakeo boasting that Egypt was superior in many areas such as glassmaking, 'the cutting of cameos' and 'carved work', the Mummy's previous incarnation as medicine ultimately undermines his position when the Westerners explain to him that the peak of civilization is now Ponnonner's

Lozenges. For all his boasting and Western dress, the Mummy falters in the face of progress, having become obsolete even at the most basic level as a form of remedy.

For both Webb and Poe, it was the contemporary world that occupied them rather than the ancient world the Mummy came from. Also significant, especially in the case of Poe (who tended to prefer his cataleptic victims female), it was men who were buried and revived in both stories. When the subject of Egyptian women was eventually undertaken in modern prose, the approach was very different. Whereas male Mummies were to be conversed with and learnt from (and in Webb's case could even instigate change for the better), female Mummies were to be fallen in love with.

Romance and the Mummy: Amorous archaeologists and comely corpses

Théophile Gautier, the poet and novelist of the French Romantic movement, added two further seminal Mummy tales to the canon in the mid-nineteenth century with the comic *Le Pied de Momie* (*The Mummy's Foot* or *Princess Hermonthis*) in 1840 and his far more solemn *Le Roman de la Momie* (*The Romance of the Mummy*) in 1857. In contrast to Webb and Poe, who had used the figure of the Mummy to explore scientific advancement and modernity, Gautier took as his central theme the moral quandaries involved in desecrating the Egyptian dead for the purposes of archaeology, progress and souvenir hunting. Both stories examine a connection that occurs across the centuries between a man of the present and a long-dead woman, for whom he comes to harbour feelings. In both stories he comes to learn to view her remains with respect and as belonging to a human being, rather than as organic residue from a distant and long forgotten past.

In *The Mummy's Foot*, a modern gentleman buys the mummified foot of an Egyptian princess as a paperweight from a merchant. The words of the merchant selling the foot immediately signify how attitudes towards body parts as souvenirs were beginning to change by the mid-nineteenth century:

> Old Pharaoh would certainly have been surprised had some one told him that the foot of his adored daughter would be used for a paper-weight after he had had a mountain of granite hollowed out as a receptacle for the triple coffin, painted and gilded – covered with hieroglyphics and beautiful paintings of the Judgment of Souls. (repr. Frayling 1992: 153)[8]

To underline her calamitous fate, Princess Hermonthis, to whom the foot belonged, visits his dreams and transports him back in time to ancient Egypt to reveal that she was once a living person who had a family just like him.[9]

Gautier's *The Romance of the Mummy* took the same sympathetic approach towards its Mummy, additionally introducing the theme of a tragic, unachievable love across the centuries that would eventually come to dominate the Mummy genre in both literature and cinema. Its story about the discovery of a tomb in the Valley of the Kings by Lord Evandale and his consequent life-long alienation from those around him because of his impossible love for the ancient queen discovered within proved hugely popular in its day and, in its melancholic delivery, prepared the way for a far more sombre story type to emerge: one in which Mummies would not simply engage in polite conversation when reawakened as in Poe, or comically request body parts returned as in *The Mummy's Foot*. It also proved to be a remarkably portentous story. The discovery of an intact tomb in the Valley of the Kings by Evandale and his colleague Dr Rumphius foreshadowed the discovery of the intact tomb of Tutankhamun by Lord Carnarvon and Howard Carter in the same place sixty-five years later. Christopher Frayling goes as far as to suggest that it is 'so uncannily like the real-life discovery of Tutankhamun's tomb ... that it goes some way towards explaining why Carter's finds were treated by the public as an exotic mix of fact and fantasy' (1992: 144).

The romantic Mummy stories inaugurated by Gautier, which, as Eleanor Dobson remarks, had a peculiar fairy-tale quality to them with their 'physically desirable and fundamentally passive' sleeping beauties (2017: 20), were followed in 1868 by Jane Austin's fundamentally different and far more frightening *After Three Thousand Years*, about a female Mummy's cursed necklace engraved with the warning 'the gods who give life also take it' (42). The necklace itself has 'golden scarabæi with diamond eyes and green enameled wings' (38) which, upon being worn, come to life and inject through their myriad 'thread-like legs' (44) lethal venom. As well as being notable for introducing terrifying flesh-attacking beetles (that would feature in later Mummy literature and films like *The Mummy* (1999)), its Mummy is also far more menacing than Gautier's fairy-tale Mummies, emphasized by the fact that this Mummy's beauty is only half retained, as its discoverer relates upon opening her sarcophagus:

> Within lay a slight, elegant figure, very dark in color, as mummies nearly always are, but retaining sufficient beauty of outline, both in face and form, to prove to my mind that a rare loveliness of the days gone by lay before me, neither preserved nor quite destroyed. (40)

Louisa May Alcott's *Lost in a Pyramid, or the Mummy's Curse* (1869) was published a year later and, as the title suggests, once more focused on a curse, this time connected to an ancient Egyptian sorceress and magical seeds that grow into deadly flowers. Although Mummies were not yet portrayed as coming back to life to avenge themselves on those who desecrated their remains, Austin and Alcott's tales reveal that they were at the very least becoming more sinister. Artefacts discovered in tombs, as well as leading to romantic encounters, were also beginning to be presented as tainted by curses that could lead to disaster.

Literature's monstrous Mummies: Dread, despair and Doyle

The Orient until the second half of the nineteenth century had largely proven a fruitful terrain for colonial conquest and achievement for the British, but from the Indian Mutiny of 1857 towards the end of the century various military setbacks began to point worryingly to a decline in British power. Just three years after the British Prime

Minister Benjamin Disraeli had sent troops into Egypt to protect British investment in the Suez Canal in 1882, General Charles Gordon had lost his life at Khartoum in the Sudan (then considered part of Egypt) during a massive Muslim revolt against British imperial rule. In the aftermath of such events, rather than being perceived as 'passive', with 'no capacity for violence' (Mercer and Julien 1988: 108), the inhabitants of the Orient became more forbidding, a change in perspective reflected in the literature of the period that simultaneously portrayed anxiety concerning Britain's own newfound sense of vulnerability.

Towards the end of the nineteenth century Stephen D. Arata argues that imperial decline and racial degeneration had become near national obsessions in Britain, evidenced in Bram Stoker's *Dracula* (1897) and his central vampire's collapsing of boundaries between Westerner and Easterner, 'between civilised and primitive, coloniser and colonised' (1990: 626). Darwinian theory added fuel to the fire by calling Britain's racial superiority into question. 'If humans could evolve,' Kathleen L. Spencer suggests 'it was thought that they could also devolve or degenerate, both as nations and individuals' (1992: 204). Concomitantly, the boundaries between civilized and primitive were being repeatedly breached in novels of the day such as Robert Louis Stevenson's *The Strange Case of Dr. Jekyll and Mr. Hyde* (1886), Oscar Wilde's *The Picture of Dorian Gray* (1891) and H. G. Wells's *The Island of Dr Moreau* (1896).

Richard Marsh's *The Beetle,* published the same year as *Dracula* and actually outselling it at the time (as well as receiving multiple reprints in the years immediately following its publication), depicted Egypt as every bit as capable as Transylvania of bringing a primitive threat to the civilized West. It told the tale of an ancient priest of the goddess Isis coming to London just as Dracula had, but blurring boundaries far more by being able to both change sex from a man into a woman and also transform into a giant flesh-eating scarab beetle.

As Marsh's novel exemplifies, the legacy of the ancient Egyptians had transformed over the course of the nineteenth century from one that bestowed valuable knowledge into one that offered secrets best left unearthed, being increasingly tainted as the years unfolded through its association 'with the mysterious and supernatural, the questionable and disreputable'. There emerged 'a persistent, dubious link of Egypt to magic' with, for example, 'the official publication of the Society of American Magicians ... named "The Sphinx"' (Lant 1997: 90).

This shift in popular understanding that the rediscovery of ancient Egypt served the supernatural as much as science is evident in two Mummy stories written by Arthur Conan Doyle towards the end of the century: *The Ring of Thoth* (1890) and *Lot No. 249* (1892).[10] In both Doyle uses the Mummy (just as Stoker would do with his Eastern vampire in *Dracula*) to portray the clandestine activities of an unnatural Oriental being in the heart of a Western city. Through portraying the West as susceptible to such incursions, Stephen D. Arata suggests such stories were an anxious counterpoint to gung-ho fictional narratives of the time, such as A. E. W. Mason's *The Four Feathers* (1901), which celebrated the ingenuity of Westerners being able to pass as Easterners in the service of Empire (1990: 638–9).

The first of Doyle's Mummy stories, *The Ring of Thoth*, is a tale close in structure to his Sherlock Holmes detective stories, yet is also romantic and sorrowful in a manner that harks back to Gautier. First published in *The Cornhill Magazine* in 1890, the plot follows the investigation of the narrator, Vansittart Smith, into the affairs of a museum attendant who is really Sosra, an ancient Egyptian priest who has lived throughout the centuries. This immortal Mummy, who has long since found life unbearable without his ancient lover, Atma, who died in ancient times, is determined to find an antidote to an elixir of life taken long ago.

Conan Doyle would later become an important figure in the press discussions surrounding the discovery of Tutankhamun in 1922, and he is clearly sympathetic towards his Mummy in this story. While evidently ancient and different from the modern Westerner, Sosra is never depicted as inhuman or merely a historical remnant. When Vansittart Smith looks at the Mummy and summons the courage to see beyond his fear and wonder of it, he recognizes that despite being from a world so far distant that it makes him almost alien, Sosra is still human enough to warrant compassion:

> 'Where have I seen such eyes?' said Vansittart Smith to himself. 'There is something saurian about them, something reptilian. There's the membrana nictitans of the snakes', he mused, bethinking himself of his zoological studies. 'It gives a shiny effect. But there was something more here. There was a sense of power, of wisdom – so I read them – and of weariness, utter weariness, and ineffable despair.' (repr. Frayling 1992: 185)

While 'passing' in Paris, Sosra is a disengaged, tragic figure who wishes harm to nobody but himself. He is never truly threatening, as the investigator initially feared, but is rather a doomed romantic who finally succeeds in joining his beloved in death.

The Mummy as a benign figure was to dramatically change two years later in *Lot No. 249* when for the very first time the Mummy itself became a truly frightening and monstrous figure.[11] In this story an Oxford student purchases a Mummy at an auction, reanimates it and sends it forth to attack all those he considers enemies. Although the auction number of the title conjures prior attitudes towards the Mummy as a harmless object or commodity to be bought and sold, the living, nameless, 'horrid, black, withered' (repr. Pronzini 1980b: 308) Mummy of *Lot No. 249* is a loathsome creature to be genuinely feared, as Doyle's description of it underlines:

> Smith stepped over to the table and looked down with a professional eye at the black and twisted form in front of him. The features, though horribly discolored, were perfect, and two little nutlike eyes still lurked in the depths of the black hollow sockets. The blotched skin was drawn tightly from bone to bone, and a tangled wrap of black, coarse hair fell over the ears. Two thin teeth, like those of a rat, overlay the shriveled lower-lip. In its crouching position, with bent joints and craned head, there was a suggestion of energy about the horrid thing which made Smith's gorge rise. (repr. Pronzini 1980b: 311)

Taken together, Doyle's stories laid the foundations for the Universal Mummy movies to come in the 1930s and 1940s. The twin themes of unwanted immortality and

Fig. 3.2 Boris Karloff as Imhotep in *The Mummy* (1932): Reminiscent of Sosra the Mummy.

the ambition to be reunited in death with an ancient lover in *The Ring of Thoth* have provided the essential elements for the plots of a great many Mummy movies and it certainly appears as a direct yet unaccredited source for *The Mummy* in 1932 (Figure 3.2).[12] Doyle's description of the Mummy is also remarkably similar to that devised by *The Mummy*'s make-up artist Jack Pierce for Boris Karloff's Mummy Imhotep:

> One could not fancy a drop of moisture upon that arid surface. From brow to chin … it was crosshatched by a million delicate wrinkles, which shot and interlaced as though nature in some Maori mood had tried how wild and intricate a pattern she could devise. (repr. Frayling 1992: 184)

The central premise of *Lot No. 249*, with its silent avenging Mummy in the thrall of another, revived through the use of leaves from a sacred plant, similarly appears to be an unaccredited source for Universal's Mummy movies of the early 1940s (whose Mummy Kharis is kept alive through a potion brewed from tana leaves). Its English countryside setting would also be utilized to striking effect by the British studio Hammer in its rendition of Kharis's story in *The Mummy* (1959).

The empire strikes back: Stoker's *Au Revoir* to the voyeur archaeologist

Bram Stoker was responsible for the next horrific Mummy text of lasting influence in his tale of the female Mummy, Tera, in *The Jewel of Seven Stars* (1903).[13] As in *Lot No. 249*, but in stark contrast to the earlier Mummy tales of Webb and Poe, the destructive potential of ancient knowledge is deeply explored. It also responds to a popular subgenre of Mummy tale that had followed Gautier's lead that featured female Mummies over whom men obsess, such as Edgar Lee's *Pharaoh's Daughter* (1889), Henrietta Everett's *Iras, a Mystery* (1896) and Clive Holland's *An Egyptian Coquette* (1898). Like the subjects of these stories Tera too is beautiful and perfectly preserved, as one of the observers of her corpse cannot help but lasciviously note:

> We all stood awed at the beauty of the figure which, save for the face cloth, now lay completely nude before us. Mr Trelawny bent over, and with hands that trembled slightly, raised this linen cloth which was of the same fineness as the robe. As he stood back and the whole glorious beauty of the Queen was revealed, I felt a rush of shame sweep over me. It was not right that we should be there, gazing with irreverent eyes on such unclad beauty: it was indecent; it was almost sacrilegious! And yet the white wonder of that beautiful form was something to dream of. ... The flesh was smooth and round, as in a living person; and the skin was as smooth as satin. (1903 repr. 1996: 203–4)

However, Stoker's Tera proves a far from passive focal point of male desire and the ancient sorceress and queen launches a spiritual attack on the desecrators of her tomb,[14] reacting violently to the common practice of Western men stripping Egyptian female Mummies that had been occurring for decades in the name of science: an act that Bradley Deane has aptly described as a form of 'imperial striptease' (2008: 381). Once awakened she also seeks possession of a modern woman's body, instigating a battle for control within between ancient and modern selves that would become an important feature of many later Mummy films including *The Mummy* (1932), *The Mummy's Ghost* (1944), *The Mummy's Curse* (1944), *Mystery and Imagination: Curse of the Mummy* (Guy Verney, UK, 1970), *Blood from the Mummy's Tomb* (1971), *The Awakening* (1980) and *The Mummy Returns* (Stephen Sommers, USA, 2001).

The Jewel of Seven Stars initial publication ended with all the major characters, except for the narrator, meeting their deaths in what Bradley Deane describes as maybe 'the most stunningly abrupt and inconclusive ending in Victorian Fiction' (2008: 404). Rather than the Mummy being defeated by men or accepting the superiority of the accomplishments of the present as in previous tales, the 'bloodless massacre' that ends the novel instead, as Meilee D. Bridges suggests, 'disturbingly presumes that the present is powerless to control or even co-exist with the past that it has resurrected' (2008: 141). When the book was reprinted in 1912, the year of Stoker's death, the publishers believed it warranted a happier ending. It received one, which, in stark contrast to the hopelessness and horror that concluded the original version, ended this time with the marriage of the hero and heroine. From extreme pessimism to blind optimism, critics continue to disagree as to whether the simplistic and anodyne new ending, so in contrast to the original, could really be Stoker's own.[15] Death in the first edition, as William Hughes suggests, 'is horrible because it is not romanticised' (2000: 36), whereas in the second edition romance wins the day.

The two endings of *The Jewel of Seven Stars* illustrate the two directions the Mummy tale had taken by the end of the nineteenth century. In some they offered readers striking accounts of otherworldly love and in others they told of ancient sorcery and terrible vengeance. Of the former, H. Rider Haggard was perhaps the most prominent, writing numerous Egyptian romances including *Cleopatra* (1889), *The Yellow Girl* (1908), *Morning Star* (1910), *Smith and the Pharaohs* (1912), *The Ancient Allan* (1920) and *Queen of the Dawn* (1923). Sax Rohmer,[16] the author best remembered today for his thirteen Dr Fu Manchu novels, became a preeminent writer of the latter with his tales of a threatening Egypt in stories such as *The Sins of Séverac Bablon* (1914), *The Brood of the Witch Queen* (1918), *Tales of Secret Egypt* (1918), *The Green Eyes of Bast* (1920) and *She Who Sleeps* (1928). Ambrose Pratt's *The Living Mummy* (1910) is a notable addition for offering a menacing Mummy in the thrall of another with a penchant for strangling victims (as Kharis the Mummy would do in the 1940s) and Agatha Christie added a title too, *The Adventure of the Egyptian Tomb* (1925), in which Hercule Poirot became embroiled in the case of a Mummy's curse supposedly claiming the lives of several archaeologists. Thus, while no one particular story or novel is identifiable as being the most influential or definitive urtext, it is also clear that the Mummy has its seminal literary texts and key authors.[17] Together, they imaginatively and incrementally created and refined many of the key characteristics and elements of the Mummy's story that have survived to this day in both literature and on screen.

Playing dead: The Mummy in the theatre

As well as literature, the theatre had a significant impact on reinterpreting and transforming the nineteenth century's literary monsters into the forms that they would eventually take on screen, providing a crucial impetus for horror to flourish and develop as a genre throughout the period. Mary Shelley's *Frankenstein*, after being rejected by three publishers and selling less than five hundred copies, did not warrant a second edition until after the work had hit the theatres as a popular melodrama (*The Frankenstein Project* 2002). So quickly did the popularity of the stage version grow that by 1823, while Richard Brinsley Peake was staging a dramatization at the English Opera House, Strand, 'there were two other versions of Mary's story playing in London, one at the Coburg, the other at the Royalty, as well as a trio of burlesque versions of *Frankenstein* at the Surrey, the Adelphi, and at Davis's Royal Amphitheatre' (Florescu 1977: 166).

As well as Frankenstein's Monster, the vampire was a popular stage presence too, well before Bram Stoker had even put pen to paper to compose *Dracula*. John Polidori's *The Vampyre* (1819) had inspired at least seven stage adaptations and a couple of operas (Skal 1996: 190) and as early as 'the mid-1820's it was possible to see a double bill of dramatic adaptations of *Frankenstein* and *The Vampire* at the English Opera House in London' (Donald 1989b: 241). The stage plays popularized the literary stories, transforming the monsters into flesh and blood characters in the process and provided many of the elements used in later films. Frankenstein went from an idealistic scientist to a madman and his monster to a grunting mute monstrosity in Peake's dramatization and it was this play that provided the lab full of generators (as opposed to the novel's candle and surgeon's table) and Frankenstein's evil assistant (Fritz in the play). Similarly, it was the stage that changed Dracula from an aged ugly fiend (complete with black moustache and pointed beard) into a clean-shaven seductive paramour, with Edmund Blake donning the evening wear and opera cape so associated with the figure in playwright-producer Hamilton Deane's 1924 production first staged in Derby, England (Haworth-Maden 1992: 19).

These plays greatly influenced the Universal horror films of the 1930s that were not, as is often assumed, directly based on the canonical literature of the nineteenth century. The structure of Stoker's *Dracula* was very complex, incorporating different viewpoints and narrative devices. Universal therefore based their film of *Dracula* (1931) on John L. Balderston's American theatrical adaptation of Deane's English stage version,[18] a source that had already ironed out many of the problems of adapting the novel for performance. A similar approach was taken with *Frankenstein* (1931), for which Peggy Whebling's stage play *Frankenstein: An Adventure in the Macabre* was adapted because, as Radu Florescu points out, 'such literary devices as the concentric tales or multiple flashbacks in Mary Shelley's novel' would otherwise have proven 'extremely difficult to adapt to the film medium' (1977: 189).

Given the huge popularity of monsters on the stage, it was to be expected that only six years after the first published Mummy story by Webb (and seven years before the second) a stage play featuring the figure appeared. *The Mummy; or, The Liquor of Life!* by William Bayle Bernard was a farce produced in London in 1833 that went on to become a hit on the American stage.[19] Burton R. Pollin explains how 'almost at once the play became a standby, sure to attract audiences' (1970: 64) and a version of it was still running in London over twenty years later in 1854 at the Olympic in London (Mullin 1987: 255). Pollin describes the original plot as follows:

> Toby Tramp, an impecunious actor in the provinces, meets his old London friend, Captain Canter. The latter, in pursuit of Fanny Mandragon, whose father conducts a private museum in the town, is in need of a Mummy to occupy the empty sarcophagus in the display and wishes Toby to impersonate one so that he can ingratiate himself with the father and court the girl. For a sum Toby agrees. (1970: 64)

Bernard's play was remarkably similar to a play entitled *Three Hours After Marriage* that had premiered over a hundred years earlier at Drury Lane in London in 1717. It was the product of three authors, John Gay, Alexander Pope and John Arbuthnot, and was an extraordinarily early prototype of what would become a recurring silent screen storyline of a male character dressing up as a Mummy in order to romance a woman under the nose of a naïve academic (although in this case it was far more risqué than what would follow later in that it was his wife he wished to seduce).

Whether Bernard's play was influenced by this or not, in a spirit of free adaptation that anticipated the practice of Mummy film production in early cinema when ideas would be liberally borrowed from each other, his own play was soon 'adapted' by Thomas Dartmouth Rice for the American stage into the *Virginia Mummy*, 'a negro farce' that premiered in Mobile, Alabama, on 22 April 1835. In this version, the basic plot is essentially the same but given a new racial dimension:

> A scientist, Dr. Galen, bans a young soldier, Captain Rifle, from courting the scientist's ward. When Rifle sees Galen's newspaper advertisement for a mummy, the soldier hires a voluble black hotel waiter, Ginger Blue, to hold his tongue and dress as the decoy. Rifle masquerades as the mummy's Egyptian owner; in that way they penetrate the household so that Rifle can court young Lucy, the ward. (Lhamon, Jr. 2003: 47)

In Rice's version the professor intends to attempt to bring the Mummy back to life, but 'his plan fails: instead of a dead Egyptian mummy, through a convoluted series of events he winds up with the "Virginny Mummy" – the blackface character "sassy Ginger Blue", packed in a box but very much alive' (Cohen 2012: 85).

Cultural attitudes towards African Americans manifestly became intertwined with contemporary ones concerning those of North African Egyptian Mummies in this version of the play. In the early part of the nineteenth century in America Mummy exhibits were proving just as popular as they had in England and formed 'an especially visible part of early American exhibition culture [often] placed alongside other motionless curiosities such as dinosaur bones and Native American artefacts' (Trafton 2004: 124). American 'unwindings of mummies in public by men of science wielding scalpels on stage for large audiences' (Lhamon, Jr. 2003: 48) were also taking place. The *Virginia Mummy* parodies such exhibitions and pseudo-scientific activities through characters variously trying to unwrap, mutilate or experiment upon the Mummy, on one occasion by attempting to bore a hole in its head. In another scene a white character decides to clip a finger off the Mummy's hand to keep as a curiosity. At this moment, the blackface Mummy Ginger Blue jumps up, butts him in the head and sends him scurrying in fright out of the room, pronouncing: 'I guess he won't want anoder finger in a hurry. Dese white folks must all be crazy' (repr. Lhamon, Jr. 2003: 172). Matthew Rebhorn reads this as a moment in the play that directly responds to the racial attitudes of the era, asserting that it is a remarkable instance of resistance to the ownership and commodification of the black body, through Ginger Blue actively objecting to being viewed as just a body that exists 'for the pleasure and profit of white society' (2012: 86). If indeed a moment of defiance and challenge, then it also foreshadows that of the Egyptian Mummy itself that would develop in Mummy literature in novels such as *The Jewel of Seven Stars*, when the Oriental body too would actively resist being so exhibited and experimented upon.

The *Virginia Mummy* became 'a long-lasting play past mid-century. Rice took it to London and around Britain during his first two European visits and he played it continually when he returned to the States' (Lhamon, Jr. 2003: 46). It was also performed widely by the Christy Minstrels in New York and the celebrated black actor Ira Aldridge throughout England in the 1850s, often alongside his performance of

Othello, and was adapted for publication in the 1870s to allow for further productions. Following the widespread and enduring success of this play in its various forms, its central premise of men dressing up as Mummies in order to secretly woo the daughters of gullible professors no doubt proved influential, as this became the most popular plot device in the early Mummy film.

In addition to The *Virginia Mummy*, the Mummy featured in numerous other theatrical productions throughout the century and throughout the world. For example, Richard Capper's 1868 *The Mummy-makers of Egypt: A Comedy in Five Acts* was staged in Australia and portrayed various husbands and wives hiding in and out of coffins. In 1896 in London D. Day and Arthur Reed's *The Mummy*, 'an unrefined farce' (Wearing 2014: 308) presented the pharaoh Rameses as a character (Mullin 1987: 255) and in 1900 in San Francisco the resurrection of Cleopatra's Mummy featured in George V. Hobart and Louis Harrison's *Broadway to Tokio* (*San Francisco Dramatic Review* 1900: 8), which Georges Méliès's *Cléopâtre* (*Robbing Cleopatra's Tomb*, France, Star, 1899) had depicted in the cinema the year before.

Richard Carle and Robert Hood Bowers's *The Maid and the Mummy: A Musical Farce in Three Acts* debuted in New York on Broadway in 1904 and went on to become a big hit around the country. It featured a plot that would be much replicated in the silent cinema era about a professor who believes he has discovered an elixir of life and a man dressing as a fake Mummy in order to fool him (*The New York Clipper* [TNYC] 1904: 522). A year later in 1905 in New York a burlesque show called *The Egyptian Mummy* played (*TNYC* 1905: 1108) and in 1907 in Chicago Matthew Ott and Albert Stedman's musical comedy *The Mummy Girl* was performed featuring a Mummy 'who comes to life in the form of shapely young woman' (*Variety* 1907: 12). In New York in the same year R. S. Durstine and H. J. van Dyke's *The Mummy Monarch: A Musical Comedy* about Ptolomy I becoming a modern ruler after being 'dynamited from his mummy case' (*The Sun* 1907: 4) was performed as a college musical by the Triangle Club at Princeton in the United States (*The Cornell Daily Sun* 1907: 6) and at the Waldorf, New York, and featured an impressive 'twenty-one musical numbers during the two acts of the play' (*The Princeton Alumni Weekly* 1907: 4). In 1910 Frank Lalor's vaudeville musical comedy *Back to Earth* (1910) played in Chicago and was about a professor 'who is too much wrapped up in a mummy which he has purchased to give heed' to his daughter's 'pleadings to marry'. He then dreams that the Mummy comes to life and dances with him (*Variety* 1910: 14.).

Pauline Perry's *The Silver Bottle*, which was staged in New York in 1911, saw a woman dressing up as a Mummy in order to test if her fiancé loved her (*Variety* 1911: 16). In 1915 Bothwell Browne's vaudeville 'girls act' *The Green Venus* was performed in Oakland and featured a secretary pretending to be a Mummy to fool the professor who employs her, as well as semi-nude dancing (*Variety* 1915: 12). Edgar Allan Woolf and Anatol Friedland's musical comedy *Bride of the Nile* played in New York in 1917 and featured a man in a Mummy case being mistaken for a revived Mummy by Egyptians and 'worshipped by them as a dead god' (*TNYC* 1917: 9). Again in New York a year later in 1918 Salem Tutt Whitney and T. Homer Tutt's '"Smarter Set" company of colored players' staged *Darkest Americans* with one of the highlights being 'a mummy dance, billed as an original creation, wherein mummies come forth from their cases in which they had been preserved and go through an Egyptian dance' (*Variety* 1918: 15).

Undulating Mummies appeared once more on the New York stage three years later in 1921 in Jack de Winters' *The Enchanted Mummy*, which saw the Mummies of the wives of a Pharaoh, who were buried alive, being brought back to life by a sacred drum before embarking on various dance routines (*Variety* 1921: 15). Again in 1921 Harry L. Dixson's *The Professor's Mummy*, written for the immensely popular American canvas playhouses that thrived during the late nineteenth century until the onset of the Great Depression, intriguingly contained very specific instructions on creating Mummy make-up for the performance, explaining how an authentic looking stage Mummy could be created through dipping bandages in coffee (4). It also had the professor waking up from a dream at the end with the events of the play but a figment of his imagination brought about by indulging in too much 'dreadful Welsh Rarebits' (29) (indigestion proving responsible for some Mummy-related encounters on the silent cinema screen too, as will be discussed in Chapter 4). In Kansas in the same year an encounter with a Mummy proved genuinely disturbing when a real Mummy being used as part of a carnival performance, billed as being that of the outlaw 'Wild Jim', was apparently recognized by an audience member as his father who had disappeared fifteen years earlier (*Variety* 1921: 4).

In 1923 Theodore Pratt's *The Revolt of the Mummies* was performed in New York and had museum Mummies coming to life after exhibition hours (*Variety* 1923a: 16) over eighty years before the *Night at the Museum* (Shawn Levy, USA, 2006, 2009, 2014) film series had them doing exactly the same thing. In the same year, but this time not translatable to the modern era because of its inherent racism, *The Explorer* had the blackface comedian Paul Nevin encountering Mummies and getting laughs from 'the negro's fear of the occult and the psychic' (*Variety* 1923b: 32), an approach repeated in 1926 in New York with Ed Daley's burlesque show *Rarin' to Go*, which featured a skit with black actors encountering a Mummy 'with negro superstition of playing around a corpse capitalized for laughs' (*Variety* 1926: 9).

What is notable about all of these productions, from Broadway to burlesque and whether refined or racist, is that they were all comedies or musical comedies: the horror of the Mummy that had begun to intermittently feature in literature not yet finding its expression on the stage.[20] This same trend for amusing or 'fake' rather than horrific Mummies was also to dominate the early years of cinema, in which the Mummy figured rarely in other than comic and light romantic roles. It was the farcical Mummy of the stage that most influenced the early screen career of the Mummy (and the Mummy on screen no doubt in turn informed further stage productions in the 1910s), mingled with the popular Mummy literary romances of the nineteenth century. Yet as the Mummy film developed in the 1910s and 1920s, flickers of horror would increasingly appear on the silent screen, with the Mummy's reworking and reinterpretation in this new medium the subject of Chapter 4.

Notes

1. In the 1990s, following the success of *Bram Stoker's Dracula* (1992), literary authors were increasingly cited in American horror film titles, such as *Mary Shelley's Frankenstein* (1994), to accentuate a literary heritage. Bram Stoker proved particularly popular, appearing in titles such as *Bram Stoker's Burial of the Rats* (Dan Golden, USA, 1995), *Bram Stoker's Legend of the Mummy* (1997) and *Bram Stoker's Shadow Builder* (Jamie Dixon, USA, 1998).
2. Webb is most commonly remembered as Loudon following her marriage to the renowned horticulturist John Claudius Loudon in 1830 and authoring a number of gardening manuals under her married name. Thus, although the novel was originally published with Jane Webb as the author, Jane Webb Loudon appears on most subsequent reprints.
3. For discussions of Webb as an early science fiction writer, see Alkon (1987, 1994) and Strickrodt (1999).
4. See Hopkins (2003) for an analysis of the various similarities between Webb's novel and Shelley's works.
5. Beaver suggests that Webb's novel was known to Poe when he wrote it (1977: 384).
6. For other Poe tales that deal with living burial, see *Berenice* (1835), *The Oblong Box* (1844), *The Premature Burial* (1844) and *The Cask of Amontillado* (1846). The dead arose in *Morella* (1835), *Ligeia* (1838), *The Fall of the House of Usher* (1839) and *Thou Art the Man* (1844). In *Ligeia* the climax is furnished by the reappearance of the Mummy-like bandaged, reanimated corpse of the narrator's first wife.
7. As well as Webb's novel, Lucille King suggests that another possible inspiration for Poe may well have been the tale *Letter from a Revived Mummy*, which appeared in the *New York Evening Mirror* on 21 January 1832. It told of an English soldier discovered on the field of battle in a comatose state and preserved in a museum. A century later, when a galvanic battery is used to revive him, he jumps to his feet shouting, 'hurrah for merry England' (1930: 130).
8. H. Rider Haggard was conceivably inspired by Gautier for a passage in *She* (1887) where one of the novel's heroes is shown a 4000-year-old, perfectly preserved woman's foot: 'Poor little foot! I set it down upon the stone bench where it had laid for so many thousand years, and wondered whose was the beauty that it had upborne through the pomp and pageantry of a forgotten civilization – first as a merry child's, then as a blushing maid's, and lastly as a perfect woman's. Through what halls of Life had its soft step echoed, and in the end, with what courage had it trodden down the dusty ways of Death!' (repr. Frayling 1992: 112–13).
9. Christopher Frayling and Kim Newman propose that this story inspired the magician Walter Booth's trick-film *The Haunted Curiosity Shop* (UK, Paul's Animatograph Films, 1901), among the earliest films to feature a Mummy (Frayling 1992: 144, Newman 1996: 224).
10. *Lot No. 249* was adapted for television in 1967 in *The Short Stories of Conan Doyle: Lot No. 249* (Richard Martin, UK), and for film in 1990 in *Tales From the Darkside: The Movie*. A radio adaptation of *The Ring of Thoth* was broadcast on CBS in America in 1947.

11. The first known Mummy of horror fiction appeared thirty years earlier in 1862, and was female, in the anonymously authored *The Mummy's Soul*, which appeared in the New York magazine *The Knickerbocker* (Day 2015: 223).
12. Conan Doyle died in 1930 and, as Carter Lupton points out, a collected edition of his works featuring his Mummy stories was published soon after. 'His name and work thus had a currency just prior to the development of this film' (2003: 35).
13. Bram Stoker partly based Tera on the female pharaoh Hatshepsut whose tomb had been found in 1902 by Howard Carter. Thus, a discovery of Carter's had already inspired a curse-based story twenty years before his unearthing of Tutankhamun would launch another.
14. Tennessee Williams continued the association of ancient Egyptian women with implacable vengeance in one of his first published works, *The Vengeance of Nitocris* (1948), which he wrote as Thomas Lanier when he was sixteen. Based on a story mentioned by the Greek historian Herodotus, it told the tale of a female pharaoh's vengeance on the murderers of her brother.
15. David Glover suggests that Stoker may well have written it himself: 'Indeed, his practice as a writer was to solicit suggestions and criticisms from friends and associates, not all of them literary figures, and to alter his manuscripts accordingly' (1996: 8). Harry Ludlam also believes that Stoker edited and rewrote the ending at the publisher's insistence (1962: 143–4). However, Nicholas Daly has pointed out that there is virtually no evidence to support such an assumption and that it could just as easily have been written by an anonymous author at the publisher's behest (1994: 42).
16. Rohmer and some other authors of Mummy stories including Conan Doyle and Algernon Blackwood (who penned a 1908 story *The Nemesis of Fire* about a fire-starting Mummy) had an interest in the supernatural that may have led them to Egyptian subjects, all having belonged to the occult society Order of the Golden Dawn (see Ashley 1987: 129). David Glover suggests Stoker could possibly be added to this list through 'his alleged membership' of the secret occult society (1996: 1). However, William Hughes points out that 'the association between Stoker and the Golden Dawn appears to stem from a highly questionable list of literary and celebrity members of the Order' first published in Pauwels and Bergier (1960: 270), (Hughes 2000: 187).
17. Many of these stories and a multitude of others can be read in various published anthologies of Mummy tales. See Ghidalia (1971), Pronzini (1980a), Haining (1988), Greenberg (1990), Stephens (2001), Davies (2004), Arment (2008), Johnston and Shurin (2013) and Guran (2017). See also Frost (2007) for an annotated bibliography of Mummy fiction and Shurin (2013) for an anthology of Mummy fiction authored especially for the collection. Mummy-related fiction also includes film and television tie-ins and children's books. For example, John Burke novelized Hammer's *The Curse of the Mummy's Tomb* (Michael Carreras, UK, 1964) in his *The Hammer Horror Omnibus* (1966). R. Chetwynd-Hayes novelized *The Awakening* (1980) despite the fact that the film was promoted as an adaptation of Bram Stoker's *The Jewel of Seven Stars*. *The Mummy* (1999), *The Mummy Returns* (2001) and *The Mummy: Tomb of the Dragon Emperor* (2008) were all novelized in the same years by Max Allan Collins. For younger readers Raymond Sibley abridged

Arthur Conan Doyle's *Lot No. 249* in *Ladybird Horror Classics: The Mummy* (1985) and R. L. Stine has written *The Curse of the Mummy's Tomb* (1993), *Return of the Mummy* (1995), *Diary of a Mad Mummy* (1998) and *The Mummy Walks* (1999) among his series of popular children's *Goosebumps* books.

18. See Skal (1990) for a detailed history of the novel's transition over time from stage play to film.
19. Harold Beaver suggests that this play may well have served as inspiration for Edgar Allan Poe's *Some Words with a Mummy* (1977: 384). Marcia D. Nichols (2015) agrees, further suggesting that the resistance on the part of the Mummy, who refuses to perform as expected for the all-white gathering, is suggestive of the tropes of the contemporary blackface theatre of the time.
20. One notable theatre work of the nineteenth century that did take a more solemn attitude towards its ancient Egyptian leads was Verdi's *Aida*, first performed at the Opera House in Cairo on 24 December 1871 following the festive opening of the Suez Canal.

4 Preserved on film: The silent Mummy of early cinema

In the silent era, Mummies in one form or another featured in at least fifty films, making the Mummy perhaps the most utilized of all modern monsters in cinema's earliest years (Glynn 2004). Its immense popularity, however, did not last and it went, virtually overnight, from being the sovereign of the screen to a cast-aside creature. In *Monsters and Mad Scientists: A Cultural History of the Horror Movie*, Andrew Tudor's research suggests that the Mummy was the least utilized horror figure in the cinema in the period between 1931 and 1984 (1989: 20).[1] Compiling a list of cinema's most used monsters, he identifies only 14 appearances of the Mummy on screen in 53 years, placing it at rock bottom of his list, while zombies are near the middle with a healthier 48 appearances and the vampire is perched near the top with 101.

The popularity of monsters rises and falls and just as the zombie was in the past a relative rarity in movies in comparison with today, when it would be near to or at the top of a rank-order of monsters, so too were many of today's horror mainstays once scarce on the screen. For instance, David Pirie has pointed out that the vampire until the late 1950s was 'in production ratio terms – simply a minor movie theme. Indeed, until that time even the most intrepid and meticulous researcher would have been hard pressed to come up with any more than two dozen titles' (1977: 6). Likewise Frankenstein's Monster, the werewolf and the zombie barely appeared at all on the silent screen. Susan D. Cowie and Tom Johnson assume the same logic would apply to the Mummy, asserting that 'before the discovery of Tutankhamun's tomb in the 1920s sparked Mummy hysteria and the genesis of the Mummy's curse, only a handful of films had used the Mummy as a player' (2002: 57). However, they greatly underestimate the Mummy's presence in early cinema. Tudor's period of study effectively begins with the sound era, but if his rank-order had instead been compiled between 1899 and 1930, rather than being at rock bottom the Mummy would be sitting near or at the top.

The Mummy as a significant presence in early cinema is far from surprising when one considers its popularity in the literature and theatre during the period immediately predating it, with their influence apparent in the predominance of Mummy romances and comedies that were made for the silent screen (romances having dominated the Mummy in literature and comedies the Mummy on stage). Such influence is notable because in all the films of the silent period, apart from the very earliest trick films, actual revived bandaged Mummies were very rare indeed and when they did appear, as in *The Temptation of Joseph* (Langford Reed, UK, Kineto, 1914) where an amorous Mummy returns to life intent on hugging its terrified owner in an antique shop, they did so for humorous and/or romantic effect.

Sinister reanimated Mummies remained uncommon in the vast literature about Egypt produced in the nineteenth century as well as in the numerous theatrical productions in which the Mummy featured, and so too did this prove to be the case on the cinema screen. Despite the Mummy itself having long been associated with magic and cinema itself appearing to have an almost magical ability to recreate the past (with flashbacks to ancient Egypt common in the early Mummy film), the silent cinema proved resistant to conjuring genuinely supernatural Mummies. Their objectification in museums and travelling shows had made them inert figures in the public's mind and so cinema, despite animating them through various conceits, held back from truly giving them life. The tendencies were for Mummies to be revealed as fakes or the products of dreams. From the early 1910s onwards the first seeds of the Mummy as a figure of horror were planted in tales of Egyptian curses, but throughout the silent era it would remain primarily a player in contemporary-set comedies and romances.

Egypt and the cinema: Monoliths, mesmerism and Mummies

The Mummy featured as a popular subject in the trick, travel, historical, comedy, romantic and fantastic films that all blossomed in the very earliest years of cinema. Antonia Lant points out that from its birth cinema had a codependent relationship with all things Egyptian, highlighting the importance of Egyptian subjects in the magic lanterns and phantasmagoria of early cinemas, in the travelogues of the Lumière Brothers (which featured river trips along the Nile and panoramic views of the Pyramids and temples)[2] and in the use of Mummies and Egyptian iconography in the décor of early cinemas.[3] She suggests that Egypt was so befitting to cinema before sound because its great monolithic structures made the country synonymous with 'silent, visual power' (1997: 85), which the cinema screen also offered.

Ancient Egypt also served to legitimate the content of early cinema and illustrate what it could achieve. Just as popular fiction by Webb, Poe and others had used Egypt to compare the past with the present as a means to contextualize modern Western accomplishment, early cinema utilized Egypt to the same ends. It presented the Western spectator with spectacular and alien worlds of greatly different values, showcasing what cinema as an art form could uniquely provide. Ella Shohat argues that films like *The Ten Commandments* (Cecil B. DeMille USA, Paramount, 1923) invited the spectator to an ethnographic tour that celebrated 'the chronotopic magical aptitude of cinema for panoramic spectacle and temporal voyeurism' (1997: 31–2), in this case by dramatically recreating the lavish and decadent world of the pharaohs.

Such an affected association with ancient Egypt was also an important constituent of the early industry's aspiration to achieve respectability because, Lant argues, 'by lashing the histories of cinema and Egypt together, dignity, legitimacy, and a heritage were bestowed both on the newest Victorian technology of narrative and spectacle and on its inventors' (1997: 89). Such reputability was further sought through the production of filmed Bible stories with Egyptian settings, including various renditions of the story of Moses such as *La Vie de Moïse* (*The Life of Moses*, d.u., France, Pathé, 1906) and *The Life of Moses* (James Stuart Blackton, USA, Vitagraph, 1909–10).

Attaining such legitimacy was crucial in the early years of cinema due to concerns about the social damage the new art form could cause. Between 1907 and 1913, while 'the new medium' had 'the approval of many' as a result of 'the film industry's deliberate attempt to upgrade perceptions of the medium' (Uricchio and Pearson 1993: 5, 195–6), there remained 'a lingering unease about the psychological effects on an audience of watching movies. There were scare stories in the press that, on the one hand, film acted as an opiate and caused lethargy and, on the other, that it led to "copycat" behavior; there were even tales that cinema-going could damage one's eyesight' (Barker and Sabin 1995: 59).[4] Egyptian subject matter was problematic in regard to the psychological effects of cinema because it offered an ineffable allure through the connotations of magic and mystery it retained from popular literature,[5] making it clearly suited to a medium with mesmeric qualities, but less welcome for interest groups trying to improve the public perception of the fledgling industry. The cinema lent itself to pseudo-superstitious fears, as its dark quiet tomblike space inhabited by gazing and transfixed patrons staring at flickering ghostlike images conjured comparisons with hypnosis and bizarre religious experience: a place, as the 1911 Sage Foundation study of commercial recreations in New York suggested, 'of darkness, physical and moral' (Davis 1911: 34). Ancient Egypt, therefore, offered a means both to approve of cinema (dealing with weighty historical material and biblical stories) and to disapprove (transfixing audiences in the dark with tales of a pagan culture and potentially dangerous mystical subjects). Just as in the nineteenth century when the Mummy proved to be a Janus-faced figure who was both educational and magical, so too in the earliest years of cinema did it feature in both instructive travelogues (with production companies such as the Lumière Brothers, Edison Company, Pathé, and Kalem all having crews in Egypt) and in less creditable trick films (themselves descended from the low end of the theatre: the stage magician's shows).

As well as form and content, the very meaning of film itself was also related back to Egypt through the hieroglyphic qualities that the movies themselves had (images juxtaposed to form a coherent syntax). It became commonplace for 'cinema's early historians to explain the newest art in terms of the oldest', as Lant explains:

> The new language of cinema would be termed hieroglyphic by theorists of the medium, and Vachel Lindsay would write in 1915 that the cinema auditorium is 'an Egyptian tomb' in which 'we realize our unconscious memories when we see the new hieroglyphs'. Sergei Eisenstein used the metaphor of the hieroglyph (as well as others, admittedly) to characterize film as visual writing. (1997: 89)

Thus, in addition to providing content and legitimization for early cinema, ancient Egypt also provided a means of explaining the distinctive quality of film as a singular art form. Later in the century the French film critic André Bazin proposed a theory that, applied to silent cinema, further helps explain why the Mummy was a figure so suitable to this medium in its infancy.

The 'Mummy Complex' and the preservative nature of film

The final phrase of the ancient Egyptian mummification ritual was 'You live again, you live again for ever, here you are young once more for ever' (Desroches-Noblecourt 1969: 163), and this phrase could serve to describe an important aspect of film too. André Bazin in his 1945 essay 'The Ontology of the Photographic Image' contended that the plastic arts and the ancient art of mummification were both consequences of a human need to transcend death, reasoning that both attempt representations of the living that will endure indefinitely. Following discussions of Mummies, sculpture and painting, he concluded that photography is significant in the long human quest for human preservation as it offers not just a resemblance but also a recorded image. This 'psychological need in man' to transcend time and oblivion, so well served by the preservative nature of the camera film, he termed the 'Mummy Complex' (repr. 1976: 9). Philip Rosen, extending Bazin's argument, further asserted that 'the imprinting of a length of time is the particular contribution of cinema to the evolution of image-production. Photography preserves an instant of time for a subject, but cinema preserves a fragment of time that can be experienced as actual duration. Time itself seems captured' (2001: 29).

Film, like mummification, preserves human beings potentially forever. Unlike mummification, it can animate them. Having already been brought to life in literature and the theatre, the Mummy became emblematic of what cinema too could achieve in its early years. For the first time the popular cultural figure rather than just being photographed, displayed or unwrapped as a stiff, immobile figure statically preserved in time could through cinema's ability to recreate the past with duration be bestowed with life and movement. Film, with its unique ability to take the past, stopped like an unwound clock and set it going again, enabled the Mummy to walk once more in the eerie projector light of the early cinemas.

The first on-screen Mummies: Short-lived moments of horror in the trick film

The magical properties of Mummies, popularized in nineteenth-century literature but attributed since the days of widespread *mummia* use, were directly referred to in the very earliest trick films that were 'designed to amuse and mystify rather than frighten'

(Haberman 2003: 13) and which were often made by former stage magicians. The first movie on record that can be loosely classed as a Mummy film is Georges Méliès's *Cléopâtre* (*Robbing Cleopatra's Tomb*, France, 1899) in which the Egyptian queen is raised from the dead. This lost film appears in a Méliès catalogue description recounting how her Mummy is chopped into pieces during a tomb robbery and burnt, but from the flames she rises as a living woman. Méliès's *La Colonne de Feu* (*The Pillar of Fire*, France, Star) from the same year provided the earliest screen rendition of H. Rider Haggard's *She* and again portrayed an ancient queen once more appearing from flames. His *L'Oracle de Delphes* (*The Oracle of Delphi*, France, Star) four years later introduced a more menacing Egyptian premise with stone sphinxes returning to life to wreak vengeance on the defiler of an Egyptian tomb, with his *Le Monstre* (*The Monster*, France, Star) from the same year continuing the sinister Oriental theme with its depiction of an Egyptian Prince witnessing his dead wife returned to life as a living, contorted skeleton (*We Put the World* 1903: 143). Méliès also made a film entitled *La Momie* (*The Mummy*) in 1906 that appears in several catalogue descriptions of his films.[6]

The Mummy first appeared in fully bandaged form very fleetingly in 1901 in Walter Booth's British short *The Haunted Curiosity Shop* in which a curio dealer is startled when 'an Egyptian mummy confronts him. Before he can recover from the surprise this occasions, the wrappings fade away and the living Egyptian stands before him. Slowly the solid flesh melts away till only the bare skeleton remains' (Paul 1903: n.p.). This was an archetypal trick film in which 'cinematic manipulation (slow motion, reverse motion, substitution, multiple exposure)' (Gunning 1990: 58–9) provided the film's novelty. With the development of the narrative film, however, the Mummy's macabre associations were transformed as quickly as the Mummy had itself been in the trick film, becoming instead a figure of fun. Having developed a narrative capacity, cinema increasingly began to draw on literature and the theatre for inspiration, and because in both of these the Mummy had been largely unthreatening, it proved well suited to early silent cinema which preferred its monsters unhorrific.

Winding people up: Pretend Mummies and Mummy mix-ups in silent comedies

Like the Mummy, most of the monsters with which we are familiar today were subjects of the silent screen: the vampire in films such as *Drakula Halála* (*The Death of Dracula*, Károly Lajthay, Hungary, Corvin, 1921) and *Nosferatu, eine Symphonie des Grauens* (*Nosferatu: A Symphony of Horror*, F. W. Murnau, Germany, Prana, 1922), Frankenstein's Monster in *Frankenstein* (J. Searle Dawley, USA, Edison, 1910), *Life Without a Soul* (Joseph W. Smiley, USA, Ocean, 1915) and *Il Mostro di Frakestein* (*The Monster of Frankenstein*, Eugenio Testa, Italy, Albertini, 1920), Jekyll and Hyde in *Dr. Jekyll and Mr. Hyde* (Lucius Henderson, USA, Thanhouser, 1912) and the Werewolf in *The Werewolf* (Henry MacRae, USA, Bison, 1913). Yet, in spite of the fact that some of these films have been retrospectively singled out because of how important these monsters would later become, horror proved to be the exception rather than the rule in British and American silent cinema. Edison himself, for example, announced that many of the grislier aspects of Mary Shelley's original story had been excised from his studio's 1910 version of *Frankenstein* (Everson 1986: 36). As John McCarty explains, 'in the early days of cinema and into the twenties literary horror was the source, but the films could hardly be called horror films ... the American silent cinema ... was decidedly light in tone with an emphasis on romance and magic as opposed to terror' (1984: 116).

It would not be until *Dracula* with its supernatural vampire in 1931 that the horror film would emerge as a recognized genre separate from the mystery film in the United States. Before then, even though British and American film producers occasionally turned to the theatre and utilized plays with horror material, they were unable to fully accommodate horror stories that accepted the existence of the supernatural. As Philip J. Riley elaborates:

> It is true that a number of sound pictures of the spine-chilling variety had preceded *Dracula*, including such popular numbers as *The Terror* [Roy Del Ruth, USA, Warner Bros., 1928], *Stark Mad* [Lloyd Bacon, USA, Warner Bros., 1929], *The Cat Creeps* [Rupert Julian, John Willard, USA, Universal, 1930], *The Bat Whispers* [Roland West, USA, Art Cinema Corporation, 1930], and *The Gorilla* [Bryan Foy, USA, First National, 1930] ... [however] most of these were adapted from Broadway plays in which the scary stuff was intermingled with comedy and anything that appeared paranormal was always revealed as the machinations of malevolent human beings. (1990: 19)

Mystical and unnatural reanimation was a possibility that even films today identified as early examples of horror seemed unprepared to offer. Edison Studio's *Frankenstein* (1910), for instance, ended with the revelation that the Monster existed only in its creator's mind, *The Headless Horseman* (Edward D. Venturini, USA, C. S. Clancy Productions, 1922) disclosed that the menace was created by a mischief-maker, and *Wolfblood: A Tale of the Forest* (Bruce Mitchell, Geo Chesebro, USA, Ryan Bros., 1925) revealed its werewolf to be a delusional man, while *London after Midnight* (Tod Browning, USA, MGM, 1927) ended with the vampire exposed as an impersonation. 'Living' Mummies in silent films adhered to similar conventions and tended to be revealed as men impersonating them, similar to Scooby-Doo cartoons where the monster is habitually revealed to be a charlatan out for personal gain. Mummy movies also proved to be highly derivative, copying and borrowing from each other to such a degree that new narrative archetypes were immediately plagiarized by following films.

By far the most popular premise in silent Mummy comedies was to have men dressing up as Mummies in order to dupe crusty, Egyptology-obsessed academics into giving them either money or, more commonly, their daughters' hands in marriage (a conceit that had been popularized in the play *The Virginia Mummy*). In 1910 there appeared the first of these, Cricks and Martin's *Wanted – A Mummy* (A. E. Coleby, UK), which the trade paper *Bioscope* describes in outline:

> Two unemployed, stoney-broke and looking for a job, pick up a newspaper and see therein an announcement that Professor Antique will give good prices for Mummies. A thought strikes Bill – Tom must be a Mummy, be sold, and trust to luck to escape. Tom agrees. (*Bioscope* 1910: 44)

Diddled! (Charles Calvert, UK, Cricks and Martin, 1912) again featured a man disguised as a Mummy, this time in order to fool a professor who refuses to allow his daughter to marry the man she loves (*Bioscope* 1912: supp.xxi), as did *The Egyptian Mummy* (d.u., USA, Kalem, 1913) with *Bioscope* describing the plot as follows:

> Professor Howe disapproves of Dick as his son-in-law. Dick sees the delivery of a Mummy, and gets inside the case. When Howe opens the case Dick cries out 'Let your daughter marry whom she chooses! Rameses demands it!' Professor Howe is so disconcerted that he removes his ban. (1913b:supp.v)

Vitagraph's *The Egyptian Mummy* (Lee Beggs, USA, 1914) offered a similar premise, featuring an aged professor desperate for a Mummy and a young man equally desperate to win his approval as a suitable suitor for his daughter. So he dresses a tramp up as a Mummy in order to impress the professor (Figure 4.1).

Too Much Elixir of Life (Bruce Mitchell, USA, Alhambra, 1915) saw a suitor this time disguising a janitor rather than a tramp as a Mummy in order to get a professor's permission to marry his daughter, the Mummy being created to 'prove' the efficacy of a life-giving potion (*Moving Picture World* [MPW] 1915b: 338). *When the Mummy Cried for Help* (A. E. Christie, USA, Nestor, 1915) had a suitor dressing himself up as a Mummy in order to win a professor's daughter, with the plan complicated by a Pasha who wants to take ownership of the Mummy, which he believes to be 'the

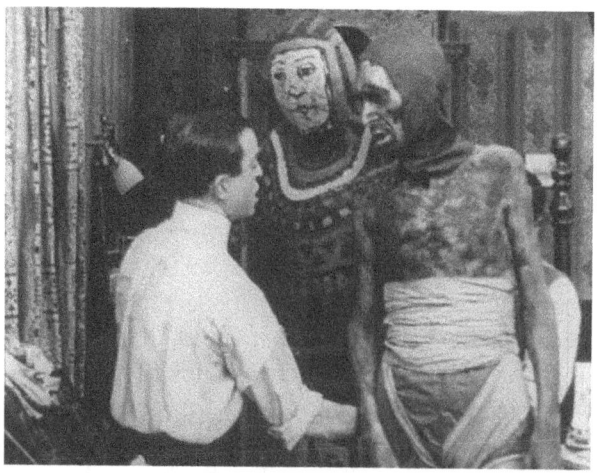

Fig. 4.1 *The Egyptian Mummy* (1914).

long looked for remains of the royal Rambastus' (*Motography* 1915: 110). In the comedy *All Bound Round* (d.u., USA, Universal, 1919), a man who has long admired a professor's daughter disguises his friend as a Mummy so he can deliver it to the aged academic and get to meet her in the process. 'Trouble starts when the old man tells another friend of his that' there may be 'hidden precious jewels' inside the Mummy's stomach and 'they get knives and saws to cut open the mummy'.[7] At this point the Mummy jumps up and the two hoaxers make a run for it 'but are caught by a policeman and taken off to jail' (*The Moving Picture Weekly* [TMPW] 1919: 25).

Occasionally men would be driven to dress as Mummies for reasons other than love or profit. In *Fritt et Plock Detectives* (*Two Clever Detectives*, d.u., France, Pathé, 1908) a detective disguises himself as a Mummy in order to lay in wait and apprehend a thief in a curio shop. (*MPW* 1908b: 201–2). In *Slim and the Mummy* (d.u., USA, Warner Bros., 1914) a cowboy guarding a Mummy is ordered not to touch it but does so, with the result that it turns to dust. To hide his mistake 'he wraps himself in what remains of the mummy cloth and plays he is it', before waking up to discover it was all a dream (*MPW* 1914d: 789). In *The Live Mummy* (d.u., France, Pathé, 1915) one professor dresses up as a Mummy in order to trick another professor (*Bioscope* 1915a: supp. iv) and in *The Missing Mummy* (William Beaudine, USA, Kalem, 1915) a watchman dresses up as a Mummy to keep his job after a Mummy is stolen on his watch. Unfortunately, he is exposed after a professor declares: 'To show that this is a real mummy I will drive a spike through its nose' (*MPW* 1915d: 2425).

An artificial Mummy rather than a dressed up man featured in *His Majesty, Bunker Bean* (William D. Taylor, USA, Lasky/Paramount, 1918) and proved to have life-changing consequences. After being told by a fortune teller that he was Ram-Tah the Great in a previous life, the eponymous hero buys what he believes is the king's Mummy (a fake actually made in America) (*Motion Picture News* [MPN] 1918a: 2523). Fancying himself a king at heart all goes well and he achieves great things because of his newfound self-assurance, including winning the affections of his boss's daughter and meeting a baseball pitcher he idolizes, until the Mummy comes 'to an untimely finish at the hands – or the paws – of Bunker's inquisitive puppy' (*Motography* 1918: 779). The film was remade in 1925 as *His Majesty, Bunker Bean* (Harry Beaumont, USA, Warner Bros., 1925) with the hero once again 'persuaded by phoney clairvoyants' into buying a counterfeit Mummy that makes him 'full of conquering confidence' (*MPN* 1925: 1514). The film was then remade for a third time in 1936 as *Bunker Bean* (Edward Killy, William Hamilton, USA).

Oh! You Mummy (d.u., USA, Crystal, 1914) showed that women could be convincing fake Mummies too and featured a young woman dressing up as a Mummy in order to get her own back on her professor uncle after he discovers her with her 'beau … and orders him out of the house' (*Motography* 1914d: 717). *The Mummy and the Cowpunchers* (d.u., USA, Kalem, 1912) again had a woman dressing up as a Mummy, this time in order for her partner in crime to profit by collecting money from delivering a sham public lecture. (*Kalem Kalendar* [KK] 1912b: 13) (Figure 4.2). *With the Mummies' Help* (A. E. Christie, USA, Christie Film Company, 1917) featured

Fig. 4.2 *The Mummy and the Cowpunchers* (1912).
Source: *Kalem Kalender* 15 November 1912. p. 13.

two women dressing up as Mummies, a wife and her friend, in order to frighten the former's husband, who is 'a "nut" on antiques', out of his obsession with collecting them (*MPW* 1917b: 1339).

Dishonesty of a more criminal bent led thieves to pretend to be Mummies in order to rob rather than dupe in *Now Watch the Professor!* (d.u., USA, Thanhouser, 1912), *The Clue of the Scarab* (d.u., USA, Apex, 1914) (*MPW* 1914c: 1830) and the Swedish *Den Levande Mumien* (*The Living Mummy*, 1917) (Figure 4.3). *Watch George* (Fred Newfield, USA, Stern Bros./Universal, 1928) offered a multitude of Mummies as thieves disguised as Mummies invade a house in order to steal a valuable Mummy, resulting in confusion as to which Mummy is which (*MPN* 1928: 754).

Mummy related mix-ups and misunderstandings were far from uncommon in the silent era. In *La Momie (The Mummy*, d.u., France, Pathé, 1908), for instance, an exhilarated professor examining a Mummy gets a little over-enthusiastic and 'taking his huge carving knife in hand begins to cut the Mummy up'. At this point his landlady 'catching a glimpse of the human form, runs out in alarm. With the cry that a man is being cut up in her house, she summons the butcher, the baker, the grocer and a score of women'. Along with the police they invade the house, discover it is only an inanimate Mummy and everyone sees the funny side (*MPW* 1908a: 193). Instead of suspicion of murder, a botched abduction leads to confusion in *A Terrible Tragedy* (Jerold T. Hevener, USA, Lubin, 1916) in which a group of nihilists mistakenly steal a box containing the Mummy of the Queen of Sheba from Professor Fobbletop thinking it contains a man who they kidnapped earlier and put in a similar box (*Motography* 1916: 109–10).

Fig. 4.3 *Den Levande Mumien* (1917).

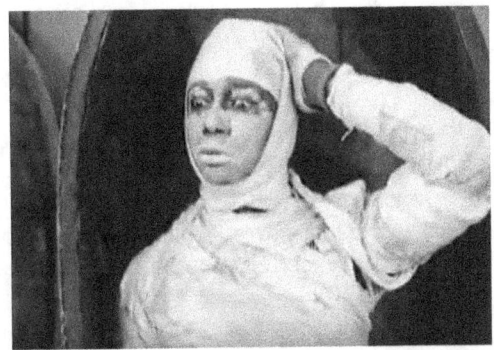

Fig. 4.4 *Mercy, the Mummy Mumbled* (1918).

One of the most intriguing Mummy films that featured fake Mummies was the all-black Ebony Corporation production *Mercy, the Mummy Mumbled* (1918), a so-called race movie produced for black audiences (Figure 4.4). Just as in The *Virginia Mummy*, a scientist is in need of a Mummy for his experiments and so a man hires a dupe to pose as one. In this case, though, Luther Pollard, the black company president of the largely white-owned Chicago-based studio, was determined for Ebony to show that 'colored players' could make 'real "honest to John" natural slapstick stuff' (*MPW* 1918: 1450) without 'any of that crap-shooting, chicken-stealing, razor-dealing, watermelon-eating stuff that the colored people generally have been a little disgusted seeing' (n.d. cited in Axmaker 2016). It is thus a rare and, thankfully, still surviving example of a Mummy movie challenging rather than drawing upon racial stereotypes.

Mummy dearest: The Mummy as romantic character

While the Mummy as a comedy character owed a great debt to the stage, the Mummy as a subject of romance was a hugely popular literary trope, with many tales written about modern academics transported back to ancient Egypt or dreaming of Egyptian romances. Such tales of love across the ages became a staple of the early Mummy film too, but because of its romantic associations these films did not tend to dwell on the more salacious aspects of the Orient that other genres of the silent era were revelling in such as its imagined propensity for cruelty and depravity. As Edward W. Said argues in *Orientalism* (1978), literature throughout the nineteenth century from the likes of Gustave Flaubert (1843 repr. 1972) and Edward William Lane (1836 repr. 1973) had contributed to the Orient becoming 'a living tableau of queerness' (103) to the Western 'Orientalist imagination' (119). Such expectations were subsequently met in movies such as *Intolerance* (D. W. Griffith, USA, Triangle, 1916) and *The Ten Commandments* (1923) with their scenes of old-world debauchery, sin and spectacle. These films overtly foregrounded imagined contrasts between East and West, featuring parallel modern stories where the opulence and orgies of Eastern lust and violence could be compared with loftier Western decency. As Kim Newman explains,

> Hollywood spectacles were only too pleased to destroy civilisations in religious epics like Griffith's *Intolerance* (1916), DeMille's first bash at *The Ten Commandments* (1923) and Michael Curtiz's *Noah's Ark* ([USA, Warner Bros.] 1929), but God-fearing audiences could relish the pagan orgies, crashing temples and smitten multitudes safe in the knowledge that they were too righteous ever to suffer the fate of the Sodomite and Babylonian extras slaughtered en masse. (1999: 25)

Such tantalizing ancient world morality tales were accompanied by the equally sexually charged Oriental tale, which appeared in the cinema as early as Méliès *Vente d'Esclaves au Harem* (*Slave Trading in a Harem*, France, Star, 1897) and *Le Palais des Milles et une Nuits* (*The Palace of the Arabian Nights*, France, Star, 1905). Harem girls proved popular, titillating subjects throughout the silent era, with *Under the Crescent* (Burton L. King, USA, Universal, 1915), for instance, promising a 'sensational succession of revelations of Oriental harem life' (*The Universal Weekly* [TUW] 1915: 32). Harem girls were joined by other disreputable but seductive Oriental figures including the sexually manipulative vamp (Cleopatra and Salome, for example) and the Arab lover well into the 1920s in films such as *The Virgin of Stamboul* (Tod Browning, USA, Universal, 1920), *Arabian Love* (Jerome Storm, USA, Fox, 1922), *Song of Love* (Chester M. Franklin, USA, Norma Talmadge/First National, 1923) and *Arab* (Rex Ingram, USA, MGM, 1924). Middle Eastern fantasies like *The Sheik* (George Melford, USA, Famous Players-Lasky/Paramount, 1921) and *Bella Donna* (George Fitzmaurice, USA, Famous Players-Lasky/Paramount, 1923) offered audiences taboo stories of rape and miscegenation, while dramas such as DeMille's *The Cheat* (USA, Lasky, 1915) and Griffith's *Broken Blossoms* (USA, Griffith/United Artists, 1919) provided similar subject matter but with Far Eastern Orientals.

In contrast to these ancient and modern-set Oriental films that gloried in the supposed immorality of the Middle and Far East and interracial desire, the silent Mummy film generally sidestepped this whole approach and instead remained in keeping with the literary association of the Mummy with romantic love, despite sharing many of the same narrative conventions of these films such as dream sequences, parallel stories and flashbacks to the ancient past. According to Gaylyn Studlar, 'prologues and dream sequences set in Egypt' did not become 'particularly popular' until 'after the discovery of King Tut's tomb in 1922' (1997: 125), but in fact these were long-established conventions of the Mummy film well before then.

Silent romantic Mummy films were inclined to be fanciful dramas about characters inspired by Mummies into fantasizing about relationships with ancient Egyptians. These gentle love stories tended to focus on the obsessions of men of the present with great Oriental beauties of the past as opposed to the sexual appetites of Orientals past and present. The female objects of desire generally proved to be apparitions, just as they were in many literary stories of modern men engaged in romantic trysts with ancient women, popularized by authors such as Théophile Gautier and H. Rider Haggard. Passion in these films is of the civilized Western kind, mainly because this passion is awakened in the Western discoverer rather than the ancient Oriental Mummy herself.

The simplest method employed to create a living Mummy to fall in love with was to simply imagine or dream of it as alive, with 1911 witnessing the first such romantic fantasy in *Le Roman de la Momie*, a fourteen-minute short based on and reasonably faithful to Gautier's story of the same name. The film version tells the tale of Lord Evendale who, while excavating in Thebes for Queen Tahoser, finds a Mummy 'perfect in all its beauty' whom he falls deeply in love with 'to the exclusion of all else'. He dreams he was a subject of the pharaohs in ancient Egypt and fears that he is losing his reason until he meets and falls in love with an American woman 'who so resembles the mummy that she seems to be its reincarnation' (*MPW* 1911c: 658).

La Momie (d.u., Éclipse), another French Mummy film, was also released in 1911 (and in America went under the title *In Ancient Days*, possibly to distinguish it from an American film called *The Mummy*, released in the same year by Thanhouser). It features a collector of antiquities, Mr Burkell, who bargains to give his daughter's hand in marriage to an aged explorer, Mr Jefferson, in exchange for the Mummy of a famous pharaoh. He then falls asleep and dreams he is a pharaoh in Egypt whose daughter poisons herself after being forced to marry against her will. He awakens and finds his daughter to tell her she can marry the man she loves. (*MPW* 1911b: 820). Yet another 1911 film called *The Mummy* is listed in *Bioscope* from the UK company Urban, but appears actually to be *La Momie* retitled for British distribution, as it has an identical plot and cast of characters, including Messrs. Burkell and Jefferson (*Bioscope* 1911:supp.vii).

Fantasizing about Egypt featured less romantically and more comically in *The Princess in the Vase* (Wallace McCutcheon, USA, Biograph, 1908)[8] in which an aged professor returns from Egypt to Boston in possession of an urn containing the ashes of a beautiful princess cremated in ancient times for having had an affair. Upon it getting broken, she materializes in his study, which he finds extremely difficult to explain to his angry wife who discovers the two of them alone there. To make matters worse, her ancient lover also pops up and in jealous rage stabs the professor with his sword, at which point he wakes up and realizes the whole episode was nothing but a dream brought about by a spate of indigestion.

In the very similar *The Dream of a Painting* (Allen Curtis, USA, Joker, 1914), a man falls in love with the painting of the beautiful 'Princess de Egyptienne', who one day steps out of the picture and proclaims her love for him and follows him home. To keep her secret from his wife he disguises her as a cook, but his subterfuge is discovered and his wife protests angrily. The princess, 'in a fit of jealous fury … bores her dagger into his ribs', at which point he wakes up to discover it was all a dream and that his wife 'is poking the point of her parasol into his ribs' (*MPW* 1914e: 1274).

Although neither of these films featured Mummies, they did have ancient Egyptian princesses who complicated modern-day relationships, which would become a popular element of numerous early Mummy films. In *And He Came Straight Home* (d.u., USA, Alta, 1915), for example, too much alcohol conjures Mummies when an intoxicated man tells his angry wife that he is only coming home at two in the morning because the Devil had brought to life the Mummy of a queen of Egypt along with her ancient husband, with the latter trying 'to chop his head off' out of jealousy after she took a shine to him. His wife does not believe a word of it and the film ends with her taking 'a wallop' at him and 'slamming the door' (*MPW* 1915c: 862).

Over-indulging in food rather than alcohol was also occasionally responsible for bringing Mummies to life. For example, in *The Perils of Pork Pie* (W. P. Kellino, UK, Homeland, 1916) a man's sleep is disturbed by indigestion, just as it had been in *The Princess in the Vase*, this time after eating too many pies before bed. In his fitful slumber he dreams that he buys a museum where a Mummy comes to life, transports him back to ancient Egypt and crowns him Pharaoh (*Bioscope* 1916: 1002).[9]

Dreaming continued to serve as a prime means to be transported through time to meet ancient Egyptian beauties on into the mid-1920s. In *Shorty Unearths a Tartar* (d.u., USA, Monogram, 1917), the final film in the series *The Adventures of Shorty Hamilton*, the hero, after unearthing a Mummy in the Egyptian desert, falls asleep and dreams she comes back to life as a dancing girl called Peopat (*MPW* 1917a: 678). In *Made for Love* (Paul Sloane, USA, Cinema Corporation of America, 1926) 'a dream episode of the days of the pharaohs' proved to be 'the most striking feature of the picture' which concerned an Egyptologist neglecting his fiancé in his blind desire to complete the excavation of a tomb at Luxor (*Bioscope* 1926: 45).

As well as men being transported backwards through time to meet ancient Egyptian women or dreaming of them, female Mummies reawakening in the present was another common convention. In *Le Miracle du Brahmane* (*The Brahmin's Miracle*, 1908), possibly an extended remake of a Méliès's film of the same name from 1901, a magician transforms a Mummy into a beautiful woman as part of his act, who then proceeds to perform magic tricks herself (*MPW* 1908c: 243). Rather than magic, the power of galvanism, which had proven such a popular feature in the literary Mummy tale as a means of resurrection, is utilized in *The Mummy* (d.u., USA, Thanhouser, 1911) where a live household electric wire accidentally brings a female Mummy back

Fig. 4.5 *The Mummy* (Thanhouser, 1911): Love despite an age difference.
Source: *The Moving Picture World*, 4 March 1911. Vol. 8. No. 9. p. 454.

to life. Just as in *Wanted – A Mummy* (1910) and *Diddled!* (1912), the hero hopes to win the daughter of a professor by bringing him a Mummy and, just as in *The Princess in the Vase* (1908), the sudden unexplainable appearance of an ancient woman in the hero's room causes a quarrel with his sweetheart. In this film, though, the Mummy enjoys a happy ending as the professor, who is 'an ardent admirer of everything antique', marries her, in spite of the fact that 'there is an age difference of several thousand years in their ages' (*MPW* 1911a: 546) (Figure 4.5).

Reincarnation generally proved a more popular method for facilitating love across the ages in the cinema than galvanism, though, probably because it offered greater romantic possibilities than electric shock. For example, in *Down Through the Ages* (Sidney Olcott, USA, Kalem 1912) a tourist who falls asleep while visiting a royal tomb at Karnak dreams of ancient Egypt and that she was once called Kama, a beggar maid, in love with a priest named Mefres. Sentenced to death while trying to escape together, she wakes up to see 'the pleasant face' of a man she recognizes as 'the Mefres of her dreams' (*KK* 1912a: 12). *When Soul Meets Soul* (J. Farrell McDonald, USA, Essanay, 1912) told the story of an Egyptian princess who swore 'to live again and through the ages' (*MPW* 1912c: 1276) until reunited with her ancient lover. Her perfectly preserved Mummy is acquired by a professor who dreams that he is her lover's reincarnation and was described by *Bioscope* as 'an extremely laudable attempt to tell a poetical story, and to present an accurate picture of life in ancient Egypt' (1913a: 523). *His Egyptian Affinity* (A. E. Christie, USA, Nestor/Universal, 1915) virtually repeated the story and concerned an Egyptian princess who meets her reincarnated lover after her Mummy is returned to life, with the story of their long 'interrupted love-making' beginning 'in the days of ancient Egypt' and finishing 'in modern times' (*Bioscope* 1915b:supp.4). *The Undying Flame* (a.k.a. *The Severed Scarabs*, Maurice Tourneur, USA, Lasky/Paramount, 1917) once again presented a comparable 'story of ancient Egypt and today' (*Bioscope* 1917a: 40) in its account of an ancient Egyptian reincarnated in the body of an English girl, with the plot unfolding as follows:

> Two unhappy lovers of ancient Egypt, a princess and a shepherd, are brutally torn asunder by an angry king. The shepherd is buried alive in the tombs and the princess, after praying to Isis to reunite her soul with that of her lover in some future age where happiness will be possible to them, is turned to stone by the deity who suffered so many matrimonial troubles herself (*Bioscope* 1917b: 72). ... The remaining three reels are devoted to the love story of these people reincarnated in modern Egypt at Wady-Halfa, in the English garrison. (*Bioscope* 1917c: 47)

In *The Image Maker* (Eugene Moore, USA, Thanhouser, 1917) a modern-day young couple realize that they may be the re-embodied spirits of an Egyptian prince and a lowly image maker (played by the same actor and actress in the parallel stories), executed for refusing to end their relationship when the pharaoh commanded him to marry royalty (*The Photo-Play Journal* 1917: 7).

So popular was this concept of Egyptian women being reborn in modern times that they featured in the cinema in the most unexpected places. In the twenty-chapter adventure serial *The Perils of Pauline* (Louis J. Gasnier, Donald MacKenzie, USA, Eclectic/Pathé, 1914),[10] for example, an Egyptian Mummy with 'the appearance of a beautiful young girl' and the possibility of reincarnation are introduced in the very first episode (*Motography* 1914a: 217). 'What did the Mummy say?' the promotional posters for the serial asked in order to garner interest and gather an audience (Figure 4.6).

Mummies appeared in other adventure serials too such as *Lord John's Journal* (Edward J. Le Saint, USA, Universal, 1915–16), which featured a society called the Grey Sisterhood whose leader is obsessed with obtaining a Mummy the heroine has in her possession (*MPN* 1916a: 104). Rather than asking 'What did the Mummy Say', 'Who is the Mummy Man?' announced the poster for the Art Acord western serial *The White Horseman* (Al Russell, USA, Universal, 1921) in relation to an enigmatic recurring character of unknown identity dressed like a Mummy who appears and reappears throughout the episodes (*TMPW* 1921: 28–9).

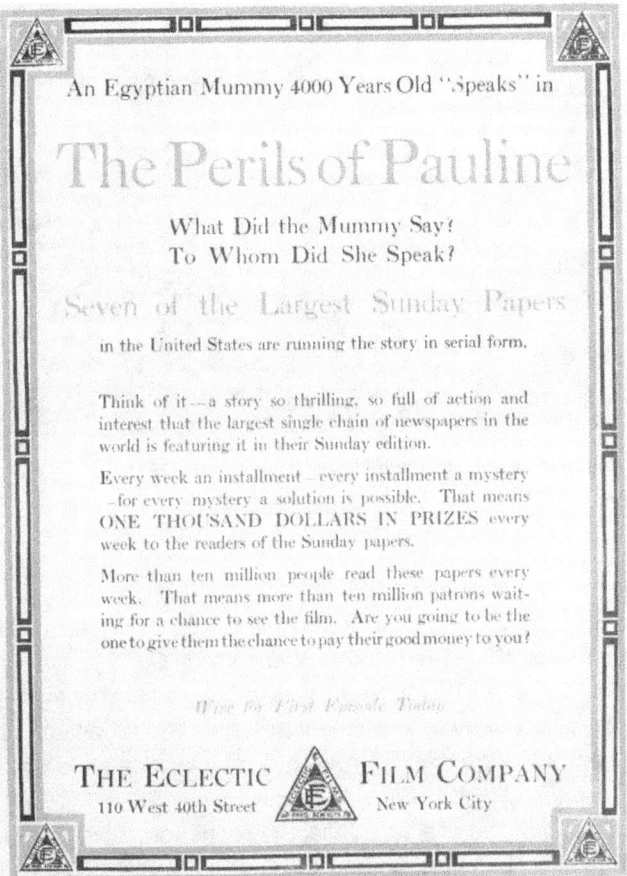

Fig. 4.6 *The Perils of Pauline* (1914): A mummy promotes Pauline's Perils.
Source: *The Motion Picture News*, 28 March 1914. Vol. 9. No. 12. p. 37.

As well as through dreams and reincarnation, Mummies were sometimes returned to life by men of great learning and scientific knowledge. Gérard Bourgeois's *La Momie du Roi* (1909) presented the story of an aged professor returning the Mummy of a pharaoh to life while in *The Egyptian Princess* (Walter C. Bellows, USA, Selig, 1914) an expert chemist revives an Egyptian princess (actually a Russian dancer who had fainted into an empty museum Mummy case) who proves appreciative of his efforts, much to the annoyance of his 'jealous wife' (*MPW* 1914b: 468,470). *Through the Centuries* (Fred W. Huntley, USA, Selig, 1914) featured 'the theory of transmigration' being 'cleverly and picturesquely worked out by two exploring Egyptologists' when they discover the body of a princess in her tomb and both fall in love with her (*TNYC* 1914: 15). It transpires that they are the reincarnations of two priests, one whom the princess loved and one that she hated. The latter punished her for loving his rival by asking the pharaoh to enforce the law for loving a priest that 'meant death or

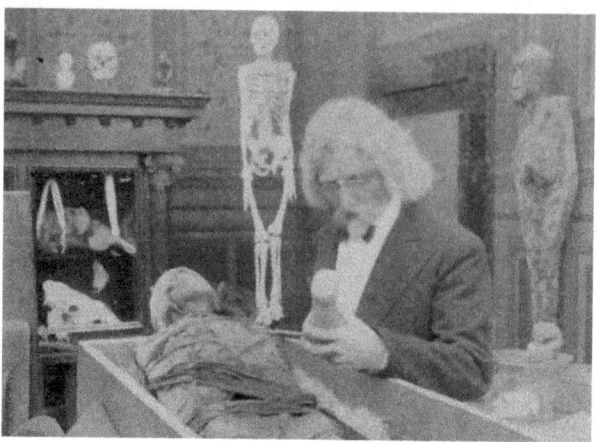

Fig. 4.7 A professor finds a potion in *If I Were Young Again* (1914).
Source: *Motography* 14 November 1914. Vol. 12. No. 20. p. 659.

burial under a hypnotic spell, which resulted in suspended animation'. Then, 'through their modern scientific cunning', they restore her to consciousness before renewing their rivalry for her (*MPW* 1914a: 1154). In the comedy *Out Again In Again* (William Beaudine, USA, Joker, 1917) a professor tries to bring a Mummy to life by applying a huge amount of electricity to it, opportunistically taking advantage of an electric chair in a prison but inadvertently providing a prisoner due for execution with an opportunity to escape (*MPW* 1917c: 1114–15).

Mysterious potions also offered an effective recipe for reviving and rejuvenating Mummies. *If I Were Young Again* (d.u., USA, Selig, 1914), for instance, told 'a weird psychological tale of an aged scientist who renewed his youth with the aid of a potion which he found in the wrappings of an Egyptian Mummy' (*Motography* 1914c:supp.2). In the film it is revealed that 'one drop with each new moon brings back youth' (*Motography* 1914c: 659), a formula very similar to the one eventually used to maintain the life of Kharis in the 1940s Universal Mummy series, although he needed three drops of potion with the moon high in the heavens (Figure 4.7).

The Dust of Egypt (George D. Baker, USA, Vitagraph, 1915), which was based on a stage play of the same name, also featured a revitalizing potion, this time drunk by a princess in ancient Egypt after a sorcerer promises that 'thou wilt be transported thru thousands of years into the future, to live thy life in another age. Thou shalt know love and kiss – once; but the second kiss shall make thee as the dust of Egypt. So Beware!' (Donnell 1915: 59). True to his word, she awakens in the modern world and 'amusing incidents and episodes arise, the young princess not being familiar with modern life wonders' (*MPW* 1915a: 94). As in several prior films in which female Mummies reawaken, the man she meets gets into trouble with his sweetheart because of her, but after being kissed twice she disappears, and the hero wakes up as if all had been a dream (Figure 4.8).

Fig. 4.8 A revived Egyptian princess puffs a cigar in *The Dust of Egypt* (1915).
Source: *Motion Picture Magazine*, May 1915. Vol 9. No. 4. p. 63.

A potion was seen again a year later in the comedy *Elixir of Life* (Allen Curtis, USA, Joker, 1916) in which an inventor, keen to try out his concoction that is so powerful it 'transforms sausages into live dogs' and 'eggs into chickens' (*MPW* 1916b: 1559), arranges for a Mummy to be stolen to test it on. Instead, he unwittingly tests it on a living woman who pretends to reawaken to humour him. Finding them together, his wife does not see the funny side and attempts to burn them both alive in revenge, before being ultimately thwarted from doing so (*TMPW* 1916: 37). Potions had far more serious consequences in *A Modern Sphinx* (Charles Bartlett, USA, American, 1916) in which Asa, a sorcerer's daughter, is punished by her father for attempting out of jealousy to poison a servant she loves by being put to sleep for 3,000 years. She reawakens in the modern age as Zaida, but after a tragic love affair in which she learns the meaning of true love commits suicide by taking poison, only to find herself reawakening once more in Egypt with her father there to welcome her home now that 'her entire nature has been transformed' (*MPW* 1916a: 1142).

In all of these films the Mummy itself was never a particularly menacing figure and functioned along clear gender lines. The male Mummies of comedies, who jumped up from examination tables or out of display cases with great regularity, offered humorous possibilities, whereas female Mummies normally offered romantic ones or complicated existing relationships. Mummies were deceitful or delightful, usually proving too lively for professors or too loving for modern men, but when cinema began to engage with the genuine origins of Mummies, these films started to become more about fear and less about fun.

Tomb raiders: Egypt and early horror

Before the advent of cinema Mummies had been appearing in display cases for decades in museums and/or travelling shows in Europe and America. Many of the silent Mummy films discussed so far emulated such practices and the ways in which audiences engaged with actual Mummies, tending to present them as already out of their tombs and out of Egypt. They reawakened in the modern West rather than in the Middle East, often in the homes of present-day Egyptology-obsessed scholars or the museums in which they worked.

The first associations of the Mummy with the sinister and the cursed began to accrue when films dwelt on where Mummies came from as opposed to where they ended up. Audiences may well have been familiar with Mummies propped up in museums, and acquainted with scholars who talked about them knowledgably within these museums, but they were not used to seeing the body parts or grave-goods of Mummies freshly dug from the earth of their far-away sacred burial places in Egypt. Unlike museums, these were sites that were clearly created with otherworldly and mystical rather than educational and entertainment purposes in mind.

Initially, a few early films parodied the concept that freshly acquired ancient Egyptian artefacts might have magical and unearthly powers. In 1909, for instance, Edison released *The Egyptian Mystery* (J. Searle Dawley, USA) about a magical pendant discovered in an Egyptian tomb that bestowed upon its wearer the power to make anything he touched disappear. The comedy *The Gloves of Ptames* (a.k.a. *Mysterious Gloves*, David Aylott, UK, Martin Films, 1914) followed suit and concerned the discovery of ancient Egyptian gloves from an Egyptian tomb that are sent to a couple who discover that, once worn, everything touched vanishes. Realizing the danger, they throw them out of the door where they are found by a carriage driver who, upon wearing them, unwittingly makes his horse disappear when he pats it, followed by his carriage and finally his passengers. Cast away, they are eventually discovered by a disreputable fellow who uses them to gain a new suit (making the tailor vanish so he need not pay him) and accumulate a lot of money (making a money lender disappear after borrowing his cash).

Amorous rather than avaricious motives featured in *The Ring of Love* (d.u., USA, Solax, 1911) about an aged professor discovering an ancient Egyptian casket, inside of which is a ring wrapped in papyrus that states: 'Who wears this ring shall be given the power to draw unto themselves the affections of whomsoever might happen to be in reach.' As a result of him wearing it his neglected wife finds newfound love for him, but then his maid wears it and he falls in love with her. His wife, understandably angry, then puts it on and becomes irresistible to everyone including her butler, butcher and baker (*The Nickelodeon* 1911: 115). In the comedy *The Man from Egypt* (Lawrence Semon, USA, Vitagraph, 1916) ancient Egyptian jewellery again causes problems as a man finds himself pursued by an Egyptian Sheik because he 'has in his possession a wonderful ruby that has been stolen from the shrine' of the sacred god Amut (*MPN* 1916b: 234).

Comedies about ancient Egyptian artefacts began to be accompanied by darker tales from 1912 onwards when disturbed tombs, appropriated grave goods and sacred places increasingly became associated with a terrible reckoning. Possibly inspired by the popularity and influence of literary tales such as Bram Stoker's *The Jewel of Seven Stars*, Sax Rohmer's *The Sins of Séverac Bablon* (1914) and *The Brood of the Witch Queen* (1918), which dealt with ancient sorcery and vengeance following on from archaeological excavations, stories pertaining to the curse of the Mummy's tomb steadily became a more prominent presence in the cinema, with relics or stolen body parts eerily being trailed by the dead in search of them.

By the time Tutankhamun's tomb was discovered in 1922, the cinema had already presented several tales equating the discovery of a tomb with curses and ancient retribution, mostly revolving around the dangers of possessing cursed treasure. In *The Vengeance of Egypt* (d.u., France, Gaumont, 1912), for example, Napoleon Bonaparte is responsible for an Egyptian Mummy being unearthed whose scarab ring then gets stolen by one of his lieutenants. 'A hundred years of disaster' follow as each eventual owner of the cursed ring dies 'through agency of plague, the strangler, poison, bullet and the wreck of aeroplane and automobile' (*MPW* 1912b: 620). At the end of the film, when the ring is finally returned to the Mummy's 'withered hands ... we see a satisfied gleam in the eyes of the mummy' (*MPW* 1912a: 251) (Figure 4.9).

The 15-chapter serial *The Silent Mystery* (Francis Ford, USA, Burston Films, 1918) featured a cursed gem called 'the Eye of the World' stolen from an Egyptian Mummy case. It is notable for introducing 'the defender of the tomb' that would become a stock plot element in many later Mummy movies, although in this film rather than sending a man 'on the discovery of the theft the priests of the temple' (*Bioscope* 1919: 73) send the malevolent Egyptian priestess Ka to recover the jewel (*MPN* 1918b: 3430).

Fig. 4.9 *The Vengeance of Egypt* (1912).
Source: *Moving Picture News*, 12 October 1912. Vol. 6. p. 9.

As well as rings and gems, necklaces also featured as cursed items, appearing in *The Necklace of Rameses* (Charles Brabin, USA, Edison, 1914), which saw ill-fated thieves steal a necklace that Rameses II once placed 'about the neck of his dying daughter and swore that whoever should dare to remove it should know no peace until it was restored' (*Bioscope* 1914: 102).[11] The Danish film *Mumiens Halsbånd* (*The Mummy's Necklace/The Fatal Necklace*, Robert Dinesen, Nordisk, 1916) told the story of a woman in possession of a pharaoh's necklace being stalked and then kidnapped because of it.

Instead of stolen jewellery, *The Avenging Hand* (a.k.a. *The Wraith of the Tomb*, Charles Calvert, UK, Cricks and Martin, 1915) told the tale of a Mummy's dismembered hand and the fates of the archaeologists who removed it from its resting place. Rather than taking the whimsical tone of Théophile Gautier's *The Mummy's Foot* (1840), this film instead adopted a horrific approach closer to Stoker's *The Jewel of Seven Stars*, which also featured a severed hand, as is clear from the outline offered in the film's press book that describes the consequences of Professor Newby and his son Harry's examination of the Egyptian princess they unearthed:

> Removing the cloth wrappings of the body he discovers a mummified hand [and places it in a box.] The mummified hand rises from the box and fastens itself on professor Newby's neck. He falls dead. ... By his father's death, Harry inherits ... the mummified hand. ... The wraith of the princess visits him in his slumbers. He wakes and reads on the wall: 'Son of the unbeliever, the curse which removed thy father will fall on thee should thou not fulfil what he ignored'. (1915: 2, 5–6)

The film concludes with Harry eventually returning the hand to the tomb after it kills another who tries to steal it. Four years later *The Beetle* (Alexander Butler, UK, Urban, 1919), based on Richard Marsh's 1897 novel of the same name, once more depicted terrible vengeance, but this time exacted by an Egyptian 'High Princess, reincarnated in the form of a loathsome beetle' (*Variety* 1920: 75).

From the early 1910s onwards, therefore, the potential existence of Egyptian curses was being explored in both American and European cinema, featuring in horror tales about Mummy's tombs and stolen treasure, but not yet in films about Mummies themselves. In one European country in particular, though, this pattern started to change and the Mummy itself began to emerge as a figure to be frightened of.

Teutonic terrors: The first Mummy horror movies

In contrast to audiences in Britain and America, those in Germany were far more acquainted with supernatural horror following the release of films such as *Der Student von Prag* (*The Student of Prague*, Paul Wegener, Stellan Rye, Germany, Deutsche Bioscop, 1913) and *Der Golem* (*The Golem*, Henrik Galeen, Paul Wegener, Germany, Deutsche Bioscop, 1915). As a result of this heritage of horror, perhaps the darkest Mummy-related films of the silent era emerged from Germany. The first of these, Ernst

Lubitsch's *Die Augen der Mumie Ma* (1918) portrays the attempts of a hypnotist, Radu, who is the leader of a fanatical sect of Mummy worshippers, to avenge himself on a dancing girl, Mafa, who has left him for a painter. Rather than ending with love conquering all, Radu unnervingly succeeds in frightening her to death. Of primary interest now because of Lubitsch's involvement, later becoming a celebrated light comedy director in America, it was very well received at the time in Germany where, after its premiere, its star Pola Negri 'could hardly reach the street because of the cheering, inescapable crowd' (*Lichtbild-Bühne* 1918, cited in Ascárate 2014: 45). However, it failed to make an impression in America, with the reviewer for the *Exhibitors Herald*, for example, stating that he 'failed to note any enthusiasm' on the part of the audience watching it (1923: 79). *Sight and Sound*, in a retrospective discussion of the film, offered a cogent argument as to why:

> [Although] a success when it came out in Germany in 1918, by the time it was released in the U.S. – to cash in on the popularity of Pola Negri, it seemed a rather crude, 'old' film. ... There were some fairly effective desert settings and interiors of an Egyptian tomb. However, in the supposedly elegant ballroom scenes, back in 'civilisation', the costumes seemed rather dowdy – which can be explained by the fact that Germany was near defeat in the last year of the war and lacked materials. (*Sight and Sound* supp. 1947: 9)

In addition to dreary mise-en-scène and 'down at the heels' gowns (*Camera! The Digest of the Motion Picture Industry* [CDMPI] 1922a: 5), perhaps another contributing factor to the film being criticized in America so strongly – one critic condemning it as 'out-and-out trash' (*CDMPI* 1922b: 3) – was that the film was horrific in effect rather than romantic or comedic, which American audiences had hitherto associated Mummy films with being. In Germany, with its own impressive history of archaeological achievement and thriving tradition of cinematic mystery and horror, Mummies were not so narrowly cinematically constricted.

Die Tophar Mumie (*The Tophar Mummy*, Johannes Guter, Decla-Bioscop 1920) was another German Mummy film that is as difficult to generically define as *Die Augen der Mumie Ma*, being a heady mix of historical drama, melodrama, horror and thriller. It tells the story of the struggle for possession of a Mummy who had died voluntarily in ancient Egypt and was perfectly preserved despite millennia in its burial chamber. The Mummy is taken from Egypt to Paris but then stolen by a man who has 'unlimited resources' and a 'peculiar, morbid ambition to buy up all the mummies he can get' (my translation) (*Die Tophar Mumie* 1920 Pressbook: 3). As the story develops there is a love triangle involving a gold-digging dancer, police chases, beatings and murder, with the unscrupulous billionaire finally getting his come-uppance by dropping dead (Figure 4.10).

Die Tophar Mumie occupied the screen alongside a host of German films that year full of 'images of a frightening, unknown territory of supernatural powers' including '*Das Blut der Ahnen* (*The Ancestors' Blood* [Karl Gerhardt, Decla-Bioscop]), *Die Augen der Maske* (*The Eyes of the Mask*, [Karl Gerhardt, Decla-Film-Ges]) ... *Das*

Fig. 4.10 *Die Tophar Mumie* (1920).
Source: Pressbook cover.

Zeichen des Malay (*The Sign of the Malay*, [Carl Heinz Boese, Decla-Bioscop]) … and *Die Jagd nach dem Tod* (*The Hunt for Death*, [Karl Gerhardt, Decla-Bioscop])' (Sudendorf 1993: 93). The same year also saw Emil Jannings star as a very different Egyptian to his role in *Die Augen der Mumie Ma* in the six-act film *Der Schädel der Pharaonentochter* (*The Skull of the Pharaoh's Daughter*, Otz Tollen, John Hagenbeck-Film), this time as the Pharaoh Osorkon. The movie initially portrays the story of the love of the pharaoh's daughter, Princess Amnertis (Erna Morena), for her lover Tirhaka (Kurt Vespermann). It then transforms into a tale about a terrible curse, as centuries later those possessing the skull of the long dead princess die violent deaths.

The following year's *Das Rätsel der Sphinx* (*The Riddle of the Sphinx*, Adolf Gärtner, UFA, 1921) told the story of a young Egyptologist, Percy Gray (Carl Günther), who discovers the location of buried treasure in a document in the grip of a Mummy's hand. While attempting to find the treasure, he meets the enigmatic Brazilian Juanita di Conchitas (Ellen Richter), but runs afoul of Amru (Erich Kaiser-Titz), a fanatical high-priest of a religious sect who still worships the old gods (a precursor of the over-zealous Egyptian high-priests that would oppose Egyptologists throughout the Mummy movies of the 1940s and beyond). The year 1921 also saw the Mummy being featured in the detective film *Das Geheimnis der Mumie* (*The Mystery of the Mummy*, Victor Janson, PAGU, 1921), an entry in a long-running German film series chronicling the adventures of the fictional 'American' detective Joe Deebs (Wlaschin 2009: 92).[12]

In Germany, as in America, Britain and other European countries, the Mummy and the Mummy's curse were proving increasingly popular cinematic subjects in an ever expanding number of genres well before Howard Carter sensationally found the tomb of Tutankhamun in 1922. The Mummy's presence in the cinema did not arise as a result of the discovery as is commonly assumed. In fact, quite the opposite appears to be the case. Despite the public fascination that surrounded the find, the subject of Mummies did not subsequently set the world of cinema alight and did not launch 'Mummy mania'. Kim Newman explains the oft-assumed effect of the astounding discovery:

> Sax Rohmer, author of the *Fu Manchu* novels as well as numerous tales of nasty goings-on in the world of Egyptian archeology (*The Brood of the Witch Queen*, 1918) rushed his *Secret Egypt* on to the London stage, while Agatha Christie jumped on the bandwagon with her play *Akhnaton* – about the life and times of the 'heretic king' who may have been Tutankhamun's father as well as his father-in-law – and *The Adventure of the Egyptian Tomb* (1924), a Poirot story about a curse which isn't really. The curse reached Hollywood with Karl Freund's *The Mummy* (1932). (1996: 223)

In spite of Newman's attempt to exemplify the obvious assumption that the theatre and the film world jumped onto the bandwagon, his evidence of two plays and a film that followed a full ten years after the event hardly suggest that it was exploited for all it was worth. In fact, the discovery of Tutankhamun, and the media frenzy that followed it, which pushed Mummies into the forefront of the public consciousness, improbably had the opposite effect to the one Newman implies it had. In the cinema, it hindered rather than helped the Mummy.

This was primarily because the discovery of Tutankhamun's tomb radically changed the public perception of the Mummy. Until 1922 in literature it had been primarily an object of Western fantasies of impossible romance. In British and American cinema it had been utilized in comedies, gentle love stories and energetic adventure serials, with the passion and danger of the Orient reserved for other genres. It was fraudsters, potions, electricity, reincarnation and dreams that invested Mummies with life, not the supernatural. Thus, the Mummy required rethinking by filmmakers following the publicity surrounding the fearsome 'curse of King Tut'. While the more horrific Mummy remembered to this day eventually stemmed from this reimagining, so too did the Mummy's comedy and light-romantic possibilities become greatly reduced, ensuring that it would never again be quite as flexible a presence in the cinema or as extraordinarily popular across such a range of genres as it had been before Tutankhamun.

Significantly, this eventual shift in the cinematic Mummy's status from romantic/comic to horror figure was not solely due to it suddenly becoming a more frightening entity following Tutankhamun's curse. It was also a result of it becoming recognizably more human. Once the enthusiasm surrounding the riches found in the tomb had died down and the curse no longer made front-page news, the body of Tutankhamun came into focus and was described in newspapers in the most tragic terms. A backlash occurred against those who had exhumed the Mummy and a great deal of public sympathy was displayed for it. Tutankhamun became an all too human victim, making the Mummy suddenly ill-suited to an entertainment industry that had repeatedly presented it in comedies and playful romances. Rather than launching the Mummy genre, the cinema for the most part kept a respectful, decade-long silence as a consequence of the aftermath of Tutankhamun's discovery.

Grave danger: Tutmania, the curse and the death of the silent Mummy

In 1921 *The Lure of Egypt* (Howard Hickman, USA, Federal Photoplays) featured an archaeologist 'whose life and fortune have been spent in search for the mummy of a renowned Egyptian king' (*CDMPI* 1921: 8). With life imitating art, Howard Carter, the man who would discover the tomb of Tutankhamun one year later and become 'arguably the most famous archaeologist of all time' (Hanlon 2012), had been in Egypt for around thirty years prior to discovering it. For five of these he had been looking for Tutankhamun's tomb in vain and he had reached his final year, virtually out of money and out of time. It had only been with great persuasion that the sponsor of the expedition, Lord Carnarvon, had been induced to fund one more season when, barely into it on 4 November 1922, the first stone step leading down to the tomb of Tutankhamun was uncovered in the Valley of the Kings, the culmination of what Christopher Frayling fittingly describes as 'the great detective story of the 1920's' (1992: 6). Carter's personal race against time, the fact that there were very few pharaohs left to find and the wealth, artistry and mystery of the discovery itself all ignited the public imagination, and Tutankhamun, his treasure and his period all became front-page news.

The sheer amount of conjecture that surrounded the archaeological discovery was in no small part due to the fact that, except for the beauty of the items in the tomb, the historical significance of what was uncovered proved less than dramatic and offered little insight into the life of Tutankhamun himself or life in his Egypt. As Joyce Tyldesley relates, 'Many academics were faintly disappointed with the contents of the tomb, but few were brave enough to express their reactions in print. Although the burial had yielded hundreds of beautiful artefacts and a multitude of fascinating items of daily use, there was virtually no written material' (1999: 81). The man and his period remained enigmas, Carter himself ruefully stating that in spite of all the artefacts found accompanying the pharaoh, 'the mystery of his life still eludes us – the shadows move but the dark is never quite uplifted' (1927: 20).

However, the dark was uplifted for many in the post-war 1920s precisely as a result of the discovery. Carter's summation that as far as could be told the only remarkable acts of Tutankhamun's life were that he died and was buried (Ceram 1971: 202) was an admission that the find had yielded few hard facts. Such lack of facts had the benefit, though, of making the man and his times open to interpretation. This enabled speculation to no longer reside solely in the realm of experts, which transformed the event into one that the public could involve themselves in. 'King Tut' quickly became 'a major cultural phenomenon, or, to use a 1920's word, a "craze"' (Frayling 1992: 10). Egypt was revived in the most spectacular of ways and 'Tutmania' influenced the design of everything from 'Nile Style' fashion, 'sculpture, vases, ashtrays, cocktail-shakers, furniture and decoration' (Jenkins 1974: 220) to architecture including, most famously, the Chrysler Building in New York. Songs were composed such as *Old King Tut* (which became a hit before it was revealed that King Tut was young when he died); the music hall discovered the sand dance and nightspots the Tutankhamun Fox Trot. It was even 'seriously proposed' that a new underground extension in London that would pass through Tooting Common and Camden Town 'should be called Tootancamden' (Graves and Hodge 1940: 114). Joyce Tyldesley describes how 'new cinemas were designed with a Nile theme, so that many a traditional town was suddenly presented with a garish replica Egyptian temple on its high street. Egypt had been fashionable before, most notably following Napoleon's 1798 expedition, but never had it had such an effect on everyday life' (1999: 83), a level of response that perhaps had as much to do with the timing of the tomb's discovery as its contents. Tyldesley recounts how

> Britain, in the aftermath of the First World War and the devastating flu epidemic which followed, was experiencing a wave of interest in all aspects of the occult as the living struggled to maintain some contact with their dead. ... Séances, automatic writing and ouija boards were more popular than ever before, while Egyptian religion, with its sinister animal-headed gods, curious writings and morbid rituals for the care of the deceased, held a great fascination for many. (1999: 85)

The fact that it was Tutankhamun who had been found, the probable son of one of Egypt's most enigmatic monarchs, the heretic king Akhenaten, only added additional fuel to the mystical aspects of the discovery.

Ultimately, there was also, of course, the treasure. Carter himself argued that

> one must suppose that at the time the discovery was made, the general public was in a state of profound boredom with news of reparations, conferences and mandates, and craved for some new topic ... the idea of buried treasure is one that appeals to most of us. (1923: 157)

Yet just as with many other stories involving buried treasure, such as Alexandre Dumas's *The Count of Monte Cristo* (1844) where a hidden hoard almost costs him his soul, or Robert Louis Stevenson's *Treasure Island* (1883) where the curse of the black spot accompanies it, so too was it perceived that Tutankhamun's treasure must come at some personal cost. As Lady Burghclere, Lord Carnarvon's sister commented, the 'story that opens like Aladdin's Cave' soon became 'like a Greek myth of Nemesis' (cited in Frayling 1992: 37). Mass circulation newspapers were more than willing to consider such ramifications for the purpose of sales. Readers were given every detail of the find and, despite the fact that Carnarvon signed an exclusive deal with *The Times*, the developing story of the excavation frequently received detailed front-page coverage in many other papers. *The Times* monopoly particularly 'encouraged rival British newspapers (notably the *Daily Express* and the *Daily Mail*), as well as *The New York Times*, to make as much mischief as they possibly could' (Frayling 1992: 29).

On the 5 April 1923, Lord Carnarvon died following a mosquito bite from which he developed blood poisoning and then pneumonia. The press reported an inexplicable power failure in Cairo for several minutes at the precise moment of his death (*Daily Express* 1923: 1), while in England his dog Susie was alleged to have howled mournfully before dropping dead. The story spread of a cobra that had devoured his 'good luck' canary just prior to his death and all were attributed to the curse of Tutankhamun. For Howard Carter it was an event of great sadness. 'One shadow was to rest upon the work, one regret, which all the world must share – the fact that Lord Carnarvon died ... and never saw the fruition of his work' (1923: 187–8). To the rest of the world it was more like a tragic drama. Christiane Desroches-Noblecourt describes how

> unlike the young lord in Théophile Gautier's *Roman de la Momie*, in the hour of his triumph Lord Carnarvon could not look upon the remains of the prince with whom his name will always be linked. To the sensation-loving public, fate, in denying him this rare satisfaction, seemed to have acted unfairly, even provocatively. So some cause had to be found for the tragedy, an invisible avenger invented, responsible for every misfortune. Why not the pharaoh himself? (1969: 16)

The stories of Sax Rohmer among others and films such as *The Necklace of Rameses* (1914) and *The Avenging Hand* (1915), by persistently associating archaeology and tombs with curses and retribution, had played their part in priming popular reaction to the discovery. Among the stories to surface was that of a clay tablet believed to have been above the tomb's entrance inscribed with the warning 'Death shall come on swift wings to any person who touches the tomb of the Pharaoh.' Although there never was such a tablet, it was reported that Carnarvon had removed it in order to put in its place his own family's coat of arms: hubris of the highest order.

The newspapers in competition with *The Times* capitalized on the sensational possibilities when misfortune struck anyone associated with the expedition because no paper had a monopoly on the supernatural aspects of the discovery. Arthur Conan Doyle added fuel to the fire by giving his view, which appeared in *The New York Morning Post*: 'An evil elemental may have caused Lord Carnarvon's fatal illness.' When asked why only Carnarvon had died out of those who had first entered the tomb, Doyle replied, 'it is nonsense to say that because "elementals" do not harm everybody, therefore they do not exist. One might as well say that because bulldogs do not bite everybody, therefore bulldogs do not exist' (cited in Tyldesley 1999: 89). In the spirit of such logic, stories of the curse grew, until finally between seventeen and twenty-five people were alleged to have fallen victim to the curse (Leca 1980: 261).[13]

Alongside the public interest in the supernatural aspects of the tomb came growing public sympathy for its occupant, whom the curse was apparently avenging. The unwavering belief and incredible lengths to which the ancient Egyptians went to ensure an undisturbed and happy afterlife struck a definite chord among the public after the deaths of so many in the First World War. Soon, therefore, came moral outrage when the rummaging through the tomb ceased to be viewed by many as archaeology but rather an excuse for robbing the dead, in clear defiance of what were known to be Tutankhamun's wishes. The final straw proved to be the examination of the Mummy itself, which in the Mummy unrollings of the nineteenth century had furnished a popular pastime, but was now seen as a step too far. Joyce Tyldesley explains how

> Carter recognized that 'the scientific examinations should be carried out as reverently as possible'. The dissection of the Mummy seemed to him an entirely natural climax to the opening of the tomb. Not everyone agreed. For the first time Egyptologists had to deal with a public backlash which they had not experienced dealing with looted tombs or isolated Mummies. Tutankhamun had been found more or less as his funeral party had left him, and that made a great deal of difference to the general public. He was recognizably a dead human being. (1999: 90)

Carter began carrying out his examination of Tutankhamun's Mummy on 11 November 1925. While doing so, although unknown at the time, he decapitated it and snapped the penis off the brittle Mummy.[14] As Ange-Pierre Leca points out, such mutilation was what the ancient Egyptians dreaded above all else. Their worst fear 'was that the corpse might be destroyed, which would also destroy its chance of eternal life. "Die not a second time" was written hopefully at the bottom of some coffins' (1980: 15). This dreaded second death was exactly the fate to which Carter's actions potentially consigned Tutankhamun and his manhandling was much objected to. H. Rider Haggard was among the first to protest at the prospect, writing:

> Now, the minor Pharaoh, Tutankhamun, is to be added to the long list of more illustrious 'dug-outs'. Presently he, too, may be stripped and, like the great Rameses and many another monarch very mighty in his day, laid half-naked to rot in a glass case of the museum at Cairo, having first been photographed as he came from the embalmer's bath. Yes, to rot ... [and] ... to be made the butt of the merry jests of tourists of the baser sort, as I have heard with my own ears. Is this decent? Is this doing as we would be done by? (1923: 13)[15]

The details that were published about the autopsy brought a disturbing reality with them, with photographs showing that the Mummy still had a recognizable human face atop the desiccated flesh and bones. After becoming a king and taking a wife at nine years of age, he was still only between seventeen and twenty years old when he died. Carter himself, when commenting upon a frieze of the king and his wife found in the tomb, believed that 'we recognise in the royal sportsman, the dog-lover, the young husband and the slender wife, creatures in human taste, emotion and affection, very like ourselves' (1927: 20).

The New York Times of 10 February 1923 also highlighted this modern aspect, comparing him to all the young soldiers who had died in the trenches of Flanders:

> As the objects have been brought out, spectators have remarked that from the manner in which they were bandaged and transported with almost tender care on the stretcher-like trays, they reminded one of casualties being brought out of the trenches or casualty clearing stations. (cited in Frayling 1992: 20)

Tutankhamun was effectively admitted into the ranks of the war dead who had similarly lost their lives tragically young. Joyce Tyldesley suggests that

> it somehow seemed easy to relate to a king – a boy, young enough to have fought and died in the recent war – who had been buried with his favourite sandals and a lock of his grandmother's hair. Lying within his golden coffin, Tutankhamun did not look like a 3,000-year-old corpse, but instead like a vulnerable young man. (1999: 84)

Tutankhamun by being perceived more as a person 'like ourselves' and less as an ancient foreign pharaoh prompted increased public criticism, with a correspondent for *The Times* comparing the ancient king to a very familiar modern counterpart in February 1923:

> I wonder how many of us, born and brought up in the Victorian era, would like to think that in the year, say, 5923, the tomb of Queen Victoria would be invaded by a party of foreigners who robbed it of its contents, took the body of the great Queen from the mausoleum in which it had been placed amid the grief of the whole people, and exhibited it to all and sundry who might wish to see it? (cited in Frayling 1992: 44)

The excavation of Egypt was clearly no longer being understood as glorifying Western civilization, as it had in the past, but instead was now seemingly dishonouring it. While Mummies had been dug up, displayed and even eaten for centuries, this time the perception of the Mummy was different. Although the treasure itself was viewed as magnificent, the Mummy that had owned it was popularly seen for the first time less as a pagan, inanimate object than as a tragic human figure, making it less and less suitable for comedy and escapism in the cinema in the way it had been. The emptying and cataloguing of the contents of the tomb were completed by 1928 and had therefore taken six years in total, but throughout this period and for a long time after it the Mummy of the cinema was strangely unresponsive. This is surprising given the fact that it was the first major dig preserved on film and any film on the subject could have capitalized on the press publicity.

There had actually been plans for a film to be made about the discovery from virtually the moment the tomb had been found. On 24 December 1922, Lord Carnarvon had written to Howard Carter with a scenario for a film with various tomb related scenes and the unveiling of the Mummy furnishing the climax. There was interest from the Goldwyn Picture Company who padded out the Earl's outline to include flashbacks to ancient Egypt. Christopher Frayling outlines how

> in a period when exotic feature-length documentaries, not to mention biblical epics with parallel stories set in the present, were packing them in, this could well become, in the Goldwyn representative's words, 'one of the biggest and most profitable events in film history'. Although the event never happened … . The Carnarvon and Goldwyn letters reveal how remarkably aware the project's sponsor was of the wider cultural implications of the discovery. (1992: 8)

In spite of the potential public interest, however, it is understandable that 'the event never happened'. Out of all the various newfound images and relics of ancient Egypt that excited the world, the one that appeared to scupper any film unproblematically cashing in was Tutankhamun himself who tainted all of the 'wonderful things' (Carter 1923: 80) Carter had discovered. The royal tomb, with all the furniture intact, gold and jewels, pictures and likenesses, gave a tableau of the past that was remarkably familiar, with Carter himself admitting that 'they told us what a short period three thousand three hundred years really was – but Yesterday and the Morrow'. They made 'that ancient and our modern civilisation kin' (1927: 53), so that finally it seemed as though a modern grave was being rifled.

Rather than this social context, Antonia Lant offers a film-industry-focused reason for the decline of the Egyptian-themed film, asserting that 'with the coming of synchronised sound, the power of the silent Egyptian past over the cinema disintegrated … the realist cinema came to the fore, while the cinema of mystery was channelled into the Mummy genre and into the avant-garde' (1997: 92–3). Although she is correct in her inference that the Mummy would become a more 'mysterious' figure in the cinema as it transformed into a monster, the Mummy genre into which she argues 'the cinema of mystery' was channelled after the coming of sound in the late 1920s did not in fact constitute a significant number of films for well over a decade until the 1940s. When one compares this absence with the sheer volume of Mummy films in the silent era and its presence in popular culture through literature and theatre before 'Tutmania', it is noteworthy that the decline of the Mummy movie, as well as Egypt's decline in the cinema, coincided with the aftermath of Tutankhamun's discovery.

Although the 'silent visual power' of Egypt suited silent cinema, as Lant suggests, the Mummy, while capitalizing on the public fascination with this ancient land, never really played any significant part in the Egyptian set epics and Bible stories that were so prevalent, instead appearing as the star of a host of alternatives to them. In fact, the Mummy itself was rarely ever 'silent' in the silent era, generally conniving or courting whereas, somewhat paradoxically, in the sound era it eventually became so, evolving into 'the most silent and unreasoning of the major horror figures' (Hogan 1986: 103).

Of as much impact as the arrival of sound on the Mummy was the erosion of interest in it as a vehicle for fun and frothy fantasies, which were its stock in trade, after the public had confronted the beautiful and yet tragic reality of Tutankhamun's entombment and been forced to reflect on its own complicity in trivializing the looting and ill-treatment of Egypt's ancient dead. It was a mood clearly reflected in the introductory intertitle of one of the final Egyptian-set silent films, *Made for Love* (1926): 'Egypt – the Valley of the Kings – where looting the tombs of the Pharaohs has been a popular outdoor sport for centuries.'

Susan Cowie and Tom Johnson, in an overall appraisal of the few silent Mummy films they identify in *The Mummy in Fact, Fiction and Film*, assert that 'cinema-going audiences were not spellbound by these forays into mummy lore ... and then Howard Carter unearthed the steps which led to the door of Tutankhamun's tomb – and mummy mania broke loose' (2002: 57). David Huckvale too in *Ancient Egypt in the Popular Imagination* states that the discovery was a cinematic starting point and inspired 'the first wave of mummy movies in Hollywood' (2012: 82). Evidently these assertions are inaccurate. 'Mummy mania' preceded 'Tutmania' in the cinema. In contrast to the plethora of Mummy-related movies discussed in this chapter that were produced prior to the discovery, there were only three in the ten years following it: a paltry figure when one considers that in 1915 alone there had been seven.

The first of these three films was the comedy *For the Love of Tut* (Eddie Lyons, USA, Arrow, 1923) in which a man disguises himself as a Mummy to be near the daughter of a collector of Mummies (*MPN* 1923b: 2405).[16] The next was *The Mummy* (Norman Taurog, USA, Fox, 1923), another comedy which tells the story of the owner of an automobile who unfortunately crashes into a telegraph pole. 'He is knocked out and dreams that a couple of thieves plan to steal an Egyptian mummy belonging to his sweetheart's father. He takes the place of the real mummy' in order to foil the plot (*The Film Daily* 1923: 15). The last was the twenty-two-minute *Mummy Love* (Marcel Perez, USA, FBO/Standard Cinema Corporation, 1926) about explorers in Egypt abducted by a sheik trying to escape the 'mummy cave' in his palace by disguising themselves as Mummies (*MPW* 1926: 797). 'Living' Mummies appear in not one of them, with all three instead preferring the long-established practice of people dressing up as Mummies to fool other people.

Perhaps more surprisingly, even the subject of the curse was not developed for all it was worth. Only two films dealt with the subject of 'the curse of King Tut' itself: *Tut-Tut and His Terrible Tomb* (Bertram Phillips, UK, Butcher, 1923) and *King Tut-Ankh-Amen's Eighth Wife* (a.k.a. *The Mystery of King Tut-Ankh-Amen's Eighth Wife*, d.u., USA, Max Cohen, 1923),[17] the latter being a drama about a curse falling on those who violate the tomb of the pharaoh and allegedly 'produced prior to the illness and death of Lord Carnarvon' (*Exhibitors Trade Review* 1923: 1086). However, rather than this unintentional prescience leading to a respectful disclaimer, it was enthusiastically pointed out on the publicity poster that so well did the film match 'the prophecy of Marie Corelli and the mystic explanations of Conan Doyle, that it would seem the Producer, the Director and Author were all three gifted with Clairvoyance and the power of Prophets' (*MPN* 1923a: 1859) (Figure 4.11). In 1924 *The Shadow of Egypt* (Sidney Morgan, UK, Astra-National, 1924) featured a man taking possession of

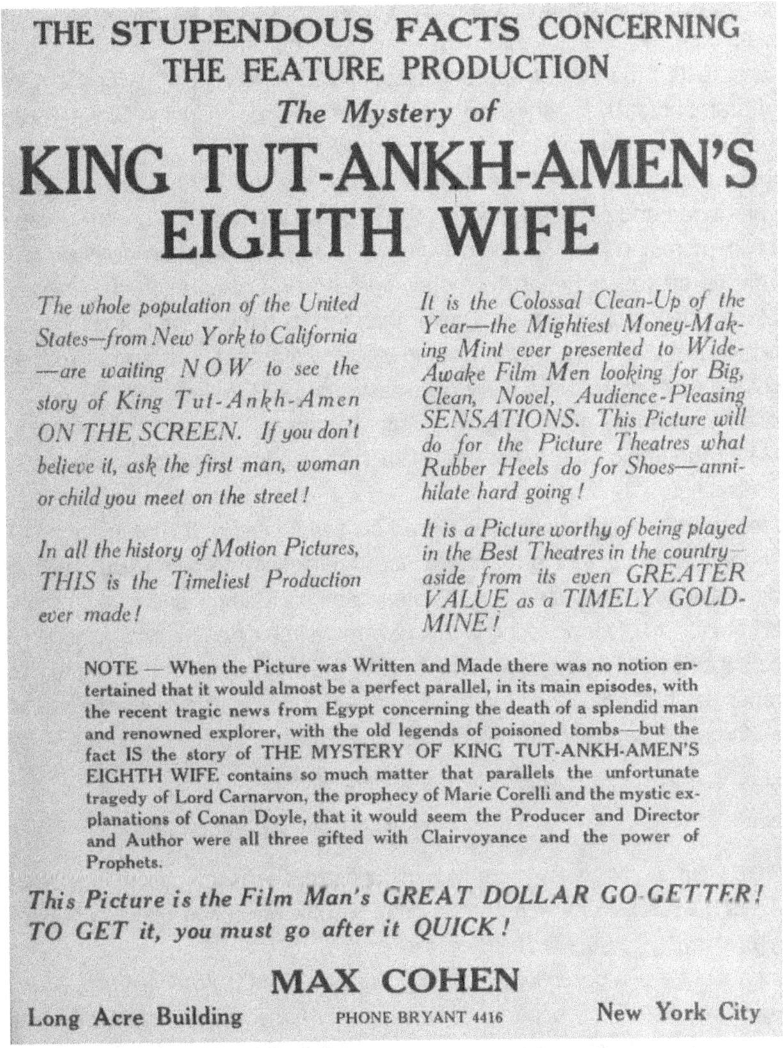

> THE STUPENDOUS FACTS CONCERNING
> THE FEATURE PRODUCTION
>
> *The Mystery of*
>
> # KING TUT-ANKH-AMEN'S EIGHTH WIFE
>
> *The whole population of the United States—from New York to California—are waiting NOW to see the story of King Tut-Ankh-Amen ON THE SCREEN. If you don't believe it, ask the first man, woman or child you meet on the street!*
>
> *In all the history of Motion Pictures, THIS is the Timeliest Production ever made!*
>
> *It is the Colossal Clean-Up of the Year—the Mightiest Money-Making Mint ever presented to Wide-Awake Film Men looking for Big, Clean, Novel, Audience-Pleasing SENSATIONS. This Picture will do for the Picture Theatres what Rubber Heels do for Shoes—annihilate hard going!*
>
> *It is a Picture worthy of being played in the Best Theatres in the country—aside from its even GREATER VALUE as a TIMELY GOLD-MINE!*
>
> NOTE — When the Picture was Written and Made there was no notion entertained that it would almost be a perfect parallel, in its main episodes, with the recent tragic news from Egypt concerning the death of a splendid man and renowned explorer, with the old legends of poisoned tombs—but the fact IS the story of THE MYSTERY OF KING TUT-ANKH-AMEN'S EIGHTH WIFE contains so much matter that parallels the unfortunate tragedy of Lord Carnarvon, the prophecy of Marie Corelli and the mystic explanations of Conan Doyle, that it would seem the Producer and Director and Author were all three gifted with Clairvoyance and the power of Prophets.
>
> *This Picture is the Film Man's GREAT DOLLAR GO-GETTER! TO GET it, you must go after it QUICK!*
>
> **MAX COHEN**
>
> Long Acre Building   PHONE BRYANT 4416   New York City

Fig. 4.11 Film fortune-tellers: Advertisement for *King Tut-ankh-amen's Eighth Wife* (1923).
Source: *Exhibitor's Trade Review* 21 April 1923. p. 7.

treasure who, rather than succumbing to a curse, instead falls foul of enraged locals after discovering 'to his sorrow' that Egypt's 'treasures are regarded as supremely sacred by all Egyptians' (Taylor 1925: 58). Two years later in 1926 *Made for Love* belatedly dealt with an Egyptian curse, although it was not Tutankhamun's but instead protected the 'royal lovers Herath and Aziru'.

Tutankhamun himself, rather than his Mummy or his curse, did feature as a character or in the title of several films, including *The Dancer of the Nile* (William P.S. Earle, USA, FBO/ William P.S. Earle Productions, 1923) and *Tut! Tut! King* (a.k.a. *Oh Mummy*, William Watson, USA, Universal, 1923), which featured a scene in which characters hiding in a sarcophagus are shocked, literally, when found by scientists who mistakenly think them Mummies and attempt to revive them in the tried and tested manner of applying electricity. *Bluebeard's 8th Wife* (Sam Wood, USA, Paramount, 1923) contained a '"King Tut" episode, in which Gloria [Swanson] as a beautiful Mummy comes to life' (*MPN* 1923c: 2584).

What is perhaps most notable is that all of the films specifically relating to 'King Tut' were produced and released quickly following his discovery, no doubt to capitalize on public interest in him. No more were made after 1923, when negative reaction towards his treatment began to mount, making on-screen interest in him a very short-lived phenomenon indeed. Rather than the Mummy genre being launched by Tutankhamun's discovery, it was instead only transformed by it and even then not straight away. After an initial flurry of releases in 1923, Mummy movie production effectively ceased in 1926 following Tutankhamun's autopsy until enough time passed for the tragic Mummy of the pharaoh to become more of a fading memory than forlorn figure.

When the Mummy hauntingly returned six years later in *The Mummy* in 1932 it would be in both frightening and tragic form, reflecting the new status established by both public and press reactions to Tutankhamun's Mummy and its accompanying curse. Yet in spite of reappearing with a new monstrous identity, it remained in many respects a cinematic figure deeply indebted to the past,[18] still conforming to many of the tropes established by the Mummy in its many guises in its remarkable and almost entirely forgotten heyday of the silent age.

Notes

1. There were a great many more Mummy appearances in the period Tudor explores, including a number of Mummy movies from Mexico, which was a country not included in his study.
2. For a list of over a dozen Egyptian-set films made in 1903 alone, see Lant (1997: 96). Egypt was also a very popular subject for the pre-cinema panoramas, dioramas and panopticons of the early nineteenth century. For a detailed account of their rise, fall and Egyptian focus, see Luckhurst (2012: 104–14).
3. For a discussion of Oriental design in cinema auditoriums, see Naylor (1981: 82–108).
4. Such public concern perhaps goes some way towards explaining early cinema's infatuation with hypnosis in films such as *The Basilisk* (Cecil M. Hepworth, UK, Hepworth, 1914) and *Trilby* (Maurice Tourneur, USA, Equitable, 1915).
5. Sax Rohmer in 1914, for instance, claimed that 'sorcery has come to us as a legacy from Ancient Egypt' (9).
6. See, for example, *Motography* (1914b: 16).
7. Such precious contents were to be found in *Cleopatra* (J. Gordon Edwards, USA, Fox, 1917) in which the queen (played by Theda Bara) is given treasure torn from the chest of a Mummy by a priest to help her escape following Caesar's death. (*Exhibitors Herald* 1917: 27).

8. The film starred D. W. Griffith, who had only just entered the movies with Biograph earlier that year as an extra. It would be the director of this film falling ill soon after that led to Griffith being given his first opportunity as a director, thereafter going on to become one of the most important figures in the history of cinema.
9. The film is very similar to Edwin S. Porter's *Dream of a Rarebit Fiend* (USA, Edison, 1906) in which a man suffers a similarly disturbed sleep after eating too much cheese on toast, which was itself based on Winsor McCay's *Dream of the Rarebit Fiend* series of cartoons.
10. The series only survives in a heavily truncated form – without the Mummy sequences.
11. For the entire plot, see *Illustrated Films Monthly* (1914: 193–8).
12. In America it would not be until 1929 that a Mummy would become the subject of a detective story in 'Menace of the Mummy', episode five of the ten-part series *The Ace of Scotland Yard* (Ray Taylor, USA, Universal) (*The Universal Weekly* 1929: 32).
13. Cursed Mummies have been credited with killing many more people than Tutankhamun's supposedly did. It was rumoured that the 1500 or so people who died in the sinking of the Titanic met their fates as a result of a curse arising from a Mummy being transported on board the vessel (Leca 1980: 247). Worse even than that, it was alleged that the many millions who died in the First World War were victims of a Mummy's wrath after her case was given to the Kaiser (Luckhurst 2012: 41).
14. There is perhaps some justification in arguing that Carter was more concerned with the treasures in the tomb than its occupant. C. W. Ceram describes how 'of the thirty-three pages that Carter uses to describe the examination of the Mummy, more than half are given over exclusively to listing precious articles found wrapped in the cerements' (1971: 203).
15. As early as 1904 Haggard had objected to 'the wholesale robbery of the ancient tombs' in 'The Debris of Majesty' and 'The Trade in the Dead', two from a series of six articles on Egypt he wrote for the *Daily Mail* (Ellis 1978: 165). His argument against displaying Tutankhamun has ultimately won out as today he 'rests still within his tomb in the Valley of the Kings; he is the only pharaoh who has been discovered and examined still to lie in his original burial place' (Cox and Davies 2006: 223).
16. The star of this film, the comedian Eddie Lyons, clearly had a penchant for Mummy movies having previously appeared in *His Egyptian Affinity* (1915), *When the Mummy Cried for Help* (1915) and *All Bound Round* (1919).
17. Richard Freeman (2009) suggests the director was Andrew Remo.
18. Robert Spadoni astutely observes that the recently expired silent past is explicitly referenced in *The Mummy* in its extended flashback scene: 'The absence of diegetic sound, the continuous non-diegetic music, the sometimes stiff gesturing of the actors, the costumes reminiscent of a biblical epic of the DeMille variety, and the undercranked camerawork all clearly mark the flashback sequence as a miniature silent film set off within the larger work' (2007: 125). Such flashback scenes were also themselves recurring elements of the silent era Mummy film.

Part 3 Universal studios and the Mummy of the 1930s and 1940s

5 *The Mummy* (1932): Overcoming the silent treatment

In addition to being a horror film, *The Mummy* (1932) is also a romance like so many Mummy films before it. Its plot is centrally concerned with the romantic trials and tribulations of a reincarnated woman of the past adjusting to modern life. The film's male lead, Frank, is an archaeologist in the present who falls in love with this beauty from the past. As such, it adheres closely to the romantic model established in Mummy literature and films such as *Le Roman de la Momie* (1911) and *The Undying Flame* (1917). It also reproduces aspects of the plot from Universal's *Dracula* of the previous year, to which it is commonly perceived, somewhat undeservedly, as little more than a copy.

Universal innovatively made the Mummy a monster and a supernatural figure rather than one revived through science, potions or dreams. There was also ingenuity displayed in the decision to explore the thoughts and feelings of Mummies themselves rather than the passions of the archaeologists of the present, which had been the focus in Mummy tales of the silent era and much Mummy literature before it. It is instead the love two reawakened people of the past have for each other that dominates the narrative of *The Mummy*. It is important to note, though, that in spite of the film's numerous qualities its monster did not prove to be influential. Contrary to popular opinion, typified by Frank Manchel's assertion that 'the conventions of almost all future Mummy movies followed the various situations in this film' (1970: 69), it did not in fact serve as the template for all Mummy films to come. More accurately, it was as much a last hurrah for a well-worn Mummy as it was a new beginning. As a lonely, romantic figure obsessed with a great love from the past the Mummy of 1932 had at least as much in common with the figures from bygone Mummy films as he would have with the rampaging monster he would become in the 1940s.

When Universal made *The Mummy* there had been a six-year hiatus in Mummy movie production, an interval unprecedented since the turn of the century. The release of *The Mummy* on 29 November 1932 was not concurrent with the media frenzy surrounding the discovery of Tutankhamun's tomb; it actually came 'almost a decade to the day after Howard Carter peeked into Tutankhamun's burial chamber' (Riley 1989: 31). It took Carter years to fully empty and catalogue the contents of the tomb in a blaze of publicity that intermittently flickered and flamed throughout this time, but he had finished completely and left Egypt altogether by the time *The Mummy* came out in 1932, by which time 'the press had moved on to other sensations' (Fritze 2016: 240). Carter's hugely popular speaking tours of Europe and North America in 1925 helped maintain the profile of Tutankhamun, as of course did the various reports of curse-related deaths. However, anything approaching 'mania' had long since dwindled, perhaps further explaining why there had been no Mummy film for six years and why, originally, *The Mummy* did not have a Mummy in it at all.

The main titles for *The Mummy* credit the story to Nina Wilcox Putnam and Richard Schayer. However, a number of drafts of very different natures were written before *The Mummy* was finally filmed, being known at various stages as *Cagliostro*, *The King of the Dead*, and *Im-Ho-Tep*. The process began life as a ten-page synopsis for a proposed original script entitled *Cagliostro* by Putnam, Schayer coming on board to help prepare a treatment early in 1932. The first version, Putnam's *Cagliostro*, told the story of an Egyptian magician who, by injecting himself with chemicals, was able to maintain his life for three thousand years, much like Sosra in Conan Doyle's *The Ring of Thoth*. In modern-day San Francisco he relentlessly pursued and attempted to murder the heroine, Helen Dorrington, who reminded him of an ancient lover who had once betrayed him. With the aid of 'a giant negro' servant called The Black Shadow (repr. Riley 2010: 16) he also used radio and television rays to enable him to rob and murder along the way. Ultimately, Helen's boyfriend, in tandem with an expert in archaeology, discovered the truth about Cagliostro's immortality and his need for chemicals to stay alive and brought about his destruction. As Ronald H. Fritze synopsizes, rather than being an effective plot it was instead 'a rather morbid story about eternal vengeance misplaced against innocent victims' (2016: 358).

In the summer of 1932 John L. Balderston took over and revised the screenplay, having already worked on *Dracula* (1931) and *Frankenstein* (1931). He revamped the muddled story, retaining some names and plot ideas while mixing in other elements. Victims were no longer attacked simply as a result of mistaken identity (in fact vengeance was removed as a motive altogether) and he changed the pseudo-scientific explanation for the Mummy's immortality in favour of the supernatural, now a more believable proposition for reviving Mummies than electricity or alchemy following the many years of publicity surrounding the curse of Tutankhamun. The film's final title, though, was apparently nothing to do with any of the writers involved, but instead resulted from a Universal inner office memo that 'went out offering $50 to whoever came up with a proper title. *The Mummy* won' (Riley 2010: 27).

Balderston's final version as filmed begins with a small group of archaeologists who discover the Mummy of Imhotep, an ancient Egyptian priest. He is inadvertently brought back to life by one of the archaeologists who reads aloud from the scroll of Thoth that had been buried in his tomb along with him, after which Imhotep promptly disappears. Eleven years later he resurfaces as the Arab Ardath Bey, determined to resurrect the Mummy of his ancient lover, the princess Anck-es-en-Amon, but his plans are thwarted when he realizes that she has been reincarnated in the person of a modern young woman, Helen Grosvenor. Bey attempts to win her over to him, all the while opposed by her boyfriend, Frank Whemple, his father Sir Joseph Whemple and an occult expert, Dr Muller. Bringing her to his home, he shows Helen in his pool of remembrance their former lives together as devoted lovers. Maddened by her premature death, Imhotep had stolen the sacred scroll of life and attempted to use it to revive her. However, he had been caught by the Pharaoh's guards and was ordered to be buried alive for the sacrilege. Back in the present, he hypnotizes Helen who, under his influence, agrees to be killed, embalmed, and finally given eternal life so that their souls can be united for all eternity. However, just as Bey, with the aid of a Nubian servant, is about to kill her she snaps out of her trance and reasserts her will. She remembers from her previous incarnation how to pray to the statue of the goddess Isis, which responds to her pleas and with a motion reduces Bey to a pile of bones.

Balderston brought to the project first-hand knowledge of Egypt and the Mummy's curse as a former London correspondent for *The New York World*, during which time he had reported from location on Howard Carter's Tutankhamun expedition. As a result, the facts and aura of the discovery permeate the film, with many props modelled on Carter's finds and dialogue directly referring to it. *The Mummy* begins in Egypt in the Valley of the Kings in 1921 with a field expedition from the British Museum unearthing the tomb of Imhotep[1] (just one year before Tutankhamun's was actually discovered). 'Permit me to present you with the most sensational find since that of Tutankhamun', the revived Imhotep says eleven years later to the British Museum archaeologists, upon revealing to them the location of the tomb of Anck-es-en-Amon (historically the wife of Tutankhamun). A telegram is sent to Sir Joseph followed by a headline announcing his return to Egypt to supervise the dig (echoing Carnarvon's journey to Tutankhamun's tomb upon being informed of the discovery). Most significantly there is also the curse itself, in the film inscribed on the lid of a small box, no doubt based on the supposed 'swift wings' curse.

However, although clearly an inspiration, the 'curse of King Tut' does not influence the story in any meaningful way. The Mummy does not seek to take revenge on those who desecrate the Egyptian dead (as it would do in the 1940s) but instead actually guides archaeologists to the tomb of Anck-es-en-Amon because he wishes her to be disentombed. His only violent actions are aimed at those who stand in the way of his being reunited with the woman he loves. The tragic overtones King Tut's Mummy developed in the popular press throughout the 1920s played as much a part as his curse did in *The Mummy*'s sad story of timeless love, restless souls and in its melancholic atmosphere: a mood widely attributed to its director, Karl Freund.

The Mummy: Art horror or production line horror?

Due to Freund's renown as a cinematographer on films like *Metropolis* (1927) and being credited with helping to bring expressionism to Hollywood with *Dracula* and *Murders in the Rue Morgue* (Robert Florey, USA, 1931), the visual style of *The Mummy* has been the aspect of the film most commonly praised by critics. His considerable reputation has resulted in Charles Stumar's involvement being largely overlooked, despite him being the actual cinematographer on the picture, as well as contributing to *The Mummy* being frequently discussed as a film closer to art cinema with a European pedigree than generic American horror. Donald F. Glut, for instance, claims that it is 'one of the few masterpieces of the horror film' because of its suggestiveness, atmosphere and visual style, in contrast to other films of the genre that 'relied on grotesque faces and shock elements' (1978: 169). S. S. Prawer places it firmly within the canon of German expressionism and the director's oeuvre by viewing it as a representative example of 'the characteristic shadow and light play of the films of Karl Freund' (1980: 167). Carlos Clarens again focuses on atmosphere when he discusses how *The Mummy* is 'notable for its sobriety and refusal to shock, concentrating instead on mood' (1967: 73). Tom Triman suggests that '*The Mummy* is a mood piece, rather than a shocker' (2001: 17), David Parkinson praises the film's 'brooding atmosphere' (2000: 19), and Leslie Halliwell refers to its 'romantic languor' (1988: 211). It appears that in this particular film, as Freund himself said, 'the mood of the scene is everything' (cited in Brunas et al. 1990: 52).

The expressionistic visual style that Freund was instrumental in bringing to Hollywood became a key feature of many American horror movies of the 1930s, serving to enhance the reputation of the horror film because it engendered an association with German art-house cinema, which had itself adopted its highly stylized approach in a deliberate attempt to 'make the cinema respectable for bourgeois audiences, and to give it the status of art' (Elsaesser 1989: 32). Andrew Tudor points out regarding horror films of the period 1931–6 that 'perhaps the most distinctive feature of the classic period is stylistic. Of the 33 films that fall within the period only two could be unproblematically described as "naturalistic" in their visual style. The remainder look variously "expressionistic"' (1989: 27). Propitiously, Freund had arrived at Universal in a period when it was still 'one of "the little three" along with Columbia and United Artists. Unlike the big five (Fox, MGM, Paramount, Warner Bros., RKO)', Universal 'did not have exhibition interests to guarantee prime bookings for their output' (Eyles 1978: 44). It was therefore a studio keen to 'establish a certain kind of "product identification" in order to sell its films to the exhibition circuits' (Cook and Bernink 1999: 32). Expressionistic style was a means to give their films a bankable quality as well as an artistic one and provided this American studio a house style that could help differentiate it from its competitors. Such industrial reasons for aspiring to art cinema perhaps help explain why *The Mummy* has tended to be viewed in one of two diametrically opposing ways: as an artistic masterpiece that conforms to Freud's auteurist vision or alternatively as formulaically and unimaginatively generic, a virtual remake of *Dracula* (1931).

Michael Brunas et al. favour the 'generic' reading, arguing that '*Dracula* was more or less remade just one year later by Universal: transposed to Egypt, the plot of *Dracula* was revamped in *The Mummy*, which is a carbon-copy of *Dracula* right down to the individual scenes' (1990: 18). Peter Haining asserts the film is little more than 'a remake' of *Dracula* 'in a different setting' (1987: 130) while Leslie Halliwell alleges that the Mummy was just '*Dracula* in another form' (1988: 214–15). David Parkinson goes so far as to suggest that the whole Egyptian theme was 'something of an afterthought' after Karl Freund was asked by Universal to rework the *Dracula* formula (2000: 18), a view which Jeremy Dyson echoes in his summation that *The Mummy* 'resembled nothing so much as a retelling of *Dracula* with Egypt standing in for Transylvania' (1997: 25). James Marriott and Kim Newman argue that the film 'is Hollywood's first conveyer-belt horror film – commissioned by a studio that knew what they were getting, patterned closely on what had worked before, and showcasing a star who was not only a proven talent but a box-office draw in this type of picture' (2010: 30).

Such views appear to be considerably supported by the fact that both Balderston and Freund had worked on *Dracula*, the former as screenwriter[2] and the latter as cinematographer. In both films an aged savant (in each case played by Edward Van Sloan) battles the malevolent designs of a fiend who is neither alive nor dead. This figure then targets a young woman and attempts to lure her away from her beloved (in both cases played by David Manners) through hypnotic influence over her will. The similarities between the two films are impossible to deny, but rather than being just a 'retelling' or 'carbon-copy', it proved instead to be an inspired reimagining.

The contrasting yet critically dominant views of *The Mummy* – as either an art film or a prime example of assembly-line studio film production – have unfortunately resulted in its own heritage and indebtedness to the Mummy genre in film and literature being largely overlooked. Significantly, *The Mummy* is also a romantic tale, in a way that *Dracula* is not, because Egypt, Mummies and tales about them had been associated with romance since the 1840s. Whereas Nina Wilcox Putman's *Cagliostro* story was originally about a fiend hunting a woman for vengeance, Balderston transformed the monster significantly in his story of 'love across the ages', making *The Mummy* quite different from *Dracula* in spite of the many similarities in story elements and cast.

Barbara Creed defines vampires as 'bodies without souls' (1996: 39) and Cynthia A. Freeland asserts that the 'vampire just wants to suck your blood; about your soul he knows and cares nothing' (2000: 123). Balderston made the concept of souls, and the memories they carry, central aspects of his screenplay with his Mummy romantically obsessed with one person: not insatiable like the vampire who, even when it gets its mate, continues its (sexual) threat upon the world by seeking further victims. Bela Lugosi's Dracula never offers love, nor has he ever suffered in the name of it; Dracula is polygamous, emphasized by his three brides, whereas the Mummy is fixated upon the extremist form of monogamy.

The importance of timeless romance in *The Mummy* can also be explained by the fact that while writing 'six drafts in as many months' (Mank 1999a: 33) in preparation for it Balderston was simultaneously preparing a film adaptation for Universal of the *fin de siècle* novel *She*, about an immortal queen and a high-priest, who like Imhotep broke his vows in the name of love in ancient times.[3] As a result, Leonard Wolf suggests that 'the grandiloquence of H. Rider Haggard's Victorian novel ... [still] ... reverberates in' *The Mummy* (1989: 152). Michael Sevastakis certainly agrees that it had a huge influence:

> *She* (1887) is about a female 'Mummy', Ayesha ... like Imhotep, Ayesha has a magic pool in which she can see what takes place. Like Imhotep, she wishes

to revive the body of her dead lover, Kallikarates, and decides not to do so when his reincarnated likeness appears. When Ayesha discovers that Leo is this reincarnation, she then, as does Imhotep, decomposes the body of her mummified lover whom she has kept with her over the centuries. (1993: 28)

The influence of *She* places *The Mummy* firmly in the tradition of Egyptian romances that dealt with eternal love, especially as this particular novel was written by the most prolific and acclaimed writer of such tales. *The Mummy* essentially reverses the gender roles in *She* in which an ancient undying woman searched for the reincarnation of her long lost love in the present day. Given such a debt to Haggard and the literature he popularized, Egypt is evidently far more than an afterthought or 'stand in' as Parkinson (2000) and Dyson (1997) have suggested. It is instead an integral aspect that served to distinguish the film from other horror films of the period. *The Mummy* is not a copy but a crystallization of disparate influences: of recent horror films, Mummy films of the past, German expressionism, popular Egyptian romances and a decade of public reaction to the discovery of Tutankhamun.

The delicate horror of *The Mummy*: A shudder not a shriek!

One means by which *The Mummy* avoided being a 'carbon copy' of *Dracula* was in its treatment of the monster. Generally, in the horror film 'enormous stress' is laid on 'the initial appearance of the monster' (Neale 1980: 45) and *Dracula* exemplifies this with Dracula's truly memorable first appearance on a staircase (Figure 5.1). *The Mummy*, by contrast, calculatingly undercuts this type of dramatic introduction. We barely see the bandaged living Mummy move on first appearance, and never see it again throughout the entire film, at least not in its bandaged form. All Freund shows of the Mummy awakening is its eyes opening slightly to signify a return to

Fig. 5.1 Dracula's grand entrance in *Dracula* (1931): A stare on the stairs.

consciousness and its arm slowly straightening. His hand is then shown taking the scroll that returned him to life and his bandages trailing out of the door as he leaves. It is the most critically celebrated scene in the film and much admired for its atmosphere and restraint, conforming to a critically oft-preferred approach to horror by being suggestive rather than exhibiting the monster as a spectacle. It also signified that in this film the monster would be less of a focus. Instead, emphasis was placed on the romance between the Mummy in his modern form as an Oriental man and a Caucasian woman and, just as with the Mummy's resurrection, their developing relationship would be carefully suggested rather than explicitly shown.

Universal had to tread carefully both in regard to how explicit they could be in portraying a mixed-race relationship and how horrific they could be in what they showed on screen. The Production Code of the Motion Picture Producers and Directors of America explicitly stated, 'miscegenation (sex relation between the white and black races) is forbidden' (Shohat 1991: 233). Although it would not be until 1934 that the industry strictly enforced this by denying distribution to any film that did not receive the Code's seal of approval, producers were fully aware as early as 1931 of the dangers in opening themselves up to censure. As David J. Skal points out in relation to Dracula, Carl Laemmle, Jr. had been 'uncomfortable with some of the homoerotic displacements of the script ("Dracula should only go for women and not men!" he wrote in his copy of the final screenplay) and sex in general was toned down' (1994: 126). In addition, there remained trepidation concerning how shocking or gruesome films should be. Although the horror genre clearly had financial potential after *Dracula's* success, there was by no means a consensus that the genre was a sure-fire moneymaker. Many associates of Universal 'considered *Dracula* a fluke and warned against flooding the market with morbid pictures bearing the Universal trademark' and 'there had been no rush on the part of competing studios to cash in' on its apparent success (Curtis 1998: 196). Although Universal's *Frankenstein* did consequently 'cash in', proving extremely profitable, it became the subject of a bitter censorship battle over its brutality (Young 1996: 320), perhaps contributing to *The Mummy's* lack of a monster or any notable violence (only the briefest glimpses being offered of the death of a guard in a museum and the destruction of the Mummy at the end). The film is, as Jack Lodge suggests, 'a little tamer than its predecessors' (1994: 57), a fact reflected in the exhibitor's campaign publicity that explicitly stated to cinema owners that *The Mummy* was not a horror film:

> 'What to play up' – *The Mummy* is very unlike in theme to any other Karloff pictures. Do NOT play it up as you did *Frankenstein*, *Dracula* and *The Old Dark House*. Avoid any mention of horror in your campaign. Play up *The Mummy* rather as a fantastic Karloff thriller – one of the strangest adventures known to man. (Riley 1989: 52)[4]

In addition to how it would be 'known to man' was the important factor of how well it would be received by women, who were increasingly being viewed as integral to maintaining admission ticket sales as the Great Depression took hold.

Paul Wells suggests that Hollywood 'responded to the poverty and hardship of the Depression by largely ignoring it, producing instead a range of escapist and utopian entertainments which served as distractions from social malaise' (2000: 50). However, one genre that is regularly identified as a response to it is horror. David J. Skal, for instance, argues that the monsters of the early 1930s

> sprung into mass consciousness in response to the trauma of the Great Depression. ... Dracula, a sanguinary capitalist, relocates from Transylvania after draining the local peasants. The bourgeois Dr. Jekyll exploits and destroys a woman of the lower classes. The freaks live in a literally unbalanced social competition – 'big people' against 'little people'. And the Frankenstein monster is a poignant symbol for an army of abject and abandoned labourers, down to his work clothes and asphalt-spreader's boots. (1994: 159)

Curtis Harrington adopts a similar position, more broadly proposing that horror movies are at their most popular in depressed periods (1972: 17–18). Thomas Elsaesser concurs, contending that this is partly due to public recognition that opportunities for social and economic advancement have been halted (1989). Robin Wood, like Skal, sees Frankenstein's monster as a representative of the proletariat (1986: 76) and so too does Noël Carroll, who asserts that the 1930s 'theme of the unjustly alienated monster, such as Frankenstein's progeny, signaled the depression anxiety of being cast out of civil society due to impoverishment' (1984: 215).

However, Rhona J. Berenstein challenges such readings that attribute the 1930s horror boom entirely to the rigours of the Depression:

> To characterise the early 1930's as an historical vacuum in which horror reigned solely because of socio-economic conditions, as some have done, is also to overlook the genre's continuum with Gothic and other artistic sources. ... Hollywood's first cycle of sound horror ... did not spring forth out of the Depression but was linked to literary and artistic precursors. *Dracula's* Broadway and touring successes ... took place in 1927 and 1928, prior to the stock market's plummet. (1996a: 16)

Berenstein's point is a cogent one as, in the case of *The Mummy*, it draws on the long tradition of romance associated with the figure that pre-dated the trend in horror of its production era. Hollywood's recent transition to sound and the decline in audiences from the Depression led to a number of studios financially restructuring and seeking a reliable income. As a result the film industry 'focused on the wooing of an upwardly mobile, middle-class audience' (Musser 1994: 41). Women were considered a crucial part of this audience and Universal, keen to attract female patrons and because they were assumed to be drawn to love stories, marketed their films as such, including the film that started the horror boom:

> The studio released *Dracula* with an explicitly romantic campaign targeted at women. The movie opened in New York City on February 14, 1931 – Valentine's Day – accompanied by suggestive outlines: 'The Story of the Strangest Passions Ever Known'; 'The Strangest Love Story of All'; and 'The Strangest Love a Man Has Ever Known'. (Berenstein 1996b: 124)

Although marketed as a 'love story' to attract female moviegoers, *Dracula* itself is not one. In contrast, *The Mummy* genuinely is primarily a romance: an important aspect accepted by numerous critics. Leslie Halliwell categorizes *The Mummy* as a 'macabre romance rather than a thriller' (1988: 211) and Gene Wright stresses that 'it is, at its purest level, a love story' (1987: 205). At the time of its release too it was regarded as a variation on romantic melodrama, the *Motion Picture Herald* arguing specifically that the film 'does not depend upon gruesomeness of horror for its entertaining punch. Weird, to be sure, and unreal, this story is ... highly imaginative melodrama about which an interesting romance is woven' (McCarthy 1932 cited in Jensen 1974: 68). Promotional posters for the film certainly attempted to appeal to both sexes. One, for instance, drew out the eerily romantic nature of the story by giving as much room to the glamorously seductive heroine as to the monster who lit up her life (Figure 5.2), another highlighted the romantic story element with the tagline 'A Love that Defied Time' (Figure 5.2), while another suggested that Karloff was 'no dumb mummy by falling madly in love with the gorgeous girl as played by Zita Johann' (Variety 1932: 16).

As Berenstein points out, 'classic horror marketing rarely took women for granted. Films often included romance at the narrative level, which was promoted as a selling point to women viewers' (1996b: 125). *The Mummy* went further still, though, by not simply including romance but also making it the focus of the story. In terms of appealing to its audience its mix of the romantic and the eerie certainly worked with the film proving a hit both at home and abroad, 'shattering records throughout Britain', for example, 'including house records set by Frankenstein' (Johnson 1997: 84).

Another promotional poster boasted that *The Mummy* was 'stranger than *Dracula* ... more fantastic than *Frankenstein* ... more mysterious than *The Invisible Man*' (Figure 5.2). While not necessarily true of the film, the film's heroine certainly lived up to such billing by being stranger, more fantastic and more mysterious than any featured in Universal horror up to that point: a complex figure who proved to be as conflicted and afflicted as the monster itself.

Fig. 5.2 Helen as Western heroine and as oriental beauty in *The Mummy* (1932).

A dichotomized damsel: A 1920s/1930s Eastern/Western woman

In contrast to *King Kong* (1933), which opens in New York where a starving woman is caught stealing an apple before embarking on an escapist fantasy in which she experiences fame, romance, an exotic far-away land and New York high-society, *The Mummy* is not grounded in its production era of the Great Depression in such a direct manner. The heroine of *The Mummy* is a glamorous and wealthy socialite who detests contemporary life and the film too prefers not to dwell on the present. Helen's lamé gown and perfectly styled hair, her life of leisure taking place within luxurious drawing rooms and ballrooms and the film's Egyptian-inspired iconography all suggest a 1920s Egyptomania-inspired glamour and decadence, with the movie offering a retreat into the recent past of the previous pre-Depression decade as well as the exotic distant past of ancient Egypt.

The film's story sets up a complex conflation of conflicting desires within its heroine that she has to resolve. On the one hand she wants to live as a virtuous woman who will eventually marry her boyfriend who evidently wants her to settle down and marry. On the other she is, through her Egyptian heritage, an Oriental seductress and vamp (the two being virtually synonymous throughout the 1920s). Unlike other heroines of horror, such as Mina Harker from *Dracula*, who are enticed by the tantalizingly new pleasures they are experiencing in their encounters with monsters, Helen, as the reincarnation of the Egyptian princess Anck-es-en-Amon, is simply reacquainting herself with old ones.

Helen can be viewed as a representative of the 'New Woman', a feminist ideal from the end of the nineteenth century that in the 1920s was embraced by women who 'believed they had a right to both education and independence from conventional ties such as matrimony' (Berenstein 1996a: 15–16). She was popularly imagined as a woman who was stylish, liberated and 'who wore her skirts shorter and her hair bobbed, who smoked, danced, drank from her beau's hip-flask and took up every fad or craze of a novelty era' (Walker 1977: 40). By the 1930s, however, the popular image had changed and, as Berenstein explains, they came to be 'described in a range of popular discourses as vixens intent on overturning social mores', colouring the depiction of women in early 1930s horror:

> Horror's heroines were lured away from convention by devious but seductive fiends only to be returned to the arms of their appropriate male mates by the closing moments of the films, thus providing a parallel saga to the New Woman's initial refusal of traditional choices and her eventual return, in many cases, to conventional ties. (1996a: 16)

Although this succinctly describes what happens to Helen in *The Mummy*, in this film her refusal to abide by convention is as much a result of her own unconventional nature as it is of the monster's influence. She is multifaceted: white but Oriental, British but also Egyptian, a Westerner but living in Cairo, a woman surrounded only by men, existing in the present but hung up on the past. As well as mirroring just the story of the New Woman, her journey from liberation to convention also more broadly parallels that of many Americans from the roaring twenties to the Depression-era thirties as she has to learn to put behind her the rediscovery of ancient Egypt and the glamour and excitement it helped stimulate and come to accept the more dour realities of the present.

To play the part of Helen, Balderston specified in his script that 'an emotional actress of high calibre' was needed and 'suggested Katherine Hepburn for a test' (1932 in Riley 1989: n.p.). In spite of not securing Hepburn for the role, Helen's 'emotional' nature was still captured on screen by the Hungarian actress Zita Johann who portrayed her from the outset as a woman who, rather than just being a target for the monster's desires, shared many of his traits and longings. Exhibitors were encouraged to market Johann 'as an actress shrouded in mystery – like Karloff's Mummy, a being whose existence defies all laws of science ... a woman with an inexplicable past' (Berenstein 1996a: 112). As opposed to the women in *Dracula*, which presented dual 'stereotypes of good and bad women through its contrast between the sexually adventurous Lucy and the pure, strong Mina' (Freeland 2000: 289), the central conceit of *The Mummy* is that these opposites coexist within Helen and the pull of each threatens to destroy her.

Upon her first appearance on screen, Helen is introduced by two gossips at a table. 'Her father is governor of the Sudan, English of course. Her mother Egyptian.' Despite the fact that she is clearly from the elite of English society, her 'foreign blood' is referred to more than once in the film.[5] We first meet her, as the script specifies, in 'the roof garden on the top of the Semiramis Hotel ... a few couples are dancing' (Riley 1989: n.p.). Yet Helen gazes wearily elsewhere while others dance and make merry as the lush 1931 waltz 'Beautiful Love' plays on the soundtrack, the modern, refined and genteel entertainment on offer evidently boring her in contrast to the pyramids, which hold her attention:

> CAMERA PANS and we see the dark Nile flowing beneath the hotel and across the narrow alluvial plain of the river the pyramids of Cheops, Chephren and Mycerinus standing out on a rocky plateau a few miles away, silhouetted against a full moon behind them which throws its light across the limitless dunes of sand. (Riley 1989: n.p.)

Her longing for the great expanse beyond Cairo is palpable. Here, she is presented as alone and troubled, distanced from modern life and drawn to the ancient past, which survives only as ruins (Figure 5.3). A physician, Dr Muller, comes over to her and asks how is his 'most interesting patient' and it is clear that she is looking for a cure for her melancholy. Instead, she gets two men obsessively intent on dragging her into their very different worlds: Imhotep who appeals to her longing for the past, but who insists on possessing her totally and Frank, who can help her fit into the present, but is determined to never leave her alone.

Fig. 5.3 Helen (re)turns to the past in *The Mummy* (1932).

Helen first encounters the Mummy while she is in a lethargic state, reclined on a couch, suggestive of Lucy who for large parts of *Dracula* is similarly exhausted and lifeless because the vampire has bitten her, and she is under his influence. However, Helen is different from Lucy in that she is weary and apathetic before the creature exerts any control over her, her languid pose in *The Mummy* instead signifying her exhausting struggle to deny the ancient Oriental urges within that have no outlet in well-mannered society. Being half-Egyptian, there is also already something seductive and vaguely vampish about her with her black hair, dark complexion and body hugging garb, the image of the vamp itself in part indebted to the popular imagery of Cleopatra and harem girls reclining on divans, 'sprawled amid cushions and draperies' (Richards 2008: 14) throughout numerous paintings and silent films. When Helen looks up to see the Mummy in the form of Ardath Bey standing over her listless frame for the first time, she does not react with alarm but instead arises from her couch with renewed vigour and responds to his tender questioning and his encroachment into her body space. She recognizes in him a kindred spirit, another Oriental from the past who similarly abhors the present. He is a man who can liberate her and her depression dissolves in his presence. 'I've never felt so alive before' she says as she gazes into his eyes (Figure 5.4).

Their meeting immediately becomes a flagrant display of attraction and devotion, made all the more transgressive by the fact that she is clearly oblivious to her suitor and guardian's disapproving presence, all of whom simply through their close proximity should have the power to inhibit such behaviour, but are in fact revealed as powerless to stop her. Colin MacCabe asserts that in any film scene 'the camera shows us what happens – it tells the truth against which we can measure the discourses' (1974: 10) and in this scene the truth of the situation is revealed

Fig. 5.4 The disapproving male gaze ignored by besotted gazers in *The Mummy* (1932).

irrespective of the polite nothings being said between the two ancient lovers. Balderston's script itself stressed the ascendancy of the image over the dialogue: 'They are looking at each other intently, the tension between them contrasting sharply with the commonplace words. ... Helen through this scene ignores the others including Frank, who keeps looking at her from time to time. She keeps her gaze on Imhotep' (Riley 1989: n.p.).

Given that there are so many gazers in this scene, some captivated and some condemning, it is worth considering Jane Gaines' arguments in 'White Privilege and Looking Relations' where she suggests that 'race could be a factor in the construction of cinematic language' (1988: 24). She offers a persuasive addendum to Laura Mulvey's influential theory that cinema plays on the 'scopophilic instinct (pleasure in looking at another person as an erotic object)' to build the image of a woman as passive material for the active gaze of men (1975: 17) by stressing that this gaze may also be racially inflected with some groups historically having the 'right to look' openly in comparison to other groups who may only have been able to look 'illicitly' (Gaines 1988: 24–5). From the stance of the white gentlemen surrounding the captivated couple it is clear that Bey does not know his place and should not be looking at Helen like this. This unease is compounded further by the next shot, which is a close-up of the lecherous-looking Bey staring with glowing eyes straight into her eyes – placing us directly in Helen's position (Figure 5.5). From this moment she is clearly under the control of a new and particularly disturbing male gaze, which in one respect gets her off the hook from here on in, but not entirely, as the very first sight of him awoke and stirred her well before he entranced her.

Fig. 5.5 Looking for a ghoul friend?: The Mummy entrances Helen and the audience in *The Mummy* (1932).

In her attraction to the Mummy, the film indulges contemporary attitudes explored also in other films of the time that white women were 'always on the verge of "slipping back" into a blackness comparable to prostitution' (Doane 1991: 214). This 'blackness' in women, Berenstein argues, was at the time equated with primitive animalistic sexuality: women controlled by their libidos (1996a: 161). Helen's struggle in the film is one in which she is battling to prevent this 'slipping back' to a more wantonly sexual and less civilized side of herself that lies within. Apparently, this inner blackness came very close to being visually depicted in the flashback scenes to ancient Egypt for which

> make-up artists debated whether to deepen the hue of Zita Johann's skin to approach an unmistakable ebony shade, or to present the actress in an olive complexion. ... No authoritative decision was reached, but as the popular conception of the reigning houses of ancient Egypt depicts them as dusky, but not actually ebon, Miss Johann's make-up was halted at that stage. (Riley 1989: 74)

As the story progresses the Mummy awakens repressed passions inside Helen to such an extent that she finally regresses into Anck-es-en-Amon and adopts the physical form of the paragon of exotic beauty and unbridled sensuality: Cleopatra (Figure 5.6). Anck-es-en-Amon once more, she conforms to the cinema's imaginary of ancient Oriental female licentiousness that had been lasciviously portrayed and simultaneously condemned since the silent era in films such as *Intolerance* (1916). Having succumbed to the call of her 'black blood' she has reverted to a more basic, degenerate sexual attitude; once more she is most at home reclining, but this time rather than being half-asleep she is fully aroused and half-dressed.

Fig. 5.6 The modern heroine gives herself over to her inner Cleopatra in *The Mummy* (1932).

A real lady-killer: *The Mummy* as Gothic romance

This creature who so enchants Helen/Anck-es-en-Amon is himself enchanted by her and her various unobtainable forms: a sacred virgin of Isis, a priestess, a princess, a dead woman and a reincarnation. His refusal to give up on love makes him a sympathetic figure in spite of him being, as Bruce Kawin suggests, so hopelessly obsessive that he is essentially a 'walking repetition compulsion' (1984: 13). Incurable he may be, but at least he is incurably romantic. In an important break from the Mummy films of the past, in spite of there being the predictable inclusion of a modern archaeologist who falls in love with an ancient beauty, it is the Mummy in this film who is for the first time the obsessed and lonely figure. As Lisa Mitchell states,

> On the surface, Dracula is the more obvious romantic figure. ... He is, after all, a rich, well-dressed Continental Gentleman offering that great seduction cocktail of mystery and flattery. But we see Ardath Bey with only one woman (in no frame of film is he found with even a female extra in the background) – an appropriate dramatic device since all that he had done, all that he is doing, is about his 3,700-year-old love for Ankhesenamun. (1994: 35)

Audience sympathy is further elicited through ceding narrative authority to the Mummy for long periods through devices such as point-of view shots and first-person narration. Just as in the novel *Frankenstein* in which the monster is made less monstrous through him narrating a good deal of the story himself, so too in the flashback sequence to ancient Egypt do we hear in the Mummy's own words how he came to be a monster. In Putnam and Schayer's earlier revised script of *The Mummy*, Imhotep and Anck-es-en-Amon had 'suffered simultaneous execution for the sin of loving under the veil' (Riley 1989: 49) and even though this scene did not appear in Balderston's final script, it remains clear that Imhotep's love for Anck-es-en-Amon was reciprocated, as displayed by the dialogue towards the end of the film when the Mummy reawakens Helen's ancient self:

> Her eyes filled with tears, a great love in her face, as she stretches out her arms to Imhotep.
>
> HELEN
>
> No man ever suffered for woman – as you suffered for me – And now – the gods have forgiven us. You say it has been four thousand years – but I can still feel your kisses – in those stolen hours before the goddess. (Riley 1989: n.p.)

In many respects Imhotep is a romantic 'hero' and conforms to a romantic model epitomized by Heathcliff in Emily Brontë's *Wuthering Heights* (1847) as a man tortured by his all-consuming and destructive passion. He is also akin to a Gothic 'hero', the film sharing elements from Gothic literature that often featured 'foreign exotic men who seem to have an uncanny knowledge of how to give pleasure' (Cherry 2002: 172). In the Gothic tradition the heroine's mother in *The Mummy* is absent and her father is incapable of protecting her (in this case because he is in the Sudan as governor). Additionally, following Gothic convention in which the focus tended to be on 'a young heroine and an older, sexualised male threat' (Benshoff 1997: 17), in *The Mummy* this threat is taken to an extreme as he could hardly be older. Yet, in spite of all his menace, the Mummy also embodies the chief characteristics of the Gothic hero, defined by Kingsley Amis as

> lonely, melancholy, of fine natural physique which has become in some way ravaged, of similarly fine but ravaged countenance, dark and brooding in expression, of a cold or cynical veneer, above all enigmatic, in possession of a sinister secret. (1965: 36)

In comparison to the complex, dignified figure of Imhotep, Helen's modern-day wooer Frank comes across poorly. He is insensitive and immature, so smitten by her that, as Michael Brunas et al. describe, he 'reverts to a whiny schoolboy, begging her favours, and mouthing the most arcane love talk this side of Harlequin romances' (1990: 57). Sometimes it is clear that even Helen finds his attentions annoying, as the script specifies:

> CLOSE-UP HELEN
>
> Hate, anger and defiance in her face as she hears Frank's name.
>
> ... HELEN
>
> [as though she wishes he weren't] *You're* here – again. (Riley 1989: n.p.)

Frank is a hero who stifles Helen in contrast to the Mummy who liberates her. She complains that 'I can't be shut up all the time' and 'I don't like the feeling that I'm always being watched'. Yet when she voices her fears to Frank he blurts out 'Now that you've asked for help I'll never leave you alone', quite oblivious to the fact that this is what she detests. Then he says, 'I'll take you to my house', his answer to her complaint that she 'can't be shut up all the time'. As Harvey Roy Greenberg says of Driscoll, the male lead in *King Kong* (1933), 'one imagines that his marriage ... will be as uninspired and as forgettable as his wooing' (1996: 349–50). Throughout the film the Mummy is by far the more interesting figure and nothing Frank says or does can compare with the images the film offers of the inconsolable Imhotep by the bedside of the dead Anck-es-en-Amon, or of his burial at night by torchlight, pitched into a hole after risking all to bring her back.

Frank's weakness is accentuated in *The Mummy* through his affinity with the archaeologists of Mummy literature, who fell in love with beauties of the past and saw in them a 'chance to be kissed rather than cursed' (Deane 2008: 384). When informing Helen of her similarity to the unwrapped Mummy of Anck-es-en-Amon, he describes how after discovering her he 'came to handle all her clothes and her jewels and her toilet things' before he came to 'unwrap the girl herself'. Helen responds reproachfully: 'How could you do that?' 'Had to – science you know', he cheerfully replies, before admitting that he 'sort of fell in love with her ... when we got the wrappings off'. After the furore that greeted the examination of Tutankhamun, such unceremonious unwrapping suggested a less than gallant act, made all the more evident from Helen's mocking reply: 'Do you have to open graves to find girls to fall in love with?' Given Frank's somewhat perverse pleasure in unclothing lifeless women, it is with Imhotep that dramatic interest lies. He, at least, loved Anck-es-en-Amon when she was alive. Once she meets the Mummy, as Berenstein points out, Helen 'looks great, feels wonderful, journeys through her past life in Egypt, and bonds with a fiend that was once the man of her dreams' (1996a: 109–10). Imhotep unlocks her inner-Oriental and from then on Frank is only a bystander.

In developing the relationship between Helen and the Mummy, the film draws not only on prior horror and the Gothic but also on Hollywood Orient-set films, wherein female characters with Caucasian fathers and missing Oriental mothers were often the protagonists (Wong 1978). These women from two worlds, as Gina Marchetti explains, had, 'since the silent era' been perennial favourites in films located in the Orient, being typically linked to 'a sinister involvement with the occult dangers' imagined to exist there (1993: 68). The Orient was a place of sexual danger for Western women too, and in the same year as *The Mummy* two other Orient-set interracial dramas, *The Bitter Tea of General Yen* (Frank Capra, USA) and *Shanghai Express* (Josef von Sternberg, USA), related similar stories about white women being abducted and coerced into obeying the will of Oriental captors.

In *The Mummy* the occult danger that threatens to overwhelm Helen emanates from Imhotep, her own Egyptian heritage and present-day Egypt too, the country being portrayed as a colony as much in flux between civilizing Western and destructively primitive Oriental influences as is the heroine of *The Mummy* herself.

Egypt, sweltering and mysterious, just like India which in the cinema was 'shown to have a claustrophobic effect especially on white women, creating abnormality in their behaviour' (Chowdhry 2000: 217), was more than just a setting but also part of the reason for Helen to lose her identity, her mind and her decency while the Mummy enticed her to do so.

The Mummy and the Nubian: Yellow peril and black brute

The majority of *The Mummy*'s running time consists of a story about a tragic doomed relationship, with the Mummy displaying utter commitment to Anck-es-en-Amon throughout. The Mummy's ultimate failure and utter destruction are therefore difficult to justify at the end of the film because he cannot easily be identified as villainous and deserving of such a terrible fate. Kim Newman suggests that in classic horror monstrous characters are 'usually given one good scene where their good manners could evaporate and they could demonstrate psychosis with facial tics, hand-wringing mannerisms and obsessional rants' in order to justify their destruction (1988: 89). Yet the Mummy never raises his voice and is never less than tender with Anck-es-en-Amon or Helen. Therefore, the transformation of the figure from a reawakened man obsessed by love to a fiend requiring annihilation is instead achieved through pairing him with another, less sympathetic character, a racial figure with very specific and different sexual associations: the black male (in this film, a Nubian).

The Mummy's focus on romantic love is foregrounded in the film by making him utterly sexless. Once reawakened, he is 'enigmatic and stiff as a hieroglyph' as Carlos Clarens put it (1967: 73), a physically non-threatening, almost androgynous figure in his robes and fez. Hollywood's films with an Oriental focus at the time tended to portray their Oriental men in one of two ways, as asexual or as rapists (Wong 1978), and towards the end of the film the Mummy veers from being the former towards becoming the latter, overcoming his androgynous frailty through association with a gigantic Nubian who provides physical sexual potency.

As Harry M. Benshoff points out, such monstrous team-ups, with servitude of one race to another, was a common feature of 1930s horror:

> Many of the classical (foreign, but still white) villains have non-white racial others as their consort(s): 'Black Janos' to Bela Lugosi's Dr Mirakie in *Murders in the Rue Morgue* ... Dr Wong to Peter Lorre's Dr Gogol in *Mad Love* [Karl Freund, USA, 1935], Dr Yogami to Henry Hull's *Werewolf of London* [Stuart Walker, USA, 1935], Fu Manchu's African bodyguards, or Murder Legendre's black zombie slaves in *White Zombie*. (1997: 59)

The Mummy and Nubian were a particularly suitable pairing considering contemporaneous racial stereotyping. Lawrence Reddick in the early 1940s, bemoaning how the complexities of racial identity were being ignored in Hollywood in favour of easily recognizable types, categorized the black 'mental inferior' as one immediately identifiable to cinema-going Americans at the time (1944 cited in Patterson 1975: 4). Elizabeth Young years later highlighted others, identifying the black 'brute' as a stereotype that 'carried particular force' in 1930s cinema as 'a monstrous beast, crazed with lust' (1996: 322, 324). The Nubian in *The Mummy*, therefore, is a native whose 'mental inferiority' makes him prone, indeed suited to, mental and physical servitude, if not outright slavery, to Ardath Bey whose stereotype, as that of an Oriental, 'is that he is cerebral' (Chao 1997: 302). As well as existing associations, contextual factors further impacted upon the resonance the Nubian would have, as *The Mummy* was made in the aftermath of the 1931 Scottsboro rape trial in which a group of black men had been accused of raping white women, becoming a case that ended up being 'publicized and debated in newspapers across the country' (Berenstein 1996a: 177). Arriving on the back of a media circus, the ending of the film depicting a black man manhandling a white woman in a semi-conscious state to make her a 'bride' both fed upon and nourished the racism of the era (with Noble Johnson, the actor who played the Nubian, being required to again be responsible for white female abduction on behalf of a monster as the tribal chief in the following year's *King Kong*) (Figure 5.7).

During the build-up to the concluding sacrificial scenes in *The Mummy*, wherein Helen's Western identity is to be murdered to free her Oriental soul, either the Nubian himself, or his shadow, are constantly within the frame. Redolent with rape imagery and racial menace, Helen in the climax is depicted as helpless in the home of two foreign fiends, an effect clearly aimed for in the script: 'Nubian comes up from behind, seizes her arm and drags her back ... the Nubian holding knife half lifted commences to walk forward ... advancing on her' (Riley 1989: n.p.).

Dressed like Cleopatra, in the company of a Nubian and about to be given over to an Egyptian, Helen has regressed as far as she can and been placed in the most extreme sexual danger under Anck-es-en-Amon's influence and so the film's climax

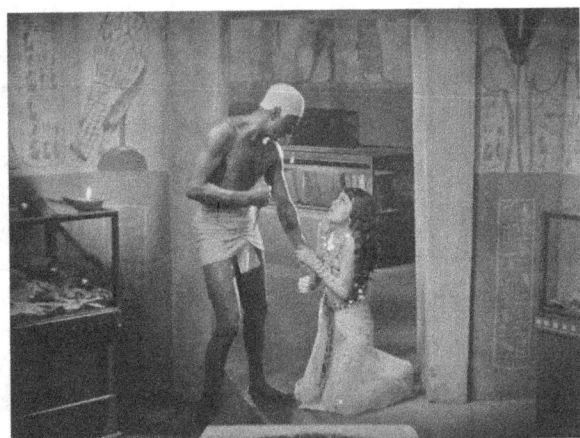

Fig. 5.7 The Nubian dominates the poster and the heroine in *The Mummy* (1932).

brings to a head the conflict that has become the locus of the film. Helen has to choose once and for all between the opposing sides of her heritage: ancient or modern, Eastern or Western, libidinous or virtuous. Like Dr. Jekyll, she has lived in fear of a person within who both terrifies and liberates her, with the Mummy ultimately making her choice clear – miscegenation by becoming his bride resulting in the destruction of her white identity, or a rejection of him and her innate Oriental desires. Given that commonly in the cinema, as Gary Hoppenstand states, 'the Oriental rape' of a 'white woman' tended to signify the 'spiritual damnation for the woman' (1983: 174), she unsurprisingly chooses the latter option. She overcomes the Mummy's spell over her and states: 'I am Anck-es-en-Amon, but I'm somebody else, too. I want to live, even in this strange new world.'

Usually, at this moment, one would expect Frank to save her. In Orient-set cinema tales, as Gina Marchetti explains, 'the romantic hero' tends to function 'as a white knight who rescues the non-white heroine from the excesses of her own culture' (1993: 109). Similarly, in horror films men typically rescued women from fiends, horror playing on a male desire to see sexually active women contained according to numerous critics. Christopher Frayling, for example, argues that after Lucy Westerna's sexual awakening in *Dracula* as a full-bloodied vampire, the only option after she 'has become a creature of erotic desire' is for her to 'be put back in her box' (1996: 103). Judith Weissman concurs, describing Dracula as a 'man's vision of a noble band of men restoring a woman to purity and passivity' (1988: 69). If the monster is not destroyed through communal male action it is, as Roger Dadoun points out, 'the scientist, the one supposed to know, who performs the operation' (1989: 57). So it is significant that in *The Mummy* it is not a group of men that kills the Mummy, nor an expert, nor Frank, but Helen herself. Anck-es-en-Amon is never fully put back in her box, but remains forever a part of Helen. Instead, she makes a choice.

The shooting script contains a scene among the sequence of flashbacks to ancient Egypt where Helen bows before the statue of Isis and prays forgiveness from the goddess for loving Imhotep. However, this does not appear in the film. What is included is a parallel scene, also described in the script, where Helen begs the statue of Isis to destroy the Mummy: 'She bumps her head three times on floor and makes gesture of scattering dust on her head, as we saw her do in the retrospect before same or similar statue' (Riley 1989: n.p.). With the first scene excised, the ending as it stands with the statue coming to life and destroying the Mummy by turning him into bones has been seen by a number of critics as overly bizarre. Leslie Halliwell, for instance, describes it as 'mumbo jumbo' that 'works well enough in terms of mood: you do not have to understand the details' (1988: 215). However, had the earlier scene been included in the released version, it would have revealed that Helen had been conflicted between passion and propriety once before when it came to Imhotep and had sought help from the goddess then too. The statue's response to Helen's prayers at the end of the film would have served as a moment of culmination with her receiving forgiveness for her ancient crime of not remaining faithful to her vows and choosing forbidden love: her prayers heard because now she rejects Imhotep in the very same place she had once kissed him, 'before the goddess' in those 'stolen hours' long ago. As it stands, however, the interconnection across scenes and across history is lost and it is only the modern relationship that is instead stressed, with the goddess solely thwarting attempted present-day miscegenation when heeding the call to destroy the Mummy. Such emphasis fitted better with the racial politics of the time, but made for a less satisfying, or logical, ending.

Following the ending, in spite of all of his crimes and desperate acts, his attempts at sexual and racial domination and his final, fatal rebuff, the Mummy remains a strangely enigmatic figure as the final credits roll. Imhotep, the film suggests, was not kept alive solely by the curses placed upon him for his ancient act of sacrilege, but also by some monstrous act of will, an obsession to see the actions begun thousands of years ago come to completion with Anck-es-en-Amon raised from the dead. Like Quasimodo, King Kong and countless other monsters, the tragedy of the Mummy lies in the monster's fixation on a woman he cannot possibly have. Such thwarted obsession was evident in the Orient-set cinema of the time too, as in *The Bitter Tea of General Yen* where the eponymous general exclaims that 'torture, real torture, is to be despised by someone you love'. This film ends with the subtle suggestion that the general and his beloved may be together in an afterlife, a hope that Imhotep also clung to in his recognition that his love would only ever be attainable after death with the passing of Helen. This notion of romantic rather than physical love allowed for the relationship between the Mummy and Helen to develop throughout the film, in spite of the racial attitudes of the time, because it clearly was a love that could never be consummated. Once the Mummy resorted to force, especially with the aid of a Nubian, he ended up doubly denied at the end of the film, losing both the prospect of eternity with his beloved and continued eternal life himself as an immortal. After millennia of devotion, the Mummy finally gets nothing but oblivion for his love, while Frank, of all people, gets to walk off with the girl.

Notes

1. Historically, Imhotep was a high-priest and architect attributed with the Step Pyramid at Sakkara, who lived in the reign of the Pharaoh Zoser a millennium before Tutankhamun.
2. The film was Balderston's second attempt at Dracula, previously adapting Hamilton Deane's British version of the play for Broadway in 1927 as *Dracula: The Vampire Play*.
3. Universal sold the property to RKO who finally produced this film in 1935, without Balderston's name on the credits. However, perhaps because Balderston had already utilized so many of the novel's elements in *The Mummy*, the setting was changed from its original location of the Egyptian-esque lost city of Kôr to the icy landscapes of the Himalayas.

4. A similar approach was adopted in Britain where Gaumont-British attempted to reproduce the success of *The Mummy* with its Egyptian-themed monster movie *The Ghoul* (T. Hayes Hunter, UK, 1933), again starring Karloff and dubbing him 'The King of the Eeries'. As with *The Mummy*, they downplayed the horrific aspects of the film by claiming that '*The Ghoul* is an intense film but it would be unfair to describe it as horrific' (Rigby 2002: 20).
5. Helen's ties to Egypt were made even more explicit in Putnam and Schayer's earlier version of the script, which appeared in story form in *Mystery Magazine* in January 1933: 'The girl always sickened when taken away from the Egypt of her maternal ancestry and returned to health only when brought back to her native soil. A case of "geographical anaemia"' (Riley 1989: 45).

6 The 1940s Mummy film: A decade of decay?

Universal did not produce a follow-up to *The Mummy* (1932) for eight years. There were some Mummy appearances in films from other studios in the years that followed *The Mummy*, but they took little from Freund's film, preferring instead to adhere to the popular silent cinema tradition of men dressing up as Mummies. Fake Mummies returned to the cinema in such films as the Eddie Cantor musical *Kid Millions* (1934), the Shemp Howard comedy *My Mummy's Arms* (Ralph Staub, USA, 1934), the Wheeler and Woolsey comedy *Mummy's Boys* (Fred Guiol, USA, 1936) and the Three Stooges' comedy *We Want Our Mummy* (Del Lord, USA, 1939) (which featured the inventively named Mummies King Rutentuten and Queen Hotsie Totsie). In episode nine of the 1933 version of *The Perils of Pauline* (Ray Taylor, USA) the villains are chased off by a walking Mummy, but this too proves to be a case of mistaken identity with a character having accidently fallen into a vat of wet plaster. Even *The Ghoul* (1933), a British attempt at recreating the success of *The Mummy* by starring Boris Karloff as a villainous Egyptologist who returns from the dead, balked at presenting an 'undead' monster with the 'ghoul' ultimately revealed to be a fraud.

Universal's decision to revive the Mummy in bona fide undead form in *The Mummy's Hand* in 1940 has been principally attributed to a horror revival and renewed interest in 1930s monsters that occurred following the double-bill reissue of *Dracula* (1931)/*Frankenstein* (1931) that played to huge success throughout America in 1938 (Rigby 2017: 175). However, although it was made to capitalize on a renewed public interest in these early 1930s monsters, *The Mummy's Hand* radically reinvented the Mummy, exploitatively redesigning it as a lumbering monster, most probably to capitalize on the popularity and box-office success of the lumbering Monster, played by Boris Karloff, that featured in the previous year's *Son of Frankenstein* (Rowland V. Lee, USA, 1939). In fact, as well as owing its form to Karloff's popular portrayal of the Monster, it has been suggested that this new Mummy may well have owed his name to the actor too, with the scriptwriters having 'subconsciously (or consciously) inverted and combined the middle two syllables' of Boris Karloff to create Kharis (Lupton 2003: 37).

The 1940s cycle of Mummy films that featured this rebooted bandaged monster (consisting of *The Mummy's Hand* (1940), *The Mummy's Tomb* (Harold Young, USA, 1942), *The Mummy's Ghost* (1944) and *The Mummy's Curse* (1944)) has found little favour with critics, Michael Brunas et al. defining them as 'far closer to juvenilia and kitsch than they are to art' (1990: 338). Jasmine Day assesses them as 'hackneyed' (2006: 67), Bob Brier adjudges them 'all dreadful' (2013: 180) and Jonathan Rigby condemns them as a 'depressing development' with each film being either a 'tired retread' of the one before or a 'by-the-numbers washout' (2017: 241). Susan D. Cowie and Tom Johnson dismiss the series as little more than an unoriginal exercise in replication 'ground out by the Universal horror factory as effortlessly and as cheaply as possible. ... They are plodding, unimaginative and repetitious, with any one picture's best moment a rip-off from a previous entry' (2002: 67, 78–9).

More broadly than this, the entire decade of 1940s Universal horror has tended not to fare well in critical discussion, Carlos Clarens denouncing them as offering 'the poorest kind of escapism' (1967: 101) and William K. Everson dismissing the period as one when the studio was 'shamelessly degrading in cheap thrillers some of their wonderful original creations' (1954: 20). However, such a division between the 'wonderful' 1930s and 'cheap', 'degrading' 1940s is a false dichotomy, not least because Universal in the 1940s did not solely produce cheap horror 'quickies'. As Tom Weaver points out, occasionally a film 'would get special treatment ... the studio's Technicolour remake of *Phantom of the Opera* [Arthur Lubin, USA, 1943] was as lavish as Universal's '40s films could get' (1991: 10). Additionally, even the 1930s horror films were sometimes hurried too, Brian Senn and John Johnson pointing out that *The Mummy* saw Freund bringing the film 'in under schedule and under budget' only after 'an incredibly rushed beginning (he received the final script on a Saturday, cast the film on Sunday, and began shooting on Monday)' (1992: 413).

Even when money was not lavished upon Universal's less prestigious 1940s productions, as was certainly the case with its Mummy films, inventiveness and originality abounded in this studio period virtually defined by its perceived repetitiveness. *Son of Dracula* (1943), for example, featured a downbeat ending as startlingly surprising and impressive as that from any 1930s horror movie. The film's hero arrives at the climax to find the woman he loves dead after becoming a vampire. He places his ring on her finger and, as a sheriff arrives, he witnesses the hero serenely standing by her flaming body, which he has burnt to free her soul. From desolation to elation, *House of Dracula* (1945) saw Lon Chaney Jr.'s Wolf Man surprisingly become a hero and find a cure for his lycanthropy. In *Frankenstein Meets the Wolf Man* (1943) it is a peripheral character, Vazec, dismissed as a drunk, who enjoys his triumphant moment by destroying the monsters and saving the town. The same film introduced the full moon as the catalyst for the Wolf Man's transformation, as previously *The Wolf Man* (George Waggner, USA, 1941) had merely specified that it occurred on nights when the wolfsbane blooms. In fact, *The Mummy's Hand* pre-dated both films in establishing the moon as having transformational powers on Universal's monsters. As the high-priest Andoheb explained in the 1940 film, the Mummy is most effective while the moon is 'high in the heavens' as his 'power to move wanes with the moon'. Yet in spite of such instances of originality and long-lasting influence, Universal's 1940s horror films have suffered critically through a focus upon repetition and disregard for original contributions,[1] with the result that a number of them remain an overlooked treasure-trove, particularly in the case of the rampaging Mummy, the period's most popular and yet misunderstood creation.

The Mummy returns: The 1940s Mummy as cadaverous copy

Universal faced a major problem when relaunching the creature from *The Mummy* in that it had displayed few memorable monstrous characteristics that could be developed. This was primarily because the bandaged monster had appeared on screen for only seconds. Thus, storylines from other Universal horror films and characteristics from other monsters were incorporated in the reboot. For instance, there were established methods for killing certain monsters, such as the wooden stake for Dracula, but as the Mummy had none (except the bizarre magic that issued from the statue of Isis) fire became the Mummy's enemy, just as with Frankenstein's Monster. Narrative outlines from previous horror films were incorporated too. Following *Son of Frankenstein*, in which the Monster began 'to assume the status of a supporting player whose activities took an increasingly secondary role to his human confederates' (Brunas et al. 1990: 179), the Mummy also become a servant to manipulative men. In the same film the Monster had lost the ability to talk that it had developed in the *Bride of Frankenstein*, and like it the Mummy was made mute. Karloff's Mummy was then essentially split in two: Imhotep, the ancient Egyptian bandaged Mummy being recast as the monstrous Kharis, while his modern fez-wearing incarnation, Ardath Bey, was re-embodied as the fanatical priest who controls the Mummy.[2] Yet in spite of the fact that the 1940s Mummy was assembled, like Frankenstein's Monster, from the bits and pieces of others, the 1940s Mummy film is largely undeserving of its enduring reputation as little more than *The Mummy*'s hideous progeny, with some, like Brunas et al., even regretful that they ever came into the world: 'It's a bit sad that Karl Freund's classic, one of the subtlest and poetic of the '30s thrillers, should spawn such formulaic and superficial sequels' (1990: 318).

Strictly speaking, the Mummy films of the 1940s were never actual sequels to *The Mummy*. Nor was *The Mummy* itself ever the urtext that critics like Brunas et al. might wish it were. It was a film that, like F. W. Murnau's *Nosferatu* (1922) and Carl Theodore Dreyer's *Vampyr* (France/Germany, 1931), offered a self-consciously artistic rendition of a popular cultural figure. While greatly admired, these artistic endeavours have not contributed to the ongoing macrotext of their subgenres to the extent their critical status would suggest, primarily because none presented a definitive version of their monsters. James Twitchell, for instance, forcefully argues that such 'artistic important' films, 'instead of advancing the myth ... promulgate one particularly self-conscious version' because 'artists are cultural architects – they don't want to just restack the blocks of myth, they want to rearrange them, create something of their own, something interesting' (1985: 141).

The 1940s Mummy films, like virtually all of Universal's 1940s horror cycle, have not been remembered as 'artistic renditions'. They have been commonly perceived as being 'written by hacks' and 'filmed by technicians' (Twitchell 1985: 141) with Brunas et al. evaluating them as being made by 'competent craftsmen who could grind 'em out on schedule within the limits of the budget' (1990: 185). Yet although Universal's 1940s horror movies were clearly designed to capitalize upon the popularity of earlier films and monsters, it is also clear (but less recognized) that the 1940s hacks and technicians, limited by the constraints of low-budget genre production, succeeded in 'grinding out' a Mummy, as well as other versions of monsters, that have in many respects eclipsed their 1930s predecessors and, in the process, managed to do so with no small amount of rearranging and cultural architecture of their own.

More than the sum of its parts: Innovation and the 1940s Mummy

James B. Twitchell's division of Universal horror into two distinct decade-based camps exemplifies how the studio's output is commonly critically regarded:

> Looking back to the 1930s and the l940s one sees the Universal deluge of horror movies coming in two waves: in the first, the individual film makers experimented with motifs, situations, and characters, and in the second, the studio executives sought to consolidate their gains by working the same sequences over and over. (1985: 188)

A distinction is drawn between 1930s art and innovation versus 1940s financially motivated production-line horror presided over by dollar-driven executives. Universal's 1940s horror is denigrated for offering little in the way of originality for audiences who took pleasure from familiar repetition: a view given substance by influential aspects of genre theory, such as Rick Altman's contention that 'the pleasure of genre film spectatorship ... derives more from reaffirmation than from novelty' (2000: 25). Nigel Andrews certainly perceived a lack of novelty in the 1940s, contending that after the 1930s 'heady heyday the horror film ... went into a long period of stagnation until the end of the 1940s. Audiences must have felt stuck in some recurring nightmare as sequel after sequel – almost invariably inferior to its original attempted to squeeze more milk from the recalcitrant udders' (1986: 38).

However, in contrast to such damning criticism, 1940s Universal horror was more than just a cycle winding down, producing pale shadows of original versions. Characters and storylines were often rethought and reinvented. While elements were borrowed, they were also experimented with and sometimes improved upon. Alongside some of the more far-fetched plot elements that were introduced to distinguish 1940s monsters from previous renditions, such as the Monster's desire to swap brains with a little girl in *The Ghost of Frankenstein* (Erle C. Kenton, USA, 1942), narratives and monsters were also reconceived and transformed in highly memorable ways. Dracula was imaginatively reinterpreted in John Carradine's performance in *House of Dracula* (1945) as an American southern gent, 'less Continental Count than Kentucky Colonel' (Brunas et al. 1990: 521) who actually wants a cure for his vampirism. Tom Weaver argues that this 'smooth, sexy new' interpretation of Dracula has proven the most influential of Universal's vampires as this 'handsome, classy, stylish Count ... has been seen in more subsequent movies than the types played by

Lugosi' (1999: 179). *Interview with the Vampire* (Neil Jordan, USA, 1994), *True Blood* (Alan Ball, USA, 2008–14) and a multitude of other Southern vampire tales knowingly or unknowingly owe a great debt to this film.

Lon Chaney Jr. also offered a novel interpretation of the vampire in *Son of Dracula* (1943), this time as a stout and physically threatening vampire that Tom Weaver aptly describes as 'a Midwestern bully' (1999: 181). Important additions to the mythology of the monsters were added too, with this film offering the first on-screen transformation of Dracula into a bat as well as his forming from and dissolving into a cloud of mist. Lon Chaney Jr. also created an original and unforgettable lycanthrope in *The Wolf Man* (1941), which both critically and commercially eclipsed Henry Hull's *Werewolf of London* that had been produced by Universal in 1935.

At Universal in the 1940s monsters tended to appear in series of films, meaning that audiences became increasingly exposed to the creatures, helping to further explain why some 1940s monsters have remained so prominently in the public consciousness. Writers were afforded ongoing opportunities to develop the characters and, in the case of the 1940s Mummy cycle, its writers were evidently fully aware of the sequential nature of the films they were working on as considered repetition became a fundamental part of their appeal. Formulaic elements were overtly foregrounded with audiences treated to an initiation scene for a new priest of Arkam (or sometimes Karnak) at the beginning of each film, the precise dosage of tana fluid needed to give life and movement to the Mummy would be provided, the recitation of the curse of Amun Ra, the repeated use of the Scripps museum as the origin of all the transgressing archaeologists – all became cherished aspects for regular attendees of the Mummy series (just as repetitive elements such as Arkham Asylum are much-loved by Batman devotees today).

Such repeated elements have led to accusations that the 1940s Mummy film was 'repetitious in the extreme' with Kim R. Holston and Tom Winchester, for example, asserting that 'each of the three sequels to *The Mummy's Hand* tells virtually the same story of some ill-advised acolyte … journeying to America to procure the lost remains of Kharis and Ananka' (1997: 342). Andrew Tudor is another who sees only duplication: 'As the pattern repeats itself … there is remarkably little change: the mummy, accidentally or deliberately revived by magic, seeks to be reunited with its lost love who is conveniently reincarnated in the person of the female lead' (1989: 166). However, to be precise, it is only in the final two films of the series that the Mummy seeks 'to be reunited with its lost love'. Only in the last two films is there reincarnation. In none of the films is the Mummy revived by magic. They do not, in fact, reprise the same story. Far from being the same film told four times, when looked at across the series, there are many striking moments and genuine surprises in Kharis' long and developing tale of love and revenge as we see him seek, gain and ultimately lose his heart's desire. In the process of telling the tale the Mummy, as a bandaged monster, for the first time ever received plenty of screen time and this decision to show rather than suggest the monster, perhaps more than anything else, has contributed to the poor standing 1940s Mummy films have among critics.

To see or not to see? That is the question that many critics have debated when it comes to identifying quality horror. William K. Everson is in no doubt that 'the most effective screen horror is … the least detailed screen horror' (1974: 7). Christopher Lee similarly contends that 'what you don't see is far more suggestive and frightening than what you do see' (cited in Lombardi 1994: 60). Carlos Clarens echoes this view in his book *An Illustrated History of the Horror Film* (1967), which Leon Hunt identifies as epitomizing 'longstanding critical orthodoxy – "good" horror movies do not show much actual horror (Universal, Lewton, Tourneur), but "bad" ones do (Hammer, the Italians) because they lack imagination, taste, and restraint' (2000: 326). Although Hammer and the Italians have been to a considerable degree critically reappraised and even rescued since Clarens's book, Hunt is only half-right regarding Universal. Whereas 1930s Universal horror is generally well-regarded, the 1940s Universal horror film has yet to be convincingly critically rescued and, perhaps, never will be because of its perceived fatal flaw, summed up in Bernard F. Dick's verdict that Val Lewton's RKO horror output 'found its place in film history by favouring the unseen over the seen (*Cat People* (1942), *The Curse of the Cat People* [Gunther V. Fritsch, Robert Wise, USA] (1944), and *Isle of the Dead* [Mark Robson, USA] (1945), Universal went the monster route' (1997:117-8). Universal appearing in cadence signifies the lowly position in which its 1940s output is commonly held, particularly in comparison with RKO's, because of going 'the monster route'.

The critical preference for films that 'suggest' the presence of monsters over those that choose to 'show' them has resulted in critics regularly getting it wrong when choosing the monster films that have provided the most definitive portrayals of monsters. Irrespective of the artistic qualities of the movies they are in, monsters have a far better chance of becoming iconic when audiences can see them. It is thus the 1940s lumbering Mummy that is the one largely remembered because, unlike the ill-defined Cat People themselves, the forgotten residents of the Isle of the Dead or the largely motionless bandaged Mummy of 1932, the 1940s Mummy was a monster who had ample on-screen time.

The Mummy's Hand (1940): Reinventing the Mummy

The Mummy appeared in full-fledged, shambling, bandaged, monstrous form for the first time in 1940 in the 67-minute-long B movie *The Mummy's Hand*. It is a film that contains comic-strip dialogue, eerie music and hokey set-ups, completely abandoning the mood of sombre romance found in *The Mummy*. As Brunas et al. note,

> With a budget set at a tight $80,000 … rampant cost-cutting is evidenced by the film's utilization of stock shots (chiefly from *The Mummy*), hand-me-down sets (most notably the extravagant temple set left over from James Whale's *Green Hell* [USA, 1940]), a musical score lifted almost entirely from *Son of Frankenstein*, a cast boasting no horror names (fifth-billed George Zucco hadn't

yet become firmly established in the genre) ... [and] ... many lines of dialogue are very obviously redubbed and the whirr of the camera can be heard in several scenes. (1990: 229-30)³

In spite of all this *The Mummy's Hand* is a film that, as well as being one of Universal's two most profitable B's of that year,⁴ has a significance that far outweighs its artistic merits because it introduced the Mummy in the form that would become seminal.⁵ Jeremy Dyson is right to an extent when he states that 'the Mummy myth started here'. Although, as he points out, the film 'is little more than a slickly made adventure based around a treasure hunt, making use of the kind of thrills and situations popular in the serials of the day, it does contain something darker and genuinely scary in the form of the lumbering Kharis' (1997: 80–1), who the film introduces in its final half hour.

Griffin Jay, a writer of radio mysteries, developed a new back story for the Mummy (and would develop the character further as writer of the next two Kharis movies, *The Mummy's Tomb* (1942) and *The Mummy's Ghost* (1944)) and a minor cowboy star from the silent era, Tom Tyler, was hired to play him, supposedly 'because Universal felt his looks were close enough to Boris Karloff's that he could easily be intercut with stock footage from *The Mummy* for the flashback scenes' (Mallory 2009: 116). However, in spite of any such resemblance, he portrayed a very changed monster to Karloff's. Unlike Imhotep, who is able to assume near human form and pass himself off as a normal man, Tyler's Kharis remains a cursed, mummified and half-crippled corpse throughout.⁶

Caught in the act of trying to resurrect his lover Ananka in ancient Egypt with stolen sacred tana leaves, Kharis' tongue was cut out so that the gods could not hear him. Cursed to protect her tomb for eternity and kept alive by the very leaves he had tried to steal, the film follows his continued enslavement in the present day. Now he is under the control of a high-priest of Karnak, Andoheb (Georgo Zucco), a man intent on killing all of the members of an archaeological expedition excavating Ananka's tomb. After much stalking and strangling on the part of the Mummy, the film ends with Kharis bested by being burnt alive, Andoheb thwarted by being shot and Ananka and her treasure being transported to a museum in America by the survivors.

In contrast to how this synopsis sounds, the film is entertaining, good-natured and full of comedy relief. One important exception, though, is the Mummy himself who is depicted as a solemn figure throughout. An impressive costume of tattered bandages and face-wrinkling make-up was greatly enhanced by the editor blacking out his eyes in post-production, resulting in black hollows that Leslie Halliwell describes as 'bottomless pools of quivering black jelly' (1988: 216-7) and David Huckvale as 'black holes of swirling, eldritch oblivion' that are 'far more frightening than the eyes of any subsequent mummy' (2012: 22). It is a subtle touch in a film not readily associated with subtlety – the empty eye-sockets effectively conveying the emptiness of Kharis' soul as an instrument of blind and mindless vengeance and standing in marked contrast to the expressiveness of Karloff's eyes so focused upon in *The Mummy*. A leg and an arm are also rendered useless because he was not given enough tana fluid to fully revive him. The end result is truly memorable: deformed, head cast downwards and silent, a servant to Andoheb's Caligari-like master, addicted to a substance that sustains his existence, Kharis is a creature of pent up frustration forced to act with little free will (an ironic fate for the Mummy who was himself the mesmeric slave-master in *The Mummy* (1932)).

Leslie Halliwell suggests that 'a living 4,000 year-old Mummy, all earth mould and dirty bandages, is a pretty loathsome concept, not a creature which even the most ardent horror fan can readily take to his heart' (1988: 184). Yet the Mummy was taken to the hearts of many filmgoers, despite the low-budget nature of the series he was in, because he was a haunting and complicated creation. As Gregory William Mank expresses, 'There was something wonderfully spooky about Kharis, sipping his Tana leaves, shuffling across Universal's back lot under the full moon, performing his weird shuffling dance to the strains of Hans J. Salter's rhapsodic music' (2000: 6). Kharis is a tortured and conflicted individual who is bound, silenced, crippled, hunted, enslaved and lovelorn, a creature that could hardly be more pathetic, more deserving of sympathy and yet who is himself quite capable, even by today's standards, of the most shocking and merciless cruelty: qualities that would be further developed in the sequels to *The Mummy's Hand*.

The Mummy's Tomb (1942): A memorably murderous Mummy

The Mummy's Hand proved so popular with audiences that it was followed in 1942 by *The Mummy's Tomb* (1942), which starred Lon Chaney Jr. as the Mummy for the first time. In this film's story, twenty years have elapsed since the events of *The Mummy's Hand* and the priest Andoheb, it is revealed, against all odds has recovered from being shot. Now aged, he inducts his young aide Mehemet Bey (Turhan Bey) into the priesthood and sends him overseas to accompany the Mummy, who has also survived, on a mission to punish those who removed Ananka from her eternal resting place.

Like prior Egyptian priests, such as the priestess Ka from *The Silent Mystery* (1918) and the zealous and ruthless priests of the Temple of Amenhotep II, who in Universal's *Detective Lloyd* (Henry Macrae, UK/USA, 1932) come to London in search of Tutankhamun's stolen Egyptian armlet (*Motion Picture Herald* 1932: 43), Mehemet seeks retribution on those he considers to be tomb robbers. However, as well as being an instrument of vengeance, Mehemet is now also charged with protecting the Mummy and to be its companion. As he himself states: 'It is my duty to offer prayers each night, so that the soul of my dear one is not left alone to wander lonely and forgotten through the spaces of time.' The spaces he and the Mummy ended up wandering are in Massachusetts, making *The Mummy's Tomb* the first film to bring a vengeful undead Mummy to America.

In spite of this significant change of location, critics have identified little new in the film, Clive Hirschhorn viewing it as one that nothing can save from 'the tedium generated by over-familiarity with the subject matter and the stereotyped characters' (2000: 132). Yet, despite some obvious similarities in plot (including the Mummy once more being set on fire at the end), *The Mummy's Tomb* is in fact very different from the light-hearted *The Mummy's Hand*, in no small part because the character of the Mummy itself is so particularly fearsome in this film. Following the fire that saw the demise of Kharis at the end of *The Mummy's Hand*, here he returns as a burnt brute. Now he is bereft of an eye on his charred face and a hand too, leaving only a scorched stump (Figure 6.1).

It is a film that sets out to frighten, with not one moment of comedy to lighten the mood, in contrast to the many such moments that occurred throughout *The Mummy's Hand*. It also offers a far subtler handling of the Mummy in the early parts of the story, with the horror to come suggested rather than shown. Aside from scenes reprising what happened in *The Mummy's Hand* at the very beginning, it is only comparatively late into the film that the Mummy is actually seen attacking anyone in its new American setting. Until then we get only partial glimpses of him in well-crafted sequences that convey his elusive and haunting moonlight progress through the landscape as he inexorably moves towards his targets: a couple of young lovers in a car feel afraid as they sense his approach, a sleeping woman senses a shadow fall across her face through a window, a horse becomes spooked, dogs bark, but nobody actually sees the Mummy. The Mummy's advance is overlaid with foreboding and because of this elaborate treatment his inevitable attacks are increasingly anticipated by both characters and audience: 'This is the first time I ever had a shadow for a suspect' says a bemused sheriff.

Babe Jenson, the comedy relief from *The Mummy's Hand*, but this time portrayed as a serious and knowledgeable figure (his change of persona perhaps reflected in his being renamed Babe Hanson), arrives to warn the townsfolk about the threat of the monster, but nobody will listen. In this respect he is a direct forerunner of Loomis (played by Donald Pleasance) in *Halloween* (John Carpenter, USA, 1978) thirty years later, whom nobody would heed either. Years ahead of its time, the film lays out

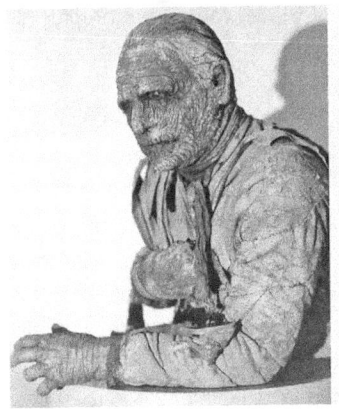 

Fig. 6.1 Kharis in *The Mummy's Tomb* (1942): Minus the Mummy's hand.

pretty much all of the ground rules for the 1970s slasher movie by presenting a killer (with a known backstory) in a small American suburban town who remains unseen by any surviving citizens until after the body count has considerably risen. This hunting monstrous executioner, just as in *Halloween* and *Friday the Thirteenth Part 2* (Steve Miner, USA, 1981), has his face hidden by a featureless mask and proves an astonishingly brutal, virtually unstoppable hands-on killing machine. He adheres to no sense of fair play and betrays no hint of mercy. He focuses on specific victims but cares not that he murders innocent bystanders along the way and, going even further than the slasher film, in this movie he succeeds in murdering all of his targets.

Brutal and graphic murder was unusual in 1940s horror, largely because of the constraints imposed by the Production Code after 1934. As Jon Towlson (2016) explains, post-production code horror saw psychological horror slowly come to the fore in order to avoid censorship issues at home. As well as American censors, there was also 'increasing resistance of foreign censors' to accept horror films after 1934 (Berenstein 1996a: 15), further promoting a reduction in explicit scenes. *The Mummy's Tomb*, however, bucked this trend and proved to be as graphic as any early 1930s horror. In the film Steve Banning, the hero of *The Mummy's Hand*, and his sister, both now aged, are strangled. Babe Hanson is next, killed in the most explicit murder in the entire series. While low-speed pursuit by a semi-crippled Mummy may now have become a comic cliché, in this film it is genuinely chilling. The climax of the extended sequence in which the Mummy tracks down Hanson is the protracted murder in a back alley of a trapped and terrified man. Hanson does not stand still in petrified fright but runs, tries to jump a fence in desperation and is dragged down. Cornered, he frantically beats his assailant with a block of wood, the only weapon he can find, but nothing is enough against the relentless Mummy. He is eventually pushed to the floor with legs kicking and arms thumping until he is overwhelmed and very slowly throttled. It is a scene that perfectly encapsulates the Mummy as an emotionless physical killer, devoid of expression or compassion: a role that Lon Chaney Jr. enhanced by investing so little of himself into playing the part. By his own admission, he lacked any real interest in the character, but this fortuitously only served to further facilitate a convincing enactment of the Mummy as a horrifyingly detached automaton.

Lon Chaney Jr.: Cursing the Mummy!

After his success as *The Wolf Man* in 1941, Chaney Jr. had been launched as 'The New Master Character Creator' in a title reminiscent of his father's 'Man of a Thousand Faces', with his casting as the Mummy a natural fit for this image: but in truth, anybody could have played the part. Jack Pierce, the celebrated make-up artist who created the look of Frankenstein's Monster in 1931, fashioned a mask (saving a great deal of make-up time) that revealed nothing but a single eye of the actor under it, enabling a stuntman, Eddie Parker, to imperceptibly stand in for Chaney Jr. for many sequences. The very fact that the features-obscuring mask allowed Parker to look like Chaney Jr. would have understandably made the role unappealing to any actor trying to promote himself. Chaney Jr. displayed little pride in being associated with the figure in the various interviews he conducted throughout his life, reserving his praise for *The Wolf Man*, which he stated was 'the best of my horror films – because he is mine' (cited in Brosnan 1976: 22):

> There wasn't anything you could do with the Mummy. You just got into the makeup and bandages and walked around dragging your leg. I liked playing the Wolf Man a lot better. … You had a chance to do some acting, and you had dialogue. All they ever wanted the Mummy to do was put his hand way out in front of him and then grab somebody, and start strangling him. (cited in Haydock 1975: 9)

Conceivably part of his antipathy towards the Mummy also stemmed from the fact that, unlike the Wolf Man, he did not feel the role was his. It was a figure already established by others and thus contributed to his own fear of being considered an inferior follow-on: a fear that proved well-founded as numerous critics felt he was precisely that. 'Lon Chaney Jr.' was 'a particularly dire sequel to Lon Chaney Sr.', Nigel Andrews bluntly put it (1986: 38), an appraisal that Brunas et al. agree with, asserting that he was ill-equipped for the role of the Mummy having 'inherited precious little of his father's legendary gift for mime' (1990: 288). Creighton Chaney had never wanted to cash in on his father's name in the first place, fully aware that comparisons would be drawn. 'I am not proud of Lon Chaney Jnr' he said later in life, 'they had to starve me to make me take this name' (cited in Brosnan 1976: 20). He had no desire to play the Mummy either: 'I didn't want to do the part, but I was under contract, so I did what they gave me' (cited in Haydock 1975: 10).

A great deal of the praise bestowed upon certain horror actors, including his father Lon Chaney, has been in recognition of the suffering undertaken to convincingly play their monster roles: for enduring hours of discomfort on a daily basis in the make-up artist's chair, most famously Jack Pierce's. As far as the critics were concerned 'the lengthier the time reported, the greater the discomfort, the better' (Peirse 2013: 34). Yet Chaney Jr. suffered also and more than most, as the Mummy proved an extremely uncomfortable part to play. He complained that the rubber mask gave him an allergy (Mank 1999a: 38), which proved particularly troublesome as the Mummy films were shot at the height of summer on the Universal back lot in the San Fernando Valley (Mank 1999b: 326). 'I sweat and I can't wipe it away. I itch and I can't scratch' (cited in Brunas et al. 1990: 431), he grumbled. He especially disliked making *The Mummy's Curse*:

> I was completely covered from head to foot with a suit and rubber mask; the only thing that was exposed was my right [sic] eye! … The temperature was in the upper nineties! It was so hot that I went to my dressing room between scenes, opened a refrigerator and lay down next to it. It was my only relief from the heat. (cited in *Castle of Frankenstein* 1966: 26)

In addition to combatting the temperature, he was also battling alcoholism. According to a colleague, the actor William Phipps, Chaney admitted to him 'that he had a container (presumably a hip flask) of vodka tucked away somewhere in his Mummy costume, with a long straw leading up inside the costume to his mouth. Chaney would suck on the end of the straw between takes, then hide it behind the bandages around his neck before each take' (Weaver 1999: 165-6).

Despite the fact that Reginald LeBorg, the director of *The Mummy's Ghost*, found his drinking problematic, he still praised him highly for his commitment to playing the Mummy, stating how in a scene set in a museum:

> There was to be a scuffle between the mummy and a guard. I had planned to have Chaney crash through the glass doors that led to the museum's Egyptian room. I asked that the plate glass be replaced with breakaway glass. But when I arrived on the set the day of shooting that scene, the breakaway glass had not been substituted. I didn't want to hold up production, so I told Chaney just to push the door open instead of crashing through. Chaney did as I suggested during the rehearsal, but when it came to the actual shooting of the scene, after the scuffle, he crashed right through the plate glass, slightly injuring one of his hands in the process. He wanted to show me he wasn't afraid to go through plate glass, and he smiled with gratification when I complimented his bravado. His father would have done it just like that, he asserted. (cited in Peary 1978: 337-8)

In spite of such commitment to a role he apparently never wanted, Chaney Jr.'s reputation was not enhanced by playing the part and some even cast doubt as to whether it was him at all beneath the Mummy's costume. William K. Everson, for instance, argued that 'certainly it didn't look like him, and beneath all that make-up it was difficult to tell whether or not Universal were using some hapless extra and exploiting the mere name of Chaney' (1955: 29). Brunas et al. suggest writer-turned-director Joe Dante was the 'first to hatch this theory in a 1962 edition of *Famous Monsters*', but repudiate it as nothing more than a baseless rumour:

> Although the horror star had various stand-ins and stunt doubles (Edwin Parker and Bob Pepper, to name two) during the shooting of these pictures, the fact that he did indeed don the wrappings is attested by Reginald LeBorg, Elyse Knox, Peter Coe, Martin Kosleck, Virginia Christine and a backlog of studio production reports. (1990: 479)

Although the reluctant star was met by critics equally reluctant to give him credit for playing the Mummy, as Michael Pitts points out, Chaney Jr. and the Mummy were nevertheless both a great success. 'During the period from 1940 to 1946, Lon Chaney, Jr., reigned as the screen's "king of horror", almost singlehandedly keeping the horror film alive. Although his productions were sometimes "B" outings, they never failed to have a huge following and make big profits' (1981: 47). So big a draw did he prove that, as David Pirie points out, 'by 1943 Universal had starred him as the Mummy, the Wolf Man and Frankenstein's monster. The studio was still blind to the enormous division that separated those parts from Count Dracula, so in 1943 they decided to build *Son of Dracula* around Chaney as well' (1977: 58). Of note here is Pirie's identification of an 'enormous division' between the Mummy and Dracula that had developed by the 1940s. As discussed in Chapter 5, *The Mummy* (1932) has regularly been accused of being a carbon copy of Tod Browning's 1931 *Dracula*, so Pirie's observation that the creatures were now poles apart demonstrates just how far the Mummy had been transformed by the early 1940s. Where Karloff's Mummy had been eloquent, hypnotic and frail, Chaney Jr.'s was now silent, obedient and virtually indestructible.

The Mummy in America: Fear and roaming in New England

It was not just Chaney as the Mummy or the brutish Mummy itself that have been remembered as unsatisfactory but also the American setting in which the Mummy was placed in *The Mummy's Tomb* and the films that followed it. William K. Everson believed it to be a 'clumsy and unworkable contrivance' (1974: 89) with Brunas et al. going further still: 'The idea of a Mummy slinking through the back alleys of New England was so ludicrously inappropriate, it engendered little fright or intrigue. Removed from the mystical trappings of Egypt, the Mummy seemed more of an anachronism than a monster, more of a curiosity than a threat' (1990: 321–2). However, Douglas Drake, a rather lonely voice among critics, disagrees:

> The mere conception of an Egyptian mummy, supposedly dead for some thousands of years, prowling through the pure Americana of a peaceful New England countryside, is horrifying in itself, and this aspect was heavily stressed – the clean white homes of the Connecticut village, the farms, the sheriff's posse hunting down the monster, the fresh, youthful college students, the very air of clean wholesomeness clouded over by the foul breath from an ancient grave, with a horrible Egyptian mummy blundering in the midst of it all, made an incongruous and frightening picture. (1966: 190–1)

Drake makes a useful point because 'incongruity' is integral to a great deal of horror and, for some, is an essential component of the genre. James B. Twitchell argues that 'what we are frightened of usually has to do with the invasion of the abnormal into the world of the normal' (1985: 10). Robin Wood offers 'a simple and obvious basic formula for the horror film: normality is threatened by the Monster' (1984: 175), while S. S. Prawer argues that horror films often play on the fear that strangers may invade our secure world and destroy us (1980: 58).

The Mummy coming to America, rather than just being 'ludicrously inappropriate', offered an effective juxtaposition between the 'abnormal' and ancient and idyllically presented modern day. The ancient monster was not parachuted into the bustling, chaotic modern big city that featured in films like *The Mystery of the Wax Museum* (1933), *King Kong* (1933) and *Cat People* (1942), but instead invaded the queasy quaintness of 'normal' and 'secure' small-town America, an effective but still largely underappreciated aspect of 1940s innovation that had a great and lasting effect on the horror genre, and most immediately on the sci-fi horror of the following decade.

A notable development in the 1950s was, as Cristina Isabel Pinedo points out, that horror films often located their scientific monsters in American small towns (1997: 15). The small town setting of *The Mummy's Tomb* and its two sequels are a 'missing link' between the old world horror located in fictitious European villages such as Visaria and Regalsberg that featured in 1930s horror and the tranquil contemporary American towns that came under threat in 1950s horror from alien or scientifically created creatures like the Body Snatchers and the Fly (to be followed in the proceeding years by more human killers such as Norman Bates, Michael Myers and Jason Vorhees) (Figure 6.2).

The 1940s Mummy itself is also significant as a 'missing link' in that it represented a step away from the supernatural monsters of the 1930s and towards the more 'scientific' monsters of the 1950s, with Kharis no longer a purely supernatural creature but one maintained by the chemical properties of tana leaves, a de-mystifying of the monster that formed part of an ongoing practice within the Universal horror cycle. As early as 1936 in *Dracula's Daughter* (Lambert Hillyer, USA) Countess Zaleska's vampirism had been presented as a psychological addiction and as late as 1945 in *House of Dracula* the Count sought a scientific cure for his vampirism, which was diagnosed as a blood disease, with the Wolf Man successfully finding a medical remedy for his affliction. Universal's 1940s horror films were thus not just a regrettable postscript to the superior horror creations of the early 1930s but also a new beginning that would have long-lasting influence on sci-fi and horror thereafter.

Fig. 6.2 The masked killer stalks small-town America decades before the slasher movie in *The Mummy's Tomb* (1942).

The Mummy's Ghost (1944): Escaping bandaged bondage

The Mummy's Tomb, like its predecessor, made a lot of money (Halliwell 1988: 221) and even ended up being released as a main attraction (Brunas et al. 1990: 318). Consequently, 1944 saw the release of two Mummy movies: *The Mummy's Ghost* and *The Mummy's Curse*, with Chaney Jr. reprising his role as the Mummy in both. As the priest Mehemet Bey had been killed in the previous film, a new priest, Yousef Bey (John Carradine), arrives in New England under new orders to help the Mummy find his 'beloved princess' (a more sympathetic description of the two given by the priest this time around). It is revealed that Ananka herself was also cursed because of her love for Kharis (the first time in the series that she has been pronounced guilty) and that a young college coed, Amina El Harun (Ramsay Ames), now walks the earth as the princess reincarnated. In a move away from the vengeful monster whose sole purpose is to punish the defilers of tombs, the Mummy returns in this film to being obsessively devoted to his ancient love, just as Imhotep had been. However, in stark contrast to Imhotep and Anck-es-en-Amon, the gods now sanctify this love, with the priests now charged with the sacred mission of ensuring that ancient lovers are reunited. The Mummy is no longer driven by his addictive craving for tana leaves, but for Ananka herself. Frustrated and enslaved for two films, Kharis breaks free of his yoke and goes after his beloved rather than her abductors.

As in *The Mummy* (1932), before he can be reunited with his Egyptian princess Kharis has to first deal with a modern rival for his ancient lover's affections. Andrew Tudor asserts that 'as the horror movies of the forties grew shorter and cheaper, the locus of formal identification shifted ... towards the ubiquitous "juvenile leads"' (1989: 86). The beginning of *The Mummy's Ghost* certainly adheres to this formula with the hero, Tom, proving a prime example: an insipid college boy who talks a lot but comprehends little. Quite clearly a grown man, he looks ridiculously old to be wearing his college jumpers, carrying schoolbooks and running around campus with his small dog Peanuts. As Bruce Kawin says of him, 'Tom is the all-time ineffectual patsy of the formula, blindly confident in the status quo of modern America and uncomplicated marriage' (1984: 16).

In contrast Amina, far from being the expected juvenile heroine, is presented as withdrawn from the normality and conformity of the modern American University whose environs Tom revels in. 'Something happens to me when I think of Egypt' she frets as she begins to have strange dreams of another life far more exotic than the one she has on campus. Soon, this other life invades her reality when Kharis arrives to stalk her. As her relationship with Kharis develops and starts to dominate the narrative, we gradually see the alienated and seemingly paranoid heroine who does not fit in begin to come to terms with who she actually is, what she wants and, rather sinisterly, where she does belong.

Of the 1940s Mummy films, this film and its follow-up are the most interesting in terms of developing the Mummy itself. In spite of the traditional stance that the 1940s

Mummy movies simply followed the same formula 'ad nauseum' (Newman 1986: 295), in actuality halfway through the cycle the formula changed. *The Mummy's Hand* and *The Mummy's Tomb* had followed the same lines as *Das Cabinet des Dr Caligari* (1919) and *Murders in the Rue Morgue* (1932) with dichotomized villains. The controlling priest schemes and lusts while the Mummy does little but follow orders. However, the Mummy in *The Mummy's Ghost* is developed along new lines (or older lines if one sees it as a return to the romance of *The Mummy*) as the instrument of vengeance transforms into a being bent on his own mission to revive and be reunited with Ananka. While still bereft of any humanizing personality traits, he was now a more sympathetic figure, so much so that the director Reginald LeBorg conceived of him as 'that poor Mummy' (cited in Weaver 1999: 165).

The Mummy's shadowy presence, established in *The Mummy's Tomb*, continues in *The Mummy's Ghost*. However, rather than signalling his arrival, this time the shadow of the Mummy serves to indicate his growing influence over his bride. When Amina and Tom profess their love for each other in his car the shadow of the Mummy falls across her and she feels uneasy. Taken home, the Mummy's shadow crosses her sleeping form and she awakens in a trance, follows him and collapses at his feet, white streaks forming in her hair. Finally, towards the end of the film, the priest announces that she is indeed Ananka in new form, the Mummy's shadow falls across her one final time, and her hair turns snow white, bringing her transformation into his ancient bride towards completion. Then, in spite of the predictability of the hero's arrival in the nick of time, events do not occur as one would anticipate. Rather than following the formula 'ad nauseum', *The Mummy's Ghost* turns formulaic aspects against themselves.

In a unique ending for cinematic horror of the period, the monster wins the girl and escapes the mob (led by Tom and his dog Peanuts). As Bruce Kawin explains,

> Aside from the St. Bartholomew's Day Massacre sequence of *Intolerance* [1916] there are very few examples of failed climactic chases in the whole history of film. One of the most troubling closes *The Mummy's Ghost*. Because the chase does fail, and in a masterful way. As Kharis carries her, Amina becomes entirely Ananka: her flesh dries, her frame contracts, but she is still alive. Imhotep's project has been fulfilled (Kharis too has returned to his origins): the two lovers are united as living mummies. This rare moment of absolute fulfilment of forbidden love, which Amina has been shrinking from and growing toward, and which Kharis has been yearning after for 3000 years, is immediately succeeded by their deaths – they drown in the swamp. The posse stands there looking beaten; Tom (who has seen Ananka's face) is a wreck; Peanuts is alone on the swampbank cocking his puzzled head. There is a sudden feeling of 'what happened!' Suddenly a real horror has asserted itself – Amina has given herself over to her unconscious drives; the Mummy has abducted her and gotten away with it; all the formulas have failed at once. (1984: 17-8)

The Mummy's Ghost finishes with an undefeated, triumphant monster and order in chaos. In many respects it is a remarkable climax because the heroine, whom we assumed would at some point break the spell over her and resist, do the right thing, never does. Rather than having boy meets girl, boy loses girl to monster, boy reclaims girl from monster, we have instead monster meets girl (in ancient Egypt), monster loses girl to boy, monster reclaims girl from boy. Heroes lose, mortal love lies unfulfilled and Kharis and Ananka achieve their hearts' desires.

While certainly a bravura ending, some caveats must be added to perceiving it as being quite as utterly unexpected or innovative as Kawin suggests. A similarly downbeat ending had already concluded *Son of Dracula* the year before in which the romantic lead had likewise been left a broken man after losing the woman he loved at the finale. It had also featured a woman intentionally giving herself over to the creature. As Peter Hutchings observes, there are also clues provided in *The Mummy's Ghost* that Amina might be susceptible to the Mummy's allure because she is presented as 'foreign (Egyptian), enigmatic and into reading books like *The Tombs of Ancient Egypt*' (2002). The sudden ageing of beautiful, intrinsically ancient women had also recently appeared in two films. In *She* (Lansing C. Holden, Irving Pichel, USA, 1935) the ancient queen Ayesha rapidly aged when she stepped into a sacred flame, as had Lo-Tsen in *Lost Horizon* (Frank Capra, USA, 1937) when she tried to leave Shangri-La. For Amina's sudden ageing, the director Reginald LeBorg admitted to being inspired by *Lost Horizon*: 'We discussed the finale ... and I said, "Why not let Amina sink with the Mummy? Why should there always be a happy ending?" Somebody else said, "No, we might make a sequel." I told him, "The Mummy is always coming up – Ananka doesn't have to!"' (cited in Brunas et al. 1990: 431). Taking into consideration this sequel to come, the ending was probably conceived of more as a cliff-hanger than a dénouement, especially as this was already the third entry in the series and it was becoming common practice at Universal to continue monsters storylines across films, with for instance, *Frankenstein Meets the Wolf Man* (1943) continuing the story where *The Ghost of Frankenstein* (1942) left off.

Yet the climax of *The Mummy's Ghost* remains a startling ending nevertheless, primarily because unlike *The Mummy* in which it was Frank who would walk off with the girl, the film inverts the ending by having the Mummy do so. It was evidently effective, being largely recreated in Universal's next horror film, *House of Frankenstein* (Erle C. Kenton, USA, 1944), which ends with the Monster, similarly chased by a mob, sinking into a swamp cradling the body of a scientist who had once shown him kindness. Unfortunately for Kharis, his ambition to remain undisturbed and united in death with his beloved would last less than a year.

The Mummy's Curse (1944): The female Mummy returns

The Mummy's Ghost was followed by *The Mummy's Curse* only eight months later, but following the convention of jumping forward in time between films, this sequel begins twenty-five years on from where the previous film left off.[7] This time Kharis and Ananka are dug out of the bog they had disappeared into together for further study, although in a moment that 'represents perhaps the biggest single continuity inconsistency in all of Universal Horror' (Mallory 2009: 123), the bog they come out of is now in Louisiana rather than in New England, which is where it had been at the end of *The Mummy's Ghost*. This dramatic licence aside, the film continues the series' record of continued innovation by this time fully developing the Mummy's bride as a character (after an initial script treatment entitled *The Mummy Returns* was jettisoned that had Kharis dug up, used as a scarecrow and becoming a carnival attraction who runs amuck).[8] *The Mummy's Curse* features a very different Ananka (literally, as this time she's played by Virginia Christine) from *The Mummy's Ghost*, one who rather than being tormented yet intrigued by dreams and who gives herself to the monster, now exists in total fear of Kharis. She prefers life to the eternal death she has sampled, or maybe it is the eternal company of the obsessed Mummy that she has now come to dread.

A withered hand erupting from beneath the earth, signalling Ananka's resurrection, marks the beginning of perhaps the most startling and influential sequence in the entire 1940s series. So potent is this image of her hand emerging from the soil that it would become a staple of horror used in films for decades thereafter, such as *Carnival of Souls* (Herk Harvey, USA, 1962), *Carrie* (Brian De Palma, USA, 1976) and *The Evil Dead* (Sam Raimi, USA, 1981). Still ancient and dirt-encrusted, she unburies herself and unsteadily walks into a lake where she washes the dirt from her skin to reveal herself as young and beautiful once more. With no memory of who she is or was, the film shows her finding a job, friends and beginning to make a new and happy life for herself. She cannot, however, escape the pursuing Kharis, who eventually tracks her down until, exhausted and afraid, she collapses at the sight of him, never to regain consciousness.

In the shooting script there is a moment where, as in *The Mummy's Ghost*, Ananka gave herself over to the monster, weakly whispering 'Kharis ... I am tired. ... (wearily) Take me with you ... so that I may know ... rest' (Mank 2000: 80). However, its omission from the finished film serves to emphasize that Ananka takes her terror of Kharis with her to the grave. Despite all her hopes for a normal life, she is unwillingly returned to death as Kharis places her in her sarcophagus wherein, within a short while, she becomes inert and ancient once more: the curse's greatest victim. After Kharis is crushed in a collapsing building and the priest is also killed, the film ends with the announcement that the pair will be exhibited in the Scripps museum. It is a sad ending to the series where this time nobody gets what they wanted. Despite Ananka being less than willing to die for love, she is doomed to rest for eternity next to the man who so frightened her, while Kharis himself is destined for public display next to her having clearly failed in his mission to guard against those who desecrate her tomb. With all the priests now dead, and with them the secret for reviving the Mummy, Kharis and Ananka are destined to remain helpless and dead forever, never to be alone or returned home.

The demise and rise of the Mummy: To buffoon and back again

After four films, most critics were probably content to see the story of Kharis finally come to an end in *The Mummy's Curse*, not least Donald F. Glut who summed up the 1940s Mummy as follows:

> It was miraculous that the Mummy managed to survive the same plot situations and character motivations through a total of four movies. The character of Kharis was simply too limited to cast him in fresh or original stories. Unlike Dracula and the Wolf Man, he was neither cunning nor tragically heroic. He simply lumbered about the countryside dragging his bad leg, moving at a cripple's pace. Somehow he always managed to overtake and strangle his victims, who either blundered into some cul-de-sac or stood in one spot shivering with fear as the Mummy casually reached out and strangled them. (1978: 182)

One cannot entirely blame Glut for this account, as the image of Kharis he recalls is the one that is popularly remembered and so often derided. However, the very fact that it is the one recalled does at the very least reveal how successful the 'hacks and technicians' of the 1940s were in developing an enduring and recognizable monster – one that owes so much to their critically maligned creativity and very little to 'Karl Freund's classic' (Brunas et al. 1990: 318). So successful were they, in fact, in redefining the 1932 Mummy that even otherwise reliable critics have become confused. Nigel Andrews, who takes the traditional line that the 1940s offered nothing but dire sequels, is clearly struck by them nevertheless when he explains how '1932, saw *The Mummy* crashing into being, with Karloff … ogre-ing into action as a 4000-year-old Egyptian corpse' (1986: 33). Wheeler Winston Dixon who dismisses the 1940s Mummy films as 'without exception cheap and shoddy affairs' describes Karloff's Imhotep as 'an undying mummy who seeks vengeance on his victims' (2010: 40–1), when, as with Andrews, he is inadvertently describing Kharis from the 1940s. Arnold Madison in *Mummies in Fact and Fiction* outlines plotlines from the 1940s cycle to describe the 1932 film (1980: 67) and Edward Edelson similarly illustrates how it is the 1940s renditions that have stuck in the memory when he describes *The Mummy* (1932) 'in which Karloff played a peculiar Egyptian archaeologist [who] … wanted to prevent the opening of the tomb of an ancient Egyptian princess named Ananka' (1973: 63).

Each film in the Mummy series of the 1940s, in spite of its derivative aspects, added important and memorable elements to the Mummy's story that lastingly contributed to the macrotext of the Mummy genre and the horror genre in general. Although there remains the common assumption that if one compares Universal horror of the 1930s and 1940s then 'clearly, it is the first wave that still surges through popular culture' (Twitchell 1985: 188), the reality is that there is just the belief that it does. Certainly, as far as the Mummy and popular culture are concerned, the second wave has to a large degree washed away the first.

After an eleven-year hiatus, *Abbott and Costello Meet the Mummy* (Charles Lamont, USA, 1955) delivered Universal's final, belated take on the Mummy in the form of Klaris (played by Eddie Parker, the stunt man who had doubled for Lon Chaney Jr. as the Mummy in the 1940s) who, unlike his 1940s predecessor, 'stomped about with four good limbs' (Willis 1997: 186) and was not especially menacing. For Leslie Halliwell, the biggest disappointment was its unfrightening costume: 'A sort of turn-of-the-century one-piece bathing suit with facial wrappings amounting to little more than a yashmak', giving the Mummy an intolerable 'teddy bear aspect' (1988: 228). He was not alone in this appraisal, as for many this descent into becoming little more than a comedy character marked an all-time low for the Mummy, along with the rest of Universal's monsters, most of whom at one time or another ended up guest-starring in Abbott and Costello movies. Even Chaney Jr. criticized the films, despite playing the Wolf Man in *Abbott and Costello Meet Frankenstein* (Charles T. Barton, USA, 1948), maintaining that the comedy duo 'ruined the horror field' because 'they made buffoons out of the monsters' (cited in Gifford 1973b: 208).

Meeting Abbott and Costello proved not to be the end of the road, but simply a detour for Universal's monsters, as a mere four years after this comedy take on the Mummy it rose again in Hammer's *The Mummy* in 1959, reimagined this time in 'terrifying technicolour'. Just as in *The Mummy's Tomb*, the Mummy once more became a fearsome and forbidding creation, but this time was provided with a worthy, principled and resolute high-priest who would not betray his calling and would eloquently and compellingly put forward a case that the Mummy was as much a victim as an aggressor. In no other film would the Mummy's revenge so convincingly be presented as deserved and in no other film would the high-priest prove such a match for the hero.

Notes

1. For a discussion of how 1940s horror critically suffered through comparison with 1930s horror films, directors and stars as well as RKO films of the 1940s, see Glynn (2009).
2. Despite these changes 'Nina Wilcox Putnam, co-author of the original story of the Freund film ... sued and received a settlement for what she felt were unjustified appropriations from her story' (Fischer 1991: 377).
3. Opportunistic utilization of available sets occurred throughout the series, with *The Mummy's Curse*, for example, using the standing set from *Tower of London* (Rowland V. Lee, USA, 1939) as a monastery as well as appropriating a jungle set built for *Gung Ho!* (Ray Enright, USA, 1943).
4. The other was *Oh, Johnny, How You Can Love* (Charles Lamont, USA, 1940), which like *The Mummy's Hand* also starred Peggy Moran (Mank 1999b: 41).
5. *The Mummy's Hand* helped lay the groundwork for the Indiana Jones films that followed over forty years later by introducing the action-hero archaeologist in the form of Steve Banning (Dick Foran) and reimagining archaeology as an action-packed occupation, in contrast to films before it such as *Hidden Valley* (Robert N. Bradbury, USA, 1932) and

Death Rides the Range (Sam Newfield, USA, 1939) wherein the archaeologist tended to be a weak character 'who required rescue, by another, more masculine heroic figure' (McGeough 2006: 176).

6. Dennis Gifford relates how 'there was horrible truth in his crippled Kharis: once athletic, Tyler was in the grip of arthritis' (1973b: 133). However, while this has become part of the Mummy's mythology – that Kharis' shuffling gait was hauntingly conveyed by a tragically crippled actor – Tyler's arthritis actually became chronic later in life. He was still in athletic form playing superheroes in the following year's *Adventures of Captain Marvel* (1941) and *The Phantom* (1943) (B. Reeves Eason, USA).

7. Given that each Mummy film began at least twenty years after the previous one, as Donald F. Glut notes, by all logic, '*The Mummy's Curse* should have been set ... [in] the middle or late 1980s!' (1978: 179).

8. This unused script treatment is summarized and discussed at length in Thomas M. Feramisco (2003: 85–97).

Part 4 Hammer Film Productions and beyond: The Mummy of the 1950s–present

7 Hammer's resurrection of the Mummy: Sex and digs and wrap and roll

Four Mummy films were made by Hammer between 1959 and 1971: *The Mummy* (1959), *The Curse of the Mummy's Tomb* (1964), *The Mummy's Shroud* (John Gilling, UK, 1967) and *Blood from the Mummy's Tomb* (1971). Unlike the Universal series of the 1940s, however, no attempt was made to create continuity across them. There was some effort made by Hammer in their Dracula and Frankenstein films to tie sequels together as a continuing story, but in regard to the Mummy each new film stood alone, with entirely different characters and stories, resulting in a collection of distinctive Mummy movies rather than a series.

The first of these films, *The Mummy* (1959), is also distinctive because it downplayed the sex and violence that became synonymous with Hammer horror. Instead, more on-screen time and greater emphasis were given to conversation and exploring the fundamental themes underlying the Mummy's motives and mythology in the cinema. The introduction of a distinctive contemporary element further contributed to the uniqueness of the film, which overtly engaged with the social and cultural aftereffects of Britain's 1956 failed invasion of Egypt: an ill-advised endeavour that ultimately proved to be 'the graveyard of the British Empire' (Luckhurst 2012: 166). A number of British sci-fi films that followed Suez have been recognized as being significantly informed by this watershed moment in British history, with Peter Hutchings (1999) and David Pirie (1973), for example, arguing that they are clearly readable as narratives of defeat. Significantly, *The Mummy* (1959) was no less influenced by this momentous occurrence, reflecting as it did upon the climate of national uncertainty that directly followed it and Britain's subsequent decline as a world power. It is a film concerned with coming to terms with change, dwelling on the positives as well as the negatives of Britain's imperial past and offering justification for it and condemnation of it in equal measure. It has a complex narrative (for which it has been criticized), gathering a number of contradictory discourses relating to science, religion, colonialism and retribution, and then ploughing a middle ground between them.

The film centrally focuses upon a clash between an archaeologist (who espouses colonialist beliefs) and a Mummy and high-priest (who feel affronted by colonial practices), and through focusing on their personal battles the film raises larger questions that relate directly to Britain's re-examination of itself following Suez and whether, essentially, Britain got what it deserved or not? Unlike the 1940s Mummy film, which implacably saw the Oriental priest as the enemy and malignant 'Other', in Hammer's film the Western hero and Oriental villain are not as clearly divided into good and evil or even right and wrong.

Following the huge box-office success of *The Curse of Frankenstein* (1957) and *Dracula* (1958), Hammer invested somewhere between £100,000 (Maxford 1996b: 48–9) and £125,000 (Hearn and Barnes 1997: 43) in making *The Mummy* in 1959. Although the Mummy was not recognizably rooted in British Gothic to quite the same degree as Frankenstein and Dracula, Hammer gave *The Mummy* the same Gothic treatment that they had given them and also retained much of the same production team. They employed the same director, Terence Fisher, along with other personnel from *The Curse of Frankenstein* and *Dracula*: the same screenwriter Jimmy Sangster was brought in, along with cinematographer Jack Asher, composer James Bernard and set designer Bernard Robinson. It also featured the same two leads, Peter Cushing and Christopher Lee.

With Terence Fisher, the Mummy for the very first time had a director who was specializing in horror, as opposed to the directors of the 1940s Mummy movies who had all been contract directors associated with any number of genres. Fisher had already tackled Frankenstein's Monster and Dracula and would take on further iconic monsters later in his career with *The Curse of the Werewolf* (1961) and *The Phantom of the Opera* (1962), understandably proving a popular subject for study as a horror auteur because of such output.[1] Yet at the point of making *The Mummy* (1959) Fisher had only a couple of years under his belt as a horror specialist. Prior to *The Curse of Frankenstein*, despite having directed over thirty films, none of them had been horror movies, his career having consisted of directing primarily low-budget genre films including light comedies, period dramas, romances and science fiction. Fisher, at this point in time, therefore, had much in common with other production-line directors, the likes of which had brought about Mummy movies before him. He himself recognized this great affinity with them throughout his career, stating that in his work 'my themes remained what I was given to translate from the written word into a visual form. You see, I'm only a working director. I'm not a director who can pick what he wants to do' (cited in Ringel 1975b: 20).

Fisher's reliance on the written word of the script is further borne out by his self-confessed lack of interest in previous cinematic interpretations of the Mummy, explaining how 'we weren't influenced at all by the old Universal horror films when we started ours. I didn't screen them or refer to them at all. I was uninterested in them. I started from scratch' (cited in Brosnan 1976: 113). With the very first Hammer horror, *The Curse of Frankenstein*, Fisher and Hammer had been left with little choice than to start from scratch. Universal were reaping the benefits from releasing their old horror films to American television in a package called *Shock!* (USA, 1957–9), which was proving 'a huge success' in terms of ratings and sales (Heffernan 2004: 156) and during pre-production for *The Curse of Frankenstein* Universal 'threatened legal action if the film went ahead as planned. ... Universal's copyright even ran as far as the name "The Monster", the reason why Christopher Lee would be playing

"The Creature". Jack Pierce's original make-up was also protected, so Hammer had to find a make-up that bore no resemblance to Karloff's' (Bradley 1996: 149).

However, such was the financial success of *The Curse of Frankenstein,* by the time Hammer came to make *Dracula* in 1958 it had secured financial backing from a number of American studios, including a newly obliging Universal, with the studio's president Alfred Daffin opening the library of Universal's classic horror subjects for Hammer to rework for American distribution by Universal itself.[2] This was a lucrative coming together that created at the time 'the biggest Anglo-American co-production deal in screen history', according to the *Daily Mail* (McKay 2007: 68). It also played to Hammer's strengths as the studio had an established track record of taking characters already popularized through prior radio, television and movie interpretations and reworking them in productions such as *Dick Barton: Special Agent* (Alfred J. Goulding, UK, 1948), *The Adventures of P.C. 49* (Godfrey Grayson, UK, 1950), *Whispering Smith Hits London* (Francis Searle, UK, 1952), *The Saint's Return* (Seymour Friedman, UK, 1952), *Men of Sherwood Forest* (Val Guest, UK, 1954) and *The Quatermass Xperiment* (Val Guest, UK, 1955).

While Fisher himself may have felt uninfluenced by Universal horror, both Hammer and *The Mummy*'s screenwriter Jimmy Sangster recognized that they were now in a position to revise rather than reinvent, as they had been forced to do with *The Curse of Frankenstein*. As a result of Universal's newfound cooperation *The Mummy* (1959) is awash with references to Universal's Mummy films of the 1930s and 1940s, with Sangster appropriating and developing story elements and characters and making them relevant to a new production era and national context.

The Mummy opens with John Banning (Peter Cushing) discovering the tomb of Queen Ananka (Yvonne Furneaux), but because of a broken leg having to leave it to his father Stephen Banning (Felix Aylmer) to excavate. Discovering the Scroll of Life, Stephen unwittingly awakens Ananka's guardian, the Mummy of the high-priest Kharis (Christopher Lee), who had been buried alive for trying to return Ananka to life 4000 years ago with the same scroll. A modern high-priest, Mehemet (George Pastell) then secretly transports the Mummy to England in order to kill, in retribution, all those who have desecrated Ananka's tomb and they succeed in murdering Stephen, who had lost his mind after seeing the Mummy brought to life. They then pursue John who, after several narrow escapes, is finally on the point of being murdered when his wife Isobel appears, her likeness to Ananka stopping the Mummy in his tracks. He turns on the priest, abducts Isobel and heads for a swamp where, as they both start sinking beneath the surface, she is successfully rescued at the last minute.

Given the combination of a director intent on starting anew and a clearly derivative screenplay, some confusion exists as to just what exactly Hammer's *The Mummy* was trying to achieve and what it was remaking. Allen Eyles et al. assert that its writer 'Jimmy Sangster made a new treatment of the old 1932 screenplay' (1981: 33), Michael R Pitts calls the film 'a colour remake of Boris Karloff's *The Mummy*' (1981: 93) and James Marriott and Kim Newman call it 'a reworking of Universal's

1932 film' (2010: 85). However, rather than being based on *The Mummy* (1932), Howard Maxford believes 'the film in fact bears more of a resemblance to Universal's 1940 sequel *The Mummy's Hand*' (1996b: 47). Andy Boot goes as far as to suggest that the film 'is an amalgam of every Universal Mummy picture ever made' (1996: 92) while Harry Ringel damns it as 'a weak pastiche of Universal Mummy clichés' (1975a: 9).

The Mummy's mish-mash of plot elements, which is actually inspired by the whole of Universal's Mummy cycle rather than any one film (the archaeologist unintentionally returning the Mummy to life by reading from the scroll and losing his mind as a result lifted directly from *The Mummy* (1932), Steve Banning, the high-priest and Kharis from *The Mummy's Hand*, the priest and the Mummy travelling overseas to take revenge from *The Mummy's Tomb*, the Mummy sinking into a swamp with the woman he loves from *The Mummy's Ghost*, the Mummy rising from a swamp from *The Mummy's Curse*) is most probably the result of the manner in which Jimmy Sangster encountered the Universal films, himself admitting that the borrowed elements formed 'a kind of *homage* to the old films which I saw in a group. It wasn't a detailed study – more a kind of mood setting' (cited in Cowie and Johnson 2002: 90). By seeing them in a group it is unsurprising that elements from them all appeared in his screenplay. Nor is it surprising, given the scope of the film's sources, that the resultant screenplay was at times a little confused even though (as he had done with *Dracula*), Sangster reduced the number of characters in favour of a more closely-knit narrative. As Peter Hutchings points out: 'Characters are ignorant of something in one scene only to be aware of it later on ... [and] ... the Mummy is impervious to gunfire early in the film but succumbs to it in the conclusion' (2001: 106).

However, such a focus on borrowed plot elements and small inconsistencies has resulted in the design and effectiveness of the story being largely overlooked. In fact, the resultant film (a combination of Sangster's *homage* to and reworking of Universal's Mummy and Fisher's desire to produce an independent interpretation) offered both a complex tribute and a novel, culturally up-to-date reappraisal of the Mummy through an emphasis on story and character development over horror. By concentrating on dramatic tensions between the film's protagonists, who are all utterly fixated on their objectives, the film recreates, purposefully or not, a classical structure whose archetype can be found in ancient Greek tragedies such as Sophocles' *Antigone* and Euripides' *Electra*: dramas that similarly focus on inflexible and corpse-obsessed characters who are utterly at odds with others over how to deal with the dead. As in such classical drama, analysed by Aristotle in his *Poetics*, *The Mummy*'s narrative consists of a series of contests between its main characters who each have valid arguments but are incapable of seeing another view and who at various points through their actions offend the gods or go too far (*hubris*), commit their acts of folly by being blinded by their passions (*ate*), realize their actions have led to the opposite effect to that intended (*anagnorisis* and *peripeteia*), contest their positions (*agon*), reveal their fatal flaw (*hamartia*) and ultimately get punished (*nemesis*).

Rather than focusing upon sex or romance, the occasional love triangle of the Mummy film is relegated to the background and the heroine barely features. Instead, *The Mummy* (1959) explores the ideological positions of its three essential characters (the Mummy, the archaeologist and the high-priest). Their three distinct philosophies are placed in opposition to each other and equal weight is given to their similarities as well as their differences. Each protagonist has two tailor-made antagonists and through their encounters important questions that the Mummy genre had been posing for decades concerning archaeology and the sanctity of the dead are thoughtfully considered, with great relevance to Britain in the late-1950s.

Show me the Mummy: Realism with restraint in *The Mummy*

Hammer chose the unstoppable, implacable Mummy from the 1940s to re-present in 1959 as opposed to the magician of the 1930s whose attacks were paranormal. Its physicality was clearly better suited to the Hammer ethos than the frail Karloff incarnation. Yet in comparison to the 1940s Mummy, Christopher Lee's interpretation of Kharis proved to be very different from Tom Tyler's 'slow shambler' (Kurta 2001: 45) or Chaney Jr.'s 'crumbling creeper' (Weaver and Gingold 1999: 19) in its athleticism and mobility. It moved far more swiftly and with much greater energy and like Lee's Frankenstein's Monster, Kharis was strong and fast enough to be a genuine threat without requiring his victims to fall down in order to be caught. Ted Newsom describes how, 'as he had done with Frankenstein's creation and Count Dracula, Lee created an original, dynamic Kharis ... striding through the night, ripping iron bars and smashing doors. Never before or since has Lee's 6'4" height been so emphasized, accentuated by Asher's ingenious camera angles' (1999: 42). Just as the physical threat of the monster was foregrounded, so too was the physical prowess of the man who opposed him. In the 1932 film, the knowledge of Dr Muller outwitted Karloff's cerebral Mummy, whereas in *The Mummy's Hand* (1940) the barroom brawling Steve Banning was required to defeat the hulking monster the Mummy had become. In Hammer's version Cushing offers a hybrid of these two types with his John Banning proving to be a scholarly yet robust monster-fighter. Cushing claimed to have had significant input into creating this action-hero aspect to his character, explaining that when 'John Banning (my part) was attacked by Kharis, the Mummy ... I asked Terry [Fisher] if I could grab a harpoon hanging on the wall of Banning's study and during the struggle for survival, drive it clear through my opponent's body' (cited in Hearn and Barnes 1997: 43).

Such brutality in the duel between John and the Mummy, alongside the hole created in the Mummy's torso that featured prominently on the film's poster (Figure 7.1), has perhaps led to the reputation *The Mummy* (1959) has among some critics for being violent and explicit and an integral part of 'the late fifties trend toward graphically presented horrific detail' (Tudor 1989: 46). However, on closer inspection,

Fig. 7.1 Poster for Hammer's *The Mummy* (1959): A hole lot of trouble.

The Mummy is actually a notable exception when compared to other Hammer horror of the period due to its lack of 'horrific detail', the result of production decisions that were taken at the time to tone down rather than ramp up the gore content.

The most notoriously violent scene within the film relates to a flashback sequence to ancient Egypt in which Kharis is punished for attempting to resurrect Ananka. A continental version of the film containing 'a gorier version of Christopher Lee's tongue-removal' was apparently filmed, 'but shots of the detached tongue and a stream of blood from Lee's mouth were cut before the film was submitted for certification' (Hearn and Barnes 1997: 43). Nothing like this actually features in the released British and American versions, even though Terence Fisher himself had little issue with such graphic approaches, arguing that explicit detail was an artistic choice and not just exploitation: 'I know that it's popular and fashionable to say that the unseen is the most scaring. I don't believe this! I believe the seen to be the most scaring thing I can think of' (cited in Wells 2000: 67). Yet in spite of this stated preference, which is evident in Fisher's preceding Hammer horrors (and later works), graphic bloodshed was not the approach taken in *The Mummy* (1959). In 1960 Christopher Lee drew attention to the comparative 'harmlessness' of his Mummy, in which 'I only kill three people, and not in a ghastly way. I just break their necks' (cited in Halliwell 1988: 228).

Violent, but hardly 'ghastly', the decision to tone down the film may well have been due to an aborted project that resulted in *The Mummy* being made in the first place. In 1957 Hammer had bought the rights to Richard Matheson's vampire novel *I Am Legend*, but 'as shooting was due to begin word came from the censor's office that, if Hammer went ahead with the film, they could expect an outright ban in Britain' (Pirie 1977: 86). Hammer had also been coming under increasing critical fire for its graphic bloodshed with attacks on its horror output 'including a call for an "SO", "Sadists Only" certificate' (Conrich 1997: 229). Fisher, no doubt aware of this growing opposition, in 1959 chose not to proclaim his preference for the 'seen' over the 'unseen' but instead offered a very different position, asserting that 'I have always strenuously tried to avoid being blatant in my pictures. Instead, whenever possible, I have used the camera to show things – especially nasty things – happening by implication' (cited in Cowie and Johnson 2002: 93).

Fisher's more measured approach towards *The Mummy* certainly appeased the critics as the film received largely favourable reviews.[3] It also managed to successfully entertain its audience, breaking 'the records for a Universal-International/Rank picture' as well as breaking 'the previous year's record set by Hammer's *Dracula*' (Cowie and Johnson 2002: 95). In addition to temporarily quietening Hammer's detractors by being markedly less graphic than *The Curse of Frankenstein* and less erotic then *Dracula*, *The Mummy*'s restraint also served to accentuate the quieter duels that take place within its story, with its brief physical battles proving secondary to battles of wits and wills. Time was afforded to reveal the reasons and motivations behind each character's actions and why adversaries were so opposed, all in the context of a credible world in which science challenged the supernatural, and was then challenged right back.

The film's focus on telling a credible story conformed to the stated preference of James Carreras, the founder and head of Hammer, who said in the studio's heyday that he wanted to make his 'films as believable as possible. None of those silly monster insects – you can always see the wires working. My Draculas and things are real' (cited in Maxford 1996b: 50). In contrast to the Universal vampire who could change into a bat and smoke, Hammer went out of its way to make the supernatural characters in its films as natural as possible by divesting them of many magical properties. Terence Fisher was comfortable with Jimmy Sangster's script for *Dracula* precisely because it denied Dracula the ability to change into a bat or a wolf or a mist. He believed that even in a horror film, once a vampire is shown doing those things, 'credibility stops' (cited in Jensen 1996: 181). Lane Roth points out further examples in relation to *Dracula*: 'Sunlight remains fatal to vampires, but is demystified when Van Helsing explains that "vampires are allergic to light". Likewise, the preventative power of garlic is attributed to vampires being "repelled by odour"' (1984: 250). By taking much of the supernatural out of horror Hammer made the monsters, as Fisher put it, 'a bit more human than they usually are' (cited in Jensen 1996: 181).

Hammer's Mummy too was made 'a bit more human' than usual, in no small part due to the expressiveness allowed to Christopher Lee through the make-up designed by Roy Ashton. For the first time he provided the Mummy with moveable eyelids that made the eyes fully visible, an addition that Lee credited with greatly enhancing his performance:

> When you are restricted from making physical effects with your face, it is much more difficult, obviously, and much more demanding. Film acting is basically

done with your mind and your eyes. If it doesn't show in your eyes, it doesn't convince anybody. But it did enable me, with movement and with eyes, to create a character. (cited in Miller 1995: 119)

The character Lee portrayed was a creature of pent up frustration, full of yearning for a woman long gone, bound from head to foot, permitted only to look through holes in bandages – prevented by ancient law, the priest who controlled him and the bindings that confined him to act on his desire. Unlike the Mummy from *The Mummy's Hand* with its blacked-out eyes, the eyes of Lee's Mummy (focused upon frequently through Fisher's close-ups) emphasize the human that exists within the monstrous trappings and the 'pathos and helplessness' (Jensen 1996: 193) of his condition. The Mummy's curse in this film is, more than ever before, on the Mummy itself over and above the defilers of tombs.

Universal's various Mummy films had already established that the Mummy was a creature who served an eternal sentence for a crime of passion and that the punishment meted out was so severe because the crime was twofold. His first offence arose from his intention to be with a woman pronounced out of bounds by the dictates of secular and religious law because she was either a priestess or a princess, or both. By modern standards this transgression was understandable and even condonable because it was solely social constraints and ancient interdicts that acted as impediments to him being with the woman he loved and thus, in this respect, one can view him as a victim who was 'unjustly murdered ... in his human life' (Curran 2003: 51). However, he broke taboos by ancient and modern standards when he committed his second offence. After failing to possess her in life, he pursued her in death. Not only did his necrophilic passion for a corpse condemn him, he exacerbated his crime by defying natural law by attempting to raise her from the dead. As a consequence, the 1940s version of Kharis the Mummy was himself condemned to exist as a creature who is both living and dead (poetic and divine justice considering this would have been the fate of his beloved had he succeeded in his ambitions). He is required to become a protector of Ananka's tomb and body and to become an agent of retribution in service to the very forces that condemned him. Further, he is charged with punishing those who attempt to commit his very own crime: the disturbance of the peaceful death and afterlife of his cherished princess. The severity with which the punishment was exacted went beyond the already intolerable imprisonment of his soul in enwrapped desiccated flesh and brutal immolation of his body with the removal of his tongue. Kharis was made an addict too, the priest ensuring his obedience through apportioning out the fluid from the drug-like tana leaves that he required to sustain him.

In Hammer's version the relationship between the high-priest and the Mummy is somewhat different. The Mummy this time is cursed simply to obey the ancient law that, when he had been a high-priest, he had disobeyed. The modern high-priest now enforces this law, faithfully, and the Mummy is both subject to and defender of it. Although Kharis clearly attempts to resist the priest's commands on several occasions, especially when ordered to return to his vault after doing the priest's bidding, he is evidently powerless to assert his own free will and repeatedly, albeit hesitantly, obeys. The religious law the Mummy is cursed to adhere to positions him, unwillingly, at the centre of the principal contest in the film, which is between religious law (where the sacred must remain inviolable) and secularism (and the freedom to pursue human knowledge). The high-priest adheres to religious law and the firm belief that the ancient dead should not be tampered with. The archaeologists in the film, in contrast, believe that such blind devotion is nothing but an obstacle to greater understanding while the Mummy occupies the middle ground, forced to protect the religious doctrines that once he himself risked all to break. The collision of these opposing ideologies recurs in various forms throughout the film: initially through warnings when Mehemet the priest cautions Stephen Banning against entering the tomb, then in articulate discussion of disparate viewpoints when Mehemet and John Banning first meet, and ultimately through combat and murder as these opposing positions are revealed to be fanatically and uncompromisingly held.

Right from the outset, Stephen Banning and his son John demonstrate an utter disregard for the sacred, while displaying an all-consuming obsession of their own to the science of archaeology. Upon breaking the seal to Ananka's tomb in the film's first scene, Stephen enters a euphoric state, oblivious to the voices around him as he is overcome by what he sees. He has to be reminded twice to inform his own injured son of the find. John is equally infatuated by the discovery and refuses to leave the expedition, even though his decision to remain, he knows, will result in a twisted leg for the rest of his life. Immediately displayed is an attitude that goes far beyond the celebration of professionalism that Peter Hutchings identifies as a defining feature of Hammer's heroes (1993: 60–6). Instead, both are revealed to be in the grip of an overwhelming, fervent desire to enter and occupy the tomb until they are satisfied it has yielded all that it can: a desire that makes them heedless of opposing voices, alternative ideologies or the rights of those who might hold them. Barry Forshaw observes that such flawed 'British characters' in foreign territory in British cinema of the time often revealed a 'crass inability to respect' what is told them by foreign nationals, which laid them open to destruction (2013: 128–9), and flawed Stephen and John certainly are, proving to be driven as much by personal ambition and sense of entitlement as by an altruistic search for knowledge. Stephen Banning disregards Mehemet's warnings at the opening of the film not only because he dismisses his words but also because he dismisses him, only interested in conversing with Egyptians who represent the government, can grant permits authorizing excavations and who are in positions to advance his archaeological ambitions.

John too shares his father's complete obsession with Egypt's buried past, made explicit when he admits: 'The best part of my life has been spent among the dead.' In his utter infatuation with the Egyptian dead John is not altogether different from the high-priest, whose mission to protect the dead has similarly dominated his life, or even the Mummy himself who has spent millennia single-mindedly guarding a corpse. John is similar also in that he displays the same indifference to the consequences of his actions that they and other Hammer's villains often do (his resemblance to the Mummy further suggested by the fact that he now has the limp that Kharis once had in the 1940s). When the Baron in *The Curse of Frankenstein*, for instance, proclaims upon first reanimating the Monster that 'we have just opened the door. Now is the time to go through that door and find what lies beyond it', he is as unconcerned about the potential ramifications of his actions as John is when the doors to Ananka's tomb are opened and he walks through.

John is ultimately exposed as less than a hero because of his resolute sense of higher purpose to the exclusion of all else, while Mehemet is revealed as more than a villain for the same reason. In the 1940s Universal cycle the high-priest had always been a dignified figure, but his fanaticism was never explained in terms other than religious devotion to a pagan god or a brutal thirst for revenge. Time and again he was ultimately shown to be morally deficient, succumbing to lust for a woman, betraying his mission and his own calling and falling in cowardly fashion after betraying the Mummy. In *The Mummy* (1959), however, the priest displays no such earthly desire or hint of betrayal. In stark contrast to the priests of the past, he carries his beliefs unflinchingly throughout the film and to the grave, to which he is finally sent for refusing to be viewed as inadequate by his god or subordinate to the Bannings.

Culture clash: The Mummy's case and the aftermath of Suez

The most noteworthy central contest in *The Mummy* (1959), perhaps surprisingly, is not the spectacular battle between the two stars of the film, Peter Cushing (John Banning) and Christopher Lee (the Mummy), which occurs near the end of the movie leaving the Mummy with a king-sized hole in his torso. While clearly an action-packed scene, the two actually have little reason to fight because both have been forced into it against their wills. There are two other encounters of greater subtlety that carry far deeper resonance because they occur between characters who are deeply opposed and signify larger social conflicts. The first is between Mehemet and the Bannings, who hold inflexible and fundamentally contrasting beliefs and the second is between Mehemet and the Mummy itself who, although on the surface seem to share the same goals, are progressively revealed to be as far apart in their beliefs as Mehemet and the Bannings.

The first confrontation between John Banning and Mehemet occurs in the high-priest's lavish English manor house and takes the form of a restrained verbal debate that occupies an on-screen running time of seven minutes. In this beautifully structured and performed dialogue-driven scene, the paradoxical nature of the archaeologist in the Mummy movie is expertly revealed: a Westerner who loves ancient Egypt, but through this love and desire to study it becomes a destructive force who displays contempt for its core beliefs. Banning discloses that he is indifferent to the wishes of the dead not to be disturbed, taking the view of the corpse as object that had dominated nineteenth-century attitudes towards the Mummy (and providing additional justification for the Victorian period-setting of the film in the process). By being so unconcerned with the final wishes of the Egyptians and so prepared to exhume their bodies, the archaeologist is exposed as being as much a curse upon the ancient dead as they themselves are feared to be upon the living.

The debate begins with Mehemet courteously welcoming Banning into his home, claiming to be honoured to meet a man responsible for unearthing 'so many of the sacred secrets' of his country. Banning replies by asking him if he is interested in archaeology, to which he replies 'academically, not commercially', a gentle first salvo that intimates that the profession serves not wholly unselfish ends. Mehemet proceeds to question the morality of 'opening the tombs of beings who are sacred', accusing those who do so of lacking respect and committing acts of desecration upon the dead. It is a view to which Banning clearly does not subscribe. He advocates a view that in the quest for knowledge nothing is inviolate. This includes dismissing the beliefs of those studied and the rights of foreign nationals to prevent him from carrying out his work. Further, he argues that Mehemet and his people benefit from his digging into their past whether they like it or not: 'If we didn't, the history of your country, indeed of a great part of civilization, would still be unknown.' Mehemet responds by pointing out that those who reap the benefits of such excavations are not his people but foreigners who rob the dead: 'Those tombs were sealed for all time. You are an intruder. You force your way in. You remove the remains of the long-dead kings and send them to places like the British Museum, where thousands of people can stare at them. Does this not trouble you at times, your conscience perhaps?' Banning responds with a simple statement of professional pride, 'No. It's my job!' He then proceeds to attack Mehemet's 'occupation' as a high-priest, mocking his religion and intelligence outright by calling his god Karnak a 'ludicrous' 'pagan', and a 'third-rate god', so 'insignificant' that he has 'nothing to commend him to anyone with the slightest degree of intelligence'. In reply, Mehemet accuses him of being the one who is narrow-minded, of being 'intolerant' of beliefs that do not conform to his own. 'Not intolerant, just practical', is Banning's controlled response.

Mehemet in the exchange openly accuses Banning of being as ardently devoted to science as he is to his own religion, drawing the battle lines between secularism versus religious law and science versus faith. These positions are further contrasted by the manner in which the opponents present their positions: Banning with the cool monotonic detachment befitting his obsessive scientist, Mehemet with barely concealed indignation befitting his religious zealot. The Tunisian critic Ferid Boughedir points out that imperial justification was commonly personified in such ways during the colonial era, with the colonizer usually 'a technician, a man of progress, from a superior culture and civilisation, while the native was a primitive, incapable of technical progress or of mastering his passions' (cited in Malkmus and Armes 1991: 16). Mehemet, his veneer of calm quickly eroding, tells Banning 'because you are unable to experience the greatness of a deity you dismiss it as of no consequence … you have scratched only the surface and you know nothing'. The archaeologist is judged as a man unable to see beyond what he wants to see, of scratching the surface as a necessity of his profession, but unable to recognize the true value of what lies revealed. While the epitome of respect in the West, in Mehemet's eyes he is the worst of criminals. 'You assume the right to disturb the everlasting peace of the gods. You pry and meddle with unclean hands and eyes. Profanity, blasphemy, religious desecration – all these you are guilty of, but the powers with which you have meddled do not rest easy. I think you shall not go unpunished.' The two remain at the end of the debate more fiercely opposed than ever, with Mehemet's immediate reaction to it being to order the Mummy to kill Banning, while Banning himself heads straight home to load his shotgun. Both have argued for their absolute right to speak on behalf of the dead and both are presented as fully prepared to create further death to enforce their positions.

The film, admirably, offers no answers to the ethical dilemmas raised and the argument is left unresolved (as well as the score to be settled between them) because the focus of the film shifts onto the second of the contests, that between Mehemet and the Mummy. The love story that had been briefly suggested earlier in the film in the flashback sequence to ancient Egypt is reintroduced when Mehemet orders Kharis to kill John's wife, Isobel, who steps into danger by trying to protect her husband when the Mummy attacks him. The Mummy becomes distressed by this command, clearly reminded by her likeness of his love for Ananka, with this moment of recognition serving as the catalyst for him to rediscover his humanity and find the strength to overcome the curse upon him. He reasserts his free will, killing the priest in the process (who in demanding the Mummy murder an innocent, especially one in the image of Ananka, has become a deserving victim himself). This romantically motivated climax constitutes quite a deviation in the narrative as up until this point neither Isobel (as a possible reincarnation of Ananka) nor the romantic subplot suggested in the flashback sequence had been developed at all in the film. In contrast to Universal's Mummy films, Isobel is simply John Banning's wife and not Ananka reborn, nor is it made clear that Ananka ever had any feelings for Kharis, only that he was infatuated with her. There is no moment where Isobel is entranced or ruled by the Mummy or her distant memories of him are rekindled. Therefore, the sequence in which she reappears, causing the Mummy to kill the high-priest, has been dismissed as a slippage in the plot. Ted Newsom, for example, bemoans the fact that 'reincarnation, so central to the Karloff original, is here a case of mistaken identity' (1999: 40).

However, it is not a quest for romantic fulfilment or lost love but rather freedom from servitude and centuries of obedience that is central to this particular Mummy's story told in the wake of Suez. The man so long hidden in time and bandages reasserts his freedom in the face of those who would oppress and dominate him. Only the Mummy, so often perceived as inflexibly the same in film after film, displays any capacity for change. Such ambiguity regarding the monster was highly unusual in a Fisher film, himself describing his cinematic universe as 'strictly dualistic, rigidly divided between Ultimate Good and Ultimate Evil, Light and Darkness' with these oppositions visually 'most often expressed in images of bourgeois splendour juxtaposed with those of madness, decay and death' (cited in Brosnan 1976: 110). While this aptly describes some of the oppositions in *The Mummy* (1959) – with the magnificent houses of John Banning and the high-priest contrasted with Stephen Banning's madness and confinement to a sanatorium, the decayed body of the Mummy and the death he brings – in this film the conflict between good and evil is also overlaid with issues of 'light and darkness' that can also be ascribed to skin colour, making it far less Manichean than other Fisher films such as *Dracula*. The dispute between the archaeologist and priest, a white man and an Arab, concerns modern scientific progress versus antiquated religious devotion, or in even more specific terms, Western advancement and the right to progress (even into foreign territory) versus assumed Oriental backwardness and the right to self-determination. It is in essence a colonial debate.

Extra-textually, the rights and wrongs of colonialism had recently been contested on the international stage. Three years before Hammer's *The Mummy* was released, the British concept of Egypt and itself radically changed as the 'ageless' North African country reasserted its place in the present. Despite being granted independence in 1922, Egypt had been occupied by Britain since 1882 until British (along with French) troops were expelled following President Nasser successfully claiming back the Suez Canal in 1956, revealing the British Empire to be perhaps as far from former glory as Egypt had itself been considered up to that point. The realization that Britain was no longer the global power it had once been had a profound effect upon British culture and its cinema, which has been much discussed. Alexander Walker (1974), for instance, considered the ways in which Suez contributed to an increased political disillusionment throughout 1960s British cinema, while John Hill (1983) argued in relation to the British New Wave that the failed confidence in male sexuality so foregrounded in this movement was a response to the failed confidence in colonial certainties that followed Suez. Peter Hutchings (1993) similarly discussed the crisis in masculinity present in post-Suez British films including Hammer's, and specifically identified a consequent Orientalist strain in British cinema linked to a 'nostalgia for a lost imperial age' in movies such as *Dr. No* (Terence Young, UK, 1962), *The Face of Fu Manchu* (Don Sharp, Germany/UK, 1965), *Invasion* (Alan Bridges, UK, 1966) and *Battle Beneath the Earth* (Montgomery Tully, UK, 1967) (1999: 45).

The Mummy (1959) too is a response to Suez, but it is not nostalgic but instead reflective and contemplates not just British but also Egyptian traditions of domination and subjugation. Egypt in the cinema had typically been the oppressor rather than the oppressed, presented in films such as Michael Curtiz's *The Egyptian* (USA, 1954), Howard Hawks' *Land of the Pharaohs* (USA, 1955) and Cecil B. De Mille's *The Ten Commandments* (1956) as powerful and imperialistic: a corrupt and immoral empire. Yet in reality Egypt had itself become a subject of empire and Suez exposed Britain as the true immoral oppressor in spite of what the cinema had been advocating. Egypt's President Nasser 'emerged as the national leader who had challenged the forces of imperialism in the interests of his own people, and gained complete victory through the support of world opinion' (Barclay 1971: 166).

In the wake of Britain's humiliation, the Bannings' imperialist attitudes ring particularly hollow in *The Mummy* (1959), while the priest's cautionary words of a reckoning to come resonate as never before in a Mummy film. The condescension Mehemet repeatedly endures from the Bannings reinforces that it is not for crimes against Ananka alone that he sends the Mummy to hunt them down. The high-priest is no longer the same quasi-supernatural figure that featured in the 1940s. He is not inducted into a secret sect in a mystical ritual in an elaborate temple, but instead lives in a manor house just like John. He is not a conventional villain because, as Bruce Lanier Wright points out, he does not '*act* like a villain' (1995: 74). He is educated, refined, pious, gently spoken, impeccably well-dressed and eloquent, and as knowledgeable in the art of Egyptology as the Bannings themselves.

With Mehemet and the Mummy coming to Britain in order to challenge imperialists on their home turf, the film, like all its main characters, looks to the past. As well as obeying a classical dramatic structure, *The Mummy* (1959) additionally conforms to a Victorian narrative of 'reverse colonization', a model perhaps most distinctively typified by Bram Stoker's *Dracula* and Rider Haggard's *She*. In his study of these texts, Stephen Arata proposes that they were responses to cultural guilt, the 'civilized' Victorian world finding itself invaded by 'primitive' forces who wreak deserved punishment for imperial sins. In each story a terrifying reversal occurs:

> The colonizer finds himself in the position of the colonized, the exploiter becomes exploited, the victimiser victimised. Such fears are linked to a perceived decline – racial, moral, spiritual – which makes the nation vulnerable to attack from more vigorous, 'primitive' peoples. ... In the marauding, invasive Other British culture sees its own imperial practices mirrored back in monstrous forms. (1990: 162)[4]

These novels were published at a time when there was a significant erosion in confidence 'in the inevitability of British progress and hegemony', due to a number of contemporary factors including the growing influence of the United States, increasing unrest in British colonies and 'growing domestic uneasiness over the morality of imperialism' (Arata 1990: 622). In the late 1950s, on the cusp of 'the wind of change' that heralded Britain's rapid decolonization, British imperial decay was at its most evident, with the same factors that beleaguered the Victorians resurfacing and warranting a resurgence of the very same narratives of reverse colonization in response, with Hammer proving responsible for also reviving *Dracula* in 1958 and *She* (Robert Day, UK) in 1965.

The Mummy (1959) became the first Hammer horror, though, to bring the monster to Britain itself. By having this monster come from the very country that had just assured the end of empire, *The Mummy* (1959) was a film with a clear subtext about Britain's relationship with colonialism. All of the film's main characters refuse to let go of Egypt's past in one form or another, and each are ultimately laid low because they cannot engage with the fact that the past is gone and they can possess it no longer. In the age-old model of tragedy, there is a plague on all their houses. The Mummy, the priest and the archaeologist are all guilty of hubris: all are presented sympathetically, offer reasonable reasons for their actions, but all are also punished. Mehemet is murdered by his own companion, ultimately abandoned by his own god, while John loses his father, uncle and mobility. The Mummy drowns in a quagmire, destined to be endlessly alone.

Yet with the submergence of the Mummy, this emblematic remnant of Egypt, a symbolic and powerful after-image of Britain's lost and tainted imperial glory briefly remains as the credits roll. For all the efforts made to govern it and learn from it, the Mummy defiantly and irreversibly slips away, leaving nothing but loss and destruction in its wake. Where Britannia once ruled the waves, it is only enveloping mist and gently rippling swamp water that remain at the end of *The Mummy*.

Notes

1. See Wheeler Winston Dixon (1991), Peter Hutchings (2001), Paul Leggett (2002) and Harry Ringel (1975a, b).
2. The first three projects were to be *The Mummy*, *The Phantom of the Opera* (not made until 1962) and *The Invisible Man* (which Hammer never remade) (Cowie and Johnson 2002: 90). The thirteen British Hammer films that were made and released in the United States through Universal were *Dracula* (1958), *The Mummy* (1959), *The Brides of Dracula* (Terence Fisher, UK, 1960), *The Curse of the Werewolf* (Terence Fisher, UK, 1961), *Captain Clegg* (Peter Graham Scott, UK, 1962), *The Phantom of the Opera* (Terence Fisher, UK, 1962), *Kiss of the Vampire* (Don Sharp, UK, 1963), *Paranoiac* (Freddie Francis, UK, 1963), *The Evil of Frankenstein* (Freddie Francis, UK, 1964), *Nightmare* (Freddie Francis, UK, 1964), *The Secret of Blood Island* (Quentin Lawrence, UK, 1965), *Hands of The Ripper* (Peter Sasdy, UK, 1971) and *Twins of Evil* (John Hough, UK, 1972) (Hirschhorn 2000: 408).
3. For a selection of reviews, see Cowie and Johnson (2002: 95).
4. See also Alok Bhalla (1990) for a discussion of the Victorian vampire story as reflective of the cultural guilt that accompanied British imperialism.

8 Wrapping up the Mummy: The last sixty years

Hammer's *The Mummy* (1959) encapsulates how the Mummy has functioned in the cinema. Many of its 'semantic components' (1996: 283), to borrow Rick Altman's useful term, were incorporated by Hammer from Mummy films of the past, while contemporary influences, domestic concerns, studio ambitions and creative decisions impacted upon how they were utilized. As a result, rather than being a changeless, repetitious archetype in the cinema, the Mummy has proven to be a highly protean one, like so many other fictional figures that circulate throughout popular culture.

Unlike these other figures, however, the Mummy's reputation for being the same, inherited from the 1940s, has stuck to it like the resin on a Mummy's bandages. The critical reception of Hammer's Mummy films that followed its version of *The Mummy* (1959) has been largely the same as the 1940s Mummy movies endured, Michael Brunas et al. adjudging them to be 'among the worst horror films Hammer ever produced' (1990: 483), James Twitchell dismissing them for offering little more than 'added colour and cleavage' (1985: 261) and Ian Cooper summarizing them as for the most part 'muddled' and 'pretty awful' (2016: 57). Even the Hammer producer Kevin Francis complained that 'there is no variation you can make with a Mummy film' and explicitly compared the pattern of Hammer's Mummy movies to Universal's: 'The first one that Universal made was okay and Hammer's first one was okay but the rest? Rubbish! It all comes down to this bloke coming out of a tomb covered in bandages' (cited in Brosnan 1976: 250).

Yet, as in the 1940s, Hammer's new Mummy cycle actually proved to be far from repetitious consisting of films that were, as Barry Forshaw argues, 'different breeds rather than direct sequels' (2013: 129), with each offering innovation and the last one avoiding a 'bloke' covered in bandages altogether. After abandoning initial plans to feature a 20-foot giant Mummy that fought planes and tanks in *The Curse of the Mummy's Tomb* (1964),[1] which would have been spectacularly different indeed, Hammer settled on a less action-packed but more violent story based around a touring show, just like P. T. Barnum's that had popularized the Mummy as an exhibit in the nineteenth century. Rather than offering the dramatically new Mummy story initially envisioned, it ended up presenting a markedly old-fashioned one, resulting in perhaps the closest the cinema has seen to an adaptation of Conan Doyle's *The Ring of Thoth*. In what is essentially a retelling of much of its story, the film focuses on an ancient Egyptian burdened with unwanted immortality whose ancient beloved, exhibited in a museum, has contained within her ring the only substance that can end his life.

The Mummy's Shroud (1967) followed, this time featuring a boy pharaoh that was potentially inspired by (or conceived to cash in on) a Tutankhamun exhibition that had been on a highly publicized world tour between 1961 and 1967 and which had 'served to re-ignite public interest' (Tyldesley 2012: 268) in him. Fittingly, if such an educational source was the film's inspiration, its Mummy was based with an impressive degree of accuracy on a Mummy on exhibition in the British Museum (although it happened to be a Roman period one). The Mummy of *The Mummy's Shroud* is Prem, an ancient mummified slave of the boy pharaoh who proves to be less brutal monster than apparition, appearing to his intended victims as a series of distorted images – mirrored in a crystal ball, reflected in a tray of chemicals, a blur to a near-sighted victim – making him as Jonathan Rigby describes, 'an almost oneiric figure' (2002: 139). He was also devilishly hard to kill, proving impervious to acid, skewering, shooting and axe attack, until the uttering of an ancient spell impelled him to crush his own head with his bare hands. Evidently the only thing that could kill this particular Mummy was itself.

Hammer's final Mummy film, *Blood from the Mummy's Tomb* (1971), 'an inventive and daring reinterpretation' (Hutchings 2008: 335) of Bram Stoker's *The Jewel of Seven Stars*, took the quasi-spectral quality of Prem from *The Mummy's Shroud* one step further when presenting its Mummy, Tera, whose spiritual life-force haunts the nightmares of a modern woman. Unusually for the studio, it updated the story to the 1970s, although as well as bringing the story forward, it simultaneously took it back to the Mummy fiction of the nineteenth century in which unwrapping female Mummies provided a frisson of eroticism. In this film once the Mummy is exposed it is revealed to be perfectly preserved and in the 'Hammer Glamour' form of Valerie Leon, but her Mummy proves to be every bit as dangerous and vengeful as in Stoker's novel, with the movie retaining its original stark downbeat ending by suggesting the ancient queen is victorious.

Stoker's female Mummy continued to prove popular well after *Blood from the Mummy's Tomb* completed Hammer's Mummy cycle. *The Jewel of Seven Stars* was adapted again in 1980 in another updated version, *The Awakening*, this time with the ancient queen renamed Kara and with a far bigger budget that allowed for shooting on location in Egypt and the Cairo Museum rather than British quarries. *The Tomb* in 1986 offered a very loose interpretation, followed by another adaptation in 1998 with *Bram Stoker's Legend of The Mummy*, with *The Mummy Resurrected* in 2014 providing yet another version. In addition to films indebted to Stoker, various other vengeful female Mummies have appeared on-screen including Nefertisia in *Evil Unleashed* (Joe Castro, USA, 2003), Aneh-Tet in *Legion of the Dead* (Paul Bales, USA, 2005) and Ahmanet in *The Mummy* (2017).

In 1999 Universal once again resurrected the male Mummy in big-budget form in Stephen Sommer's *The Mummy*. Perhaps because of Kharis' chequered past with critics, it was Imhotep who was revived, brought to life in the film as a result of the words from the Book of Amun-Ra being read aloud after its discovery within his tomb, adhering to what Carter Lupton has shrewdly identified as perhaps the most illogical constant of virtually all Mummy films: 'Why the means of reviving these destructive mummies is universally buried with them' (2003: 39). Despite his conventional resurrection, however, Imhotep himself was radically reimagined for a new generation, partly through necessity after *Bram Stoker's Dracula* (1992) had co-opted Imhotep's original narrative in its story of love across the ages. Dracula, as Imhotep had been in 1932, was presented less as 'tyrannical and demonic and more victim and sufferer' (Botting 1996: 178), transforming into a monster following the loss of his beloved in a bygone era and becoming obsessed with her reincarnation. Rather than Imhotep being a carbon-copy of Dracula as in 1932, this time around Dracula had borrowed shamelessly from the Mummy.

While still driven by love, the Imhotep of 1999 was less victim and sufferer than millennial menace who threatened to rain down the plagues of Egypt apocalyptically onto the world, when not transforming into sandstorms or directing swarms of beetles. The air or romanticism that so dominated Coppola's and Freund's films was replaced by action and adventure: the movie inspired as much by Indiana Jones and the *Tomb Raider* video games as Universal's Mummy movies of the past. Such was its box-office success that it once more instigated a cycle of Mummy films that featured Mummies in a variety of different forms. These included the resurrection of a creature that is half scorpion in *The Mummy Returns* (2001) and a Mummy who can transform into a dragon in *The Mummy: Tomb of the Dragon Emperor* (2008). The latter of these, set in the Far East rather than the Middle East, revived the 1940s tradition of continuing the story from the previous film many years later, with Alex (Luke Ford), the son of the hero of *The Mummy* (1999), now an adult adventurer following in his father's footsteps (Alex's adventures as a youth having also previously featured in *The Mummy: The Animated Series* (2001–2)).

The shuffling, bandaged Mummy, as most would identify it, has increasingly had to compete with alternative Mummies with differing abilities. In 1997 it took the form of a malevolent disembodied spirit in *Bram Stoker's Legend of the Mummy* (1997), in 1998 it became a collection of flying, fluttering empty bandages that enwraps its victims in *Talos the Mummy* (1998) and in 1999 a rotten corpse who slowly regenerates into a man in *The Mummy* (1999). In Universal's *The Mummy* (2017), designed to be the beginning of an all-new monster cycle to feature its classic monsters under the umbrella title 'Dark Universe' and become a parallel to Marvel's Cinematic Universe – or 'some Famous Monsters of Filmland version of the Justice League' (Gleiberman 2017: 102) – the Mummy is a tattooed (hieroglyphed) woman. This Mummy blockbuster shares many similarities with the studio's 1999 blockbuster, such as its Mummy again being in control of sandstorms, sucking the life-force from the living in order to regenerate and being opposed by a mercenary adventurer (this time a sergeant and American war profiteer operating in Iraq, reflecting how the United States today has as much political, economic and military investment and moral uncertainty in the Middle East as Britain once had when Hammer made *The Mummy* in 1959). Despite being derivative, however, as the Mummy film does, it also offers freshness to the musty monster. Once bereft of their life-forces, the husks of the Mummy's victims do not become withered remains as in *The Mummy* (1999), but instead transform into undead slaves, this Mummy being able to reproduce more undead like the vampire or zombie. In place of beetles, it is spiders, crows and rats that the Mummy commands. Rather than her crime being an attempt to resurrect a dead lover, this time she is buried alive (with liquid mercury keeping her contained) for committing familicide, including regicide and infanticide, in a quest for power and to give human form to a god.

As even the critically maligned 2017 version of *The Mummy* demonstrates, solely by introducing a monstrous feminine version of the figure, the Mummy is not 'inflexibly the same, film after film', but rather remains, as it has always been, a mutating figure within the cinema. In fact, so much has the Mummy changed, that this long derided figure is today, somewhat ironically, being criticized for having deviated too much from its much-criticized roots. Hunt, Lockyer and Williamson, for instance, complain that it is now just 'the supernatural heavy in an action-adventure franchise' rather than a horror film creature (2014: 2–3). Griselda Pollock similarly dislikes Mummy movies becoming 'swashbuckling adventure films full of technical wizardry', losing, in her view, their effectiveness because they have become little more than '*boy's own fantasies based on infant dreams*' (2007: 63).

However, by changing and adapting, as it always has, the Mummy has arguably found itself the subject of more blockbusters since 1999 than any other classic monster. Yet even so, the Mummy remains in the critical crosshairs as a cinematic concept, whether as a figure of horror or as an action-adventure 'heavy'. It seems the Mummy film can never win, but just like its star, it will always return. Although hardly Chopin, the Mummy's artistry has, like this composer, resided in variations on a theme. Its narratives of colonial invasion and romantic transgression have been constantly transformed in relation to changing notions of the Orient and imperialism and varying attitudes towards relations with other races and interracial relationships.

It is the Mummy's malleability, rather than the stiff lifelessness with which it has been characterized, that has ensured its continued popularity in the cinema in which it has featured in virtually every form: as hero and villain, as archetypal romantic and opponent of love, as bandaged hideous brute and unbandaged beautiful seductress, as ethereal force and shapeshifting sorcerer, as comedic buffoon and tragic obsessive, as victim and avenger. Although identified as a clearly defined archetype – and a deeply flawed one – the Mummy's protean nature has resulted in it lacking any sense of fixed, restricting personality. To repeat Peter Hutchings' appraisal, it appears to possess 'neither the charisma of Dracula, the pathos of Frankenstein's monster, nor the sexualized rage of the Wolf Man' (2002). Largely, it is this indeterminate identity that is the creature's primary strength, as it is a monster that is, at its frightening heart, unknowable and like 'the Orient' itself, irrepressible, ultimately unconquerable and forever changing.

Critics are correct in that the Mummy does borrow heavily, but it seldom repeats itself, instead being redefined in relation to each new production period and context. Not all Mummy films feature reincarnation (of the ones focused upon in this book, not even most of them). Not all of them feature a love-obsessed Mummy, especially in the case of Hammer's Mummy films. To view the Mummy as a static archetype or the subject of an unchanging genre that offers little and is influenced by little, except an obsessive desire, like the Mummy itself, to return again and again, is both limiting and distorting. Yet considered as such it has been, resulting in the Mummy proving to be the most neglected of all classic cinematic monsters.

In this book it has been necessary to skirt around or skim over a great deal, including a vast variety of Mummy movies which, if discussed, would have allowed little space for anything other than an encyclopaedic account of the Mummy as a figure of horror (and other genres) in films from all over the world. I have chosen to only briefly discuss the last sixty years of Mummy film production in order to afford space for meaningful discussion of the genre and the growth and development, from its roots, of the Mummy movie's key tropes. As well as significant films left under-analysed or not analysed at all, important aspects of the Mummy have also had to be neglected, such as the development and transformation of the female Mummy genre, which deserves a book of its own. The Mexican Mummy deserves a book too, not least because, as Andrew Syder and Dolores Tierney point out, it 'embodies a specific cultural threat quite different from that of its Egyptian cousin' (2005: 39).

What has been attempted, instead of trying to cover all films, is to offer a revaluation of the Mummy by reconstructing some of its forgotten history and through analysing various important moments in the figure's development. By placing particular renditions of the Mummy in their social and cultural contexts, I have sought to illustrate how its various narratives of colonial and/or interracial encounters have revealed contemporary attitudes towards both. Rather than focusing upon the repetitious elements so often foregrounded, I have attempted to show how synchronic influences at each moment have impacted upon and added to the diachronic development of the Mummy, stressing the differences in each telling that have made each depiction of the Mummy distinct from the version preceding it. This approach has been adopted to counter the claims of so many critics who have focused upon the repetitive elements in the genre and then, unsurprisingly, claimed that the Mummy genre is repetitive. The Mummy, rather than being maddeningly repetitious, has actually been incredibly varied in its on-screen manifestations. Perhaps the only truly stable element of the Mummy's cinematic history has been the disdain in which it has been held, a reputation so long-standing that it has resulted in the figure being as misrepresented and misunderstood by academia and cultural commentators as perhaps any in the entire history of the cinema.

Note

1. For details of the aborted plot, see Hearn and Barnes (1997: 84).

Bibliography

Ackerman, Forrest J. (1959). 'Mummy's the Word'. *Famous Monsters of Filmland* 4: 32–9, 62–5.
Alcott, Louisa May (1869). 'Lost in a Pyramid, or the Mummy's Curse'. *The New World* January 16: 33–42.
Alkon, Paul K. (1987). *The Origin of Futuristic Fiction*. Athens: U of Georgia P.
Alkon, Paul K. (1994). *Science Fiction before 1900*. New York: Twayne.
Altman, Rick (1996). 'Cinema and Genre'. *The Oxford History of World Cinema*. Ed. Geoffrey Nowell-Smith. Oxford: Oxford UP: 276–85.
Altman, Rick (2000). *Film/Genre*. London: BFI.
Amis, Kingsley (1965). *The James Bond Dossier*. London: Jonathan Cape.
Andrews, Carol (1998). *Egyptian Mummies*. 2nd ed. London: BM.
Andrews, Carol (2002). 'The Fascination with Mummies: From Herodotus to the 20th Century'. *Eternal Life?: Images of Mummies*. British Museum assn. BFI, London. 18 May.
Andrews, Nigel (1986). *Horror Films*. London: Admiral.
Arata, Stephen D. (1990). 'The Occidental Tourist: *Dracula* and the Anxiety of Reverse Colonisation'. *Victorian Studies* 33: 621–45.
Arment, Chad, Ed. (2008). *Out of the Sand: Mummies, Pyramids, and Egyptology in Classic Science Fiction and Fantasy*. Greenville, OH. Coachwhip Publications.
Ascárate, Richard John (2014). '"The Eyes Are Alive!:" Envisioning History in Ernst Lubitsch's *The Eyes of the Mummy* (1918)'. *Film & History* 44.2: 45–65.
Ashley, Mike (1977). *Who's Who in Horror and Fantasy Fiction*. New York: Taplinger.
Ashley, Michael (1987). 'The Supernatural'. *The Encyclopaedia of Horror*. Ed. Richard Davis. London: Hamlyn: 112–33.
Atkins, Rick (1997). *Let's Scare 'Em!: Grand Interviews and a Filmography of Horrific Proportions, 1930–1961*. Jefferson, NC: McFarland.
Austin, Jane G. (1868). 'After Three Thousand Years'. *Putnam's Monthly Magazine of American Literature, Science and Art* 12.7: 38–46.
The Avenging Hand (1915). Pressbook.
Aylesworth, Thomas G. (1972). *Monsters from the Movies*. New York: J.B. Lippincott.
Barbour, Alan G. (1971). *A Thousand and One Delights*. New York: Macmillan.
Barbour, Alan G., Alvin H. Marill and James Robert Parish (1969). *Karloff*. New York: Cinefax.
Barclay, Glen St. J. (1971). *20th Century Nationalism: Revolutions of Our Time*. London: Weidenfeld & Nicolson.
Barker, Martin and Roger Sabin (1995). *The Lasting of the Mohicans: History of an American Myth*. Jackson: UP of Mississippi.

Barnes, Alan (1994). 'Eddie Powell, a Double Life'. *Hammer Horror* May: 14–18.
Barron, Neil, Ed. (1999). *Fantasy and Horror: A Critical and Historical Guide to Literature, Illustration, Film, TV, Radio and the Internet*. Lanham, MD: Scarecrow.
Bazin, André (1945). 'The Ontology of the Photographic Image' repr. *What Is Cinema? Vol. 1*. Trans. Hugh Gray. Berkeley, LA: U of California P, 1967: 9–16
Beaver, Harold (1977). *The Science Fiction of Edgar Allan Poe*. Comp. and Ed. Harold Beaver. Harmondsworth: Penguin.
Beck, Calvin Thomas (1975). *Heroes of the Horrors*. New York: Macmillan.
Beck, Calvin Thomas (1978). *Scream Queens: Heroines of the Horrors*. New York: Collier.
Bennett, Tony and Janet Woollacott (1987). *Bond and Beyond: The Political Career of a Popular Hero*. New York: Methuen.
Benshoff, Harry M. (1997). *Monsters in the Closet: Homosexuality and the Horror Film*. Manchester: Manchester UP.
Berenstein, Rhona J. (1996a). *Attack of the Leading Ladies: Gender, Sexuality, and Spectatorship in Classic Horror Cinema*. New York: Columbia UP.
Berenstein, Rhona J. (1996b). 'It Will Thrill You, It May Shock You, It Might Even Horrify You: Gender, Reception, and Classic Horror Cinema'. *The Dread of Difference: Gender and the Horror Film*, Ed. Barry Keith Grant. Austin: U of Texas: 117–42.
Bernstein, Matthew and Gaylyn Studlar, Eds. (1997). *Visions of the East: Orientalism in Film*. New Brunswick, NJ: Rutgers UP.
Bhalla, Alok (1990). *Politics of Atrocity and Lust: The Vampire Tale as a Nightmare History of England in the Nineteenth Century*. New Delhi: Sterling.
Bioscope (1910). 3 March: 44.
Bioscope (1911). 14 September, supp.: vii.
Bioscope (1912). 12 December, supp.: xxi.
Bioscope (1913a). 13 February: 523–5.
Bioscope (1913b). 24 July, supp.: v.
Bioscope (1914). 2 April: 102.
Bioscope (1915a). 15 April, supp.: iv.
Bioscope (1915b) 4 November, supp.: 4.
Bioscope (1916). 14 September: 1002.
Bioscope (1917a). 15 November: 40.
Bioscope (1917b). 29 November: 72.
Bioscope (1917c). 6 December: 47.
Bioscope (1919). 3 July: 73.
Bioscope (1926). 4 March: 45.
Bojarski, Richard (1966). 'The Horror Worlds of Boris Karloff'. *For Monsters Only* November: 8–17.
Bojarski, Richard and Kenneth Beale (1974). *The Films of Boris Karloff*. Secaucus, NJ: Citadel.
Boot, Andy (1996). *Fragments of Fear: An Illustrated History of British Horror Films*. London: Creation.
Botting, Fred (1996). *Gothic*. London: Routledge.
Bradley, Doug (1996). *Sacred Monsters: Behind the Mask of the Horror Actor*. London: Titan.
Bridenthal, Reanate, Susan M. Stuard and Merry E. Weisner, Eds. (1998). *Becoming Visible: Women in European History*. 3rd ed. Boston, MA: Houghton Mifflin.

Bridges, Meilee D. (2008). 'Tales from the Crypt: Bram Stoker and the Curse of the Egyptian Mummy'. *Victorians Institute Journal* 36: 137–65.

Brier, Bob (2013). *Egyptomania: Our Three Thousand Year Obsession with the Land of the Pharaohs*. New York: Palgrave.

Brosnan, John (1976). *The Horror People*. London: Macdonald & Jane's.

Brosnan, John (1978). 'Terror from the Tomb'. *Hammer Halls of Horror* July: 42–5.

Brunas, John (1983). 'Martin Kosleck: Memorable Menace of the Screen'. *Midnight Marquee* Fall: 17–21.

Brunas, Michael, John Brunas and Tom Weaver (1990). *Universal Horrors: The Studio's Classic Films, 1931-1946*. Jefferson, NC: McFarland.

Buehrer, Beverley Bare (1993). *Boris Karloff: A Bio-Bibliography*. Bio-Bibliographies in the Performing Arts 39. London: Greenwood.

Burke, John (1966). *The Hammer Horror Omnibus*. London: Pan.

Butler, Ivan (1967). *The Horror Film*. London: A.S. Barnes.

Byron, George Gordon, Lord (1821). *Don Juan*. Ed. T. G. Steffan, E. Steffan and W. W. Pratt. London: Penguin, 1973.

Camera! The Digest of the Motion Picture Industry (1921). 3.46. 26 February: 8.

Camera! The Digest of the Motion Picture Industry (1922a). 5.15. 22 July: 5.

Camera! The Digest of the Motion Picture Industry (1922b). 5.17. 5 August: 3.

Cardin, Matt, Ed. (2015). *Mummies around the World: An Encyclopedia of Mummies in History, Religion, and Popular Culture*. Santa Barbara, CA: ABC-CLIO.

Carroll, Noël (1984). '*King Kong*: Ape and Essence'. *Planks of Reason: Essays on the Horror Film*. Ed. Barry Keith Grant. Metuchen, NJ: Scarecrow: 215–44.

Carroll, Noël (1990). *The Philosophy of Horror, or, Paradoxes of the Heart*. London: Routledge.

Carter, Howard and A. C. Mace (1923). *The Tomb of Tut-Ankh-Amen: Discovered by the Late Earl of Carnarvon and Howard Carter*. 3 vols. 1. Reprinted 2010. Cambridge: Cambridge UP.

Carter, Howard and A. C. Mace (1927). *The Tomb of Tut-Ankh-Amen: Discovered by the Late Earl of Carnarvon and Howard Carter*. 3 vols. 2. Reprinted 2010. Cambridge: Cambridge UP.

Castle of Frankenstein (1966). 'An Interview with Lon Chaney, Jr.', 10 February: 26–7.

Cawelti, John G. (1985). 'The Question of Popular Genres'. *Journal of Popular Film and Television* 13.2: 55–61.

Cawelti, John G. (1986). '*Chinatown* and Generic Transformation in Recent American Films'. *Film Genre Reader*. Ed. Barry Keith Grant. Austin: U of Texas P: 183–201.

Ceram, C. W. (1971). *Gods, Graves and Scholars*. Trans. E. B. Gabside and Sophie Wilkins. 2nd ed. London: Book Club.

Chao, Phebe Shih (1997). 'Reading *The Letter* in a Postcolonial World'. *Visions of the East: Orientalism in Film*. Eds. Matthew Bernstein and Gaylyn Studlar. New Brunswick, NJ: Rutgers UP: 292–313.

Chaudhuri, Napur and Margaret Strobels (1992). *Western Women and Imperialism: Complicity and Resistance*. Bloomington: Indiana UP.

Cherry, Brigid (2002). 'Refusing to Refuse to Look: Female Viewers of the Horror Film'. *Horror: The Film Reader*. Ed. Mark Jancovich. London: Routledge: 169–78.

Cherry, Brigid (2009). *Horror*. London: Routledge.

Chetwynd-Hayes, R. (1980). *The Awakening*. London: Magnum.
Chibnall, Steve and Julian Petley, Eds. (2002). *British Horror Cinema*. London: Routledge.
Chowdhry, Prem (2000). *Colonial India and the Making of Empire Cinema: Image, Ideology and Identity*. Manchester: Manchester UP.
Clarens, Carlos (1967). *An Illustrated History of the Horror Film*. New York: Capricorn.
Clover, Carol J. (1992). *Men Women and Chainsaws: Gender in the Modern Horror Film*. London: BFI.
Cohen, Lara Langer (2012). *The Fabrication of American Literature: Fraudulence and Antebellum Print Culture*. Philadelphia: U of Pennsylvania P.
Collins, Max Allan (1999). *The Mummy*. London: Ebury.
Collins, Max Allan (2001). *The Mummy Returns*. New York: Berkley.
Collins, Max Allan (2008). *The Mummy: Tomb of the Dragon Emperor*. New York: Berkley.
Conrich, Ian (1997). 'Traditions of the British Horror Film'. *The British Cinema Book*. Ed. Robert Murphy. London: BFI: 226–34.
Cook, Pam and Mieke Bernink (1999). *The Cinema Book*. 2nd ed. London: BFI.
Cooper, Ian (2016). *Frightmares: A History of British Horror Cinema*. Leighton Buzzard: Auteur.
Cormack, Mike (1994). *Ideology and Cinematography in Hollywood, 1930-39*. London: Macmillan.
The Cornell Daily Sun (1907). 'University Calendar'. xxvii.105, 20 February: 6.
Coubro, Gerry (1991). *Hammer and Horror: Bad Taste and Popular British Cinema*. Culture Matters 2. Sheffield: PAVIC.
Cowie, Susan D. and Tom Johnson (2002). *The Mummy in Fact, Fiction and Film*. Jefferson, NC: McFarland.
Cox, Simon and Susan Davies (2006). *An A to Z of Ancient Egypt*. Edinburgh: Mainstream.
Crane, Jonathan Lake (1994). *Terror and Everyday Life: Singular Moments in the History of the Horror Film*. Thousand Oaks, CA: Sage.
Creed, Barbara (1996). 'Horror and the Monstrous-Feminine: An Imaginary Abjection.' *The Dread of Difference: Gender and the Horror Film*. Ed. Barry Keith Grant. Austin: U of Texas P: 35–65.
Curran, Angela (2003). 'Aristotelian Reflections on Horror and Tragedy in *An American Werewolf in London* and *The Sixth Sense*'. *Dark Thoughts: Philosophic Reflections on Cinematic Horror*. Eds. Steven Jay Schneider and Daniel Shaw. Lanham, MD: Scarecrow: 47–64.
Curran, James and Vincent Porter, Eds. (1983). *British Cinema History*. London: Weidenfeld & Nicolson.
Curtis, James (1998). *James Whale: A New World of Gods and Monsters*. London: Faber.
Cushing, Peter (1988). *Past Forgetting: Memoirs of the Hammer Years*. London: Weidenfeld & Nicolson.
Dadoun, Roger (1989). 'Fetishism in the Horror Film'. *Fantasy and the Cinema*. Ed. James Donald. London: BFI: 39–61.
Daily Express (1923). 'Lord Carnarvon's Last Hours'. 6 April: 1.
Daly, Nicholas (1994). 'That Obscure Object of Desire: Victorian Commodity Culture and Fictions of the Mummy'. *Novel* 28.1: 24–51.
Daniels, Les (1977). *Fear: A History of Horror in Mass Media*. London: Paladin.

Daugherty, Walt (1994). 'Wrapping on the Mummy'. *Famous Monsters of Filmland* Spring: 26–34.

David, Rosalie and Rick Archbold (2000). *Conversations with Mummies*. London: Harper.

Davies, David Stuart, Ed. (2004). *Return from the Dead: Classic Mummy Stories*. London: Wordsworth.

Davis, Michael (1911). *The Exploitation of Pleasure*. New York: Russell Sage Foundation.

Davis, Richard, Ed. (1987). *The Encyclopaedia of Horror*. London: Hamlyn.

Day, Jasmine (2006). *The Mummy's Curse: Mummymania in the English-Speaking World*. London: Routledge.

Day, Jasmine (2015). 'Repeating Death: The High Priest Character in Mummy Horror Films'. *Histories of Egypt: Interdisciplinary Measures*. Ed. William Carruthers. London: Routledge: 215–26.

Deane, Bradley (2008). 'Mummy Fiction and the Occupation of Egypt: Imperial Striptease'. *English Literature in Transition, 1880-1920* 51.4: 381–410.

DeGiglio-Bellemare, Mario, Charlie Ellbé and Kristopher Woofter, Eds. (2014). *Recovering 1940s Horror Cinema: Traces of a Lost Decade*. Lanham: Lexington.

Del Vecchio, Deborah and Tom Johnson (1992). *Peter Cushing: The Gentle Man of Horror and His 91 Films*. Jefferson, NC: McFarland.

Derry, Charles (1977). *Dark Dreams: A Psychological History of the Modern Horror Film*. South Brunswick, NJ: A. S. Barnes.

Desroches-Noblecourt, Christiane (1969). *Tutankhamun*. London: World.

Dettman, Bruce and Michael Bedford (1976). *The Horror Factory: The Horror Films of Universal 1931-1955*. New York: Gordon.

Dick, Bernard F. (1997). *City of Dreams: The Making and Remaking of Universal Pictures*. Lexington: UP of Kentucky.

Dillard, R. H. W. (1967). 'Even a Man Who Is Pure at Heart: Poetry and Danger in the Horror Film'. *Man and the Movies*. Ed. W. R. Robinson. Baton Rouge: Louisiana State UP: 60–96.

Dillard, R. H. W. (1976). *Horror Films*. New York: Monarch.

Dixon, Wheeler Winston (1991). *The Charm of Evil: The Life and Films of Terence Fisher*. Scarecrow Filmmakers Ser. 26. Metuchen, NJ: Scarecrow.

Dixon, Wheeler Winston (2010). *A History of Horror*. New Brunswick, NJ: Rutgers UP.

Dixson, Harry L. (1921). *The Professor's Mummy. Portfolio of Dixson Plays*. Memphis, TN: The National Drama Company: 3–29.

Doane, Mary Ann (1991). *Femmes Fatales: Feminism, Film Theory, Psychoanalysis*. New York: Routledge.

Dobson, Eleanor (2017). 'Sleeping Beauties: Mummies and the Fairy-Tale Genre at the Fin de Siècle'. *Journal of International Women's Studies* 18.3: 19–34. http://vc.bridgew.edu/jiws/vol18/iss3/3/ (21 February 2018).

Donald, James, Ed. (1989a). *Fantasy and the Cinema*. London: BFI.

Donald, James (1989b). 'The Fantastic, the Sublime and the Popular or, What's at Stake in Vampire Films?'. *Fantasy and the Cinema*. Ed. James Donald. London: BFI: 233–52.

Donne, John D. (1972). 'Society and the Monster'. *Focus on the Horror Film*. Eds. Roy Huss and T. J. Ross. Englewood Cliffs, NJ: Prentice Hall: 125–31.

Donnell, Dorothy (1915). 'The Dust of Egypt'. *Motion Picture Magazine*. 9.4 May: 57–66.

Doyle, Arthur Conan (1890). *'The Ring of Thoth'*. *The Face of Tutankhamun*. Ed. Christopher Frayling. London: Faber, 1992: 183–94.

Doyle, Arthur Conan (1892). 'Lot No. 249'. *Tales of the Dead*. Ed. Bill Pronzini. London: Book Club, 1980: 301–36.

Drake, Douglas (1966). *Horrors*. New York: Macmillan.

Dudley, Keith (1993). 'Censored Hammer'. *Dark Terrors* October/December: 24–5.

Dyson, Jeremy (1997). *Bright Darkness: The Lost Art of the Supernatural Horror Film*. London: Cassell.

Edelson, Edward (1973). *Great Monsters of the Movies*. New York: Doubleday.

Ellis, Peter Berresford (1978). *H. Rider Haggard: A Voice from the Infinite*. London: Routledge & Kegan Paul.

Elsaesser, Thomas (1989). 'Social Mobility and the Fantastic: German Silent Cinema'. *Fantasy and the Cinema*. Ed. James Donald. London: BFI: 23–38.

Evans, Walter (1975). 'Monster Movies and Rites of Initiation'. *Journal of Popular Film* 4.2: 353–65.

Everson, William K. (1954). 'Horror Films: Though Their Ingredients Vary They All Depend upon the Manipulation of Fear'. *Films in Review* 5.1: 12–23.

Everson, William K. (1955). 'A Family Tree of Monsters'. *Film Culture* 1.1: 24–30.

Everson, William K. (1974). *Classics of the Horror Film*. Secaucus, NJ: Citadel.

Everson, William K. (1986). *More Classics of the Horror Film*. Secaucus, NJ: Citadel.

Exhibitors Herald (1917). 5.19. 3 November: 27.

Exhibitors Herald (1923). 16.18. 28 April: 79.

Exhibitors Trade Review (1923). 13.22. 28 April: 1086.

Eyles, Allen (1978). 'Universal and International'. *Focus on Film* 30: 42–7.

Eyles, Allen, Robert Adkinson and Nicholas Fry, Eds. (1981). *The House of Horror: The Complete Story of Hammer Films*. 2nd ed. London: Lorrimer.

Fellner, Chris (1967). 'The Intriguing World of Hammer Films'. *Monster Mania* January: 18–31.

Fenton, Louise (2014). 'The Demise of the Cinematic Zombie: From the Golden Age of Hollywood to the 1940s'. *Recovering 1940s Horror Cinema: Traces of a Lost Decade*. Mario DeGiglio-Bellemare, Charlie Ellbé and Kristopher Woofter. Lanham: Lexington: 225–37.

Feramisco, Thomas M. (2003). *The Mummy Unwrapped: Scenes Left on Universal's Cutting Room Floor*. Jefferson, NC: McFarland.

Feuer, Jane (1993). *The Hollywood Musical*. 2nd ed. Bloomington: Indiana UP.

The Film Daily (1923). 24.70. 10 June: 15.

Fischer, Dennis (1991). *Horror Film Directors, 1931-1990*. Jefferson, NC: McFarland.

Fisher, Terence (1967). 'Horror Is My Business'. *Monster Mania* January: 6–11.

Fitzgerald, Michael (1977). *Universal Pictures: A Panoramic History in Words, Pictures and Filmographies*. New York: Arlington.

Flaubert, Gustave (1972). *Flaubert in Egypt*. Ed. and trans. Francis Steegmuller. Harmondsworth: Penguin.

Flint, David (2009). *Zombie Apocalypse: How the Living Dead Devoured Pop Culture*. London: Plexus.

Florescu, Radu (1977). *In Search of Frankenstein*. London: New English Library.

Forshaw, Barry (2013). *British Gothic Cinema*. Basingstoke: Palgrave Macmillan.

Fox, Julian (1976a). 'The Golden Age of Terror: Part One'. *Films and Filming* 261.22: 16–23.
Fox, Julian (1976b). 'The Golden Age of Terror: Part Two'. *Films and Filming* 262.22: 18–24.
Fox, Julian (1976c). 'The Golden Age of Terror: Part Three'. *Films and Filming* 263.22: 20–4.
Fox, Julian (1976d). 'The Golden Age of Terror: Part Four'. *Films and Filming* 264.22: 21–5.
Fox, Julian (1976e). 'The Golden Age of Terror: Part Five'. *Films and Filming* 265.22: 18–25.
The Frankenstein Project (2002). Narr. Richard Holmes. Radio 3. 17 February.
Frayling, Christopher (1992). *The Face of Tutankhamun*. London: Faber.
Frayling, Christopher (1996). *Nightmare: The Birth of Horror*. London: BBC.
Freeland, Cynthia A. (2000). *The Naked and the Undead: Evil and the Appeal of Horror*. Boulder, CO: Westview.
Freeman, Richard (2009). 'The Mummy in Context'. *European Journal of American Studies* 4.1: 1–13. http://ejas.revues.org/7566 (21 February 2018).
Freud, Sigmund (1958). 'The Uncanny'. *The Standard Edition of the Complete Psychological Works of Sigmund Freud 1917-1919 Vol. 12*. Ed. and trans. James Strachey. London: Hogarth, 1994: 217–56.
Friedman, Lester D., Ed. (1991). *Unspeakable Images: Ethnicity and the American Cinema*. Chicago: U of Illinois P.
Fritze, Ronald H. (2016). *Egyptomania: A History of Fascination, Obsession and Fantasy*. London: Reaktion.
Frost, Brian J. (2007). *The Essential Guide to Mummy Literature*. Plymouth: Scarecrow P.
Gaines, Jane (1988). 'White Privilege and Looking Relations: Race and Gender in Feminist Film Theory'. *Screen* 29.4: 12–27.
Gautier, Théophile (1840). '*The Mummy's Foot*'. *The Face of Tutankhamun*. Ed. Christopher Frayling, London: Faber, 1992: 151–9.
Gelder, Ken, Ed. (2000). *The Horror Reader*. London: Routledge.
Ghidalia, Vic, Ed. (1971). *The Mummy Walks among Us*. Middletown, CT: American Education.
Gifford, Denis (1969). *Movie Monsters*. London: StudioVista; New York: E.P. Dutton.
Gifford, Denis (1973a). *Karloff: The Man, the Monster, the Movies*. New York: Curtis.
Gifford, Denis (1973b). *A Pictorial History of Horror Movies*. London: Hamlyn.
Gliddon, George Robins (1843). *Ancient Egypt: Her Monuments, Hieroglyphics, History and Archaeology, and Other Subjects Connected with Hieroglyphical Literature*. New York: J. Winchester.
Gleiberman, Owen (2017). '*The Mummy*'. *Variety* 13 June: 101–2.
Glover, David (1996). *Vampires, Mummies, and Liberals: Bram Stoker and the Politics of Popular Fiction*. Durham, NC: Duke UP.
Glut, Don (1975). 'The Mummy's Hammer'. *Monsters of the Movies* April: 64–71.
Glut, Donald F. (1978). *Classic Movie Monsters*. Metuchen, NJ: Scarecrow.
Glynn, Basil (2004). 'Preserved on Film: The Mummy, Silent Cinema and Egyptomania'. *Screen Studies Conference*, 2–4 July, U of Glasgow.
Glynn, Basil (2009). 'Sex and Digs and Wrap and Roll: Orientalism, Transgressive Romance and the Resurrection of the Mummy'. *Beyond Life: The Undead in Global Cult Media, Cine Excess: The Third International Conference on Cult Film Traditions*. London: Curzon Soho Cinema, 30 April–2 May.

Grant, Barry Keith, Ed. (1984). *Planks of Reason: Essays on the Horror Film*. Metuchen, NJ: Scarecrow.
Grant, Barry Keith, Ed. (1986). *Film Genre Reader*. Austin: U of Texas P.
Grant, Barry Keith, Ed. (1996). *The Dread of Difference: Gender and the Horror Film*. Austin: U of Texas P.
Graves, Robert and Alan Hodge (1940). *The Long Weekend: A Social History of Great Britain 1918-1939*. 2nd ed. 1994. New York: Norton.
Green, Peter (1992). 'The Treasures of Egypt'. *The Face of Tutankhamun*. Ed. Christopher Frayling. London: Faber: 263–76.
Greenberg, Harvey Roy (1996). '*King Kong*: The Beast in the Boudoir - or, "You Can't Marry That Girl, You're a Gorilla!"'. *The Dread of Difference: Gender and the Horror Film*. Ed. Barry Keith Grant. Austin: U of Texas P: 338–51.
Greenberg, Martin H., Ed. (1990). *Mummy Stories*. New York: Ballantine.
Guerrero, Edward (1990). 'AIDS as Monster in Science Fiction and Horror Cinema'. *Journal of Popular Film and Television* 1.18: 86–93.
Gunning, Tom (1990). 'The Cinema of Attractions: Early Film, Its Spectator and the Avant-Garde'. *Early Cinema: Space, Frame, Narrative*. Ed. Thomas Elsaesser with Adam Barker. London: BFI: 56–62.
Guran, Paula (2007). 'The Mummy'. *Icons of Horror and the Supernatural: An Encyclopedia of Our Worst Nightmares*. Ed. S. T. Joshi. 2 vols. 1. Westport, CT: Greenwood: 375–407.
Guran, Paula, Ed. (2017). *The Mammoth Book of the Mummy: 19 Tales of the Immortal Dead*. Germantown, MD: Prime.
Haberman, Steve (2003). *Chronicles of Terror: Silent Screams*. Baltimore, MD: Luminary P.
Haggard, H. Rider (1887). *She*. Reprinted. Oxford: Oxford UP, 1991.
Haggard, H. Rider (1912). 'Smith and the Pharaohs' *The Strand* December 1912. *Into the Mummy's Tomb*. Ed. John Richard Stephens. New York: Berkley, 2001: 137–78.
Haggard, H. Rider (1923). 'King Tutanhhamen. Reburial in the Great Pyramid. Sir Rider Haggard's Plan'. *The Times*. 13 February: 13.
Haining, Peter (1987). *The Dracula Centenary Book*. London: Souvenir.
Haining, Peter, Ed. (1988). *The Mummy: Stories of the Living Corpse*. Surrey: Severn House.
Halberstam, Judith (1995). *Skin Shows: Gothic Horror and the Technology of Monsters*. Durham, NC: Duke UP.
Hallenbeck, Bruce G. (1994). 'Terence Fisher'. *The Fearmakers: The Screen's Directorial Masters of Suspense and Terror*. Ed. John McCarty. New York: St. Martin's: 85–93.
Halliwell, Leslie (1988). *The Dead That Walk*. London: Paladin.
Hamam, Iman (2006). '"A Race for Incorporation:" Ancient Egypt and its Mummies in Science and Popular Culture'. *The Victorians and the Ancient World: Archaeology and Classicism in Nineteenth-Century Culture*. Ed. Richard Pearson. Newcastle-upon-Tyne: Cambridge Scholars P: 25–40.
Hamam, Iman (2007). 'Al Momia'. *The Cinema of North Africa and the Middle East*. Ed. Gönül Dönmez-Colin. London: Wallflower: 31–40.
Hanlon, Chris (2012). 'Nobody Is Allowed to Open the Coffin'. *MailOnline* 18 May. http://www.dailymail.co.uk/news/article-2146458/Nobody-allowed-open-coffin-The-seen-letters-curse-Tutankhamun-sent-Howard-Carter--brave-buy-them.html (3 March 2018).

Harper, Sue (1998). 'The Scent of Distant Blood: Hammer Films and History'. *Screening the Past: Film and the Representation of History*. Ed. Tony Barta. Westport, CT: Praeger: 109–25.

Hardy, Phil, Ed. (1993). *Horror: The Aurum Film Encyclopedia*. London: Aurum.

Harrington, Curtis (1972). 'Ghoulies and Ghosties'. *Focus on the Horror Film*. Eds. Roy Huss and T. J. Ross. Englewood Cliffs, NJ: Prentice Hall: 14–23.

Harrington, Curtis (1978). 'Boris Karloff: His Reign of Terror'. *Close-Ups: The Movie Star Book*. Ed. Danny Peary. New York: Simon & Schuster: 329–32.

Harrison, Tony (1991). 'Preface to *Phaedra Britannica*'. *Bloodaxe Critical Anthologies 1: Tony Harrison*. Ed. Neil Astley. Newcastle upon Tyne: Bloodaxe: 174–91.

Haworth-Maden, Clare (1992). *The Essential Dracula: The Man, the Myths and the Movies*. Leicester: Magma.

Haydock, Ron (1975). 'The Mummy Chronicles'. *Monsters of the Movies* April: 5–18.

Hearn, Marcus and Alan Barnes (1997). *The Hammer Story*. London: Titan.

Heffernan, Kevin (2004). *Ghouls, Gimmicks and Gold: Horror Films and the American Movie Business, 1953-1968*. Durham, NC: Duke UP.

Hélene-Huet, Marie (2000). 'Introduction to Monstrous Imagination'. *The Horror Reader*. Ed. Ken Gelder. London: Routledge: 84–9.

Herodotus (1988). *The Histories*. Trans. Aubrey de Sélincourt. Harmondsworth: Penguin.

Hill, John (1983). 'Working Class Realism and Sexual Reaction: Some Theses on the British "New Wave"'. *British Cinema History*. Eds. James Curran and Vincent Porter. London: Weidenfeld & Nicolson: 303–11.

Hirschhorn, Clive (2000). *The Universal Story*. London: Hamlyn.

Hogan, David J. (1981). *Who's Who of the Horror and Other Fantasy Films*. London: Tantivy.

Hogan, David J. (1986). *Dark Romance: Sexuality in the Horror Film*. Jefferson, NC: McFarland.

Holston, Kim R. and Tom Winchester (1997). *Science Fiction, Fantasy and Horror Film Sequels, Series and Remakes*. Jefferson, NC: McFarland.

Hopkins, Lisa (2003). 'Jane C. Loudon's "The Mummy!:" Mary Shelley Meets George Orwell, and They Go in a Balloon to Egypt. *Cardiff Corvey: Reading the Romantic Text* 10: 5–15. http://sites.cardiff.ac.uk/romtextv2/files/2013/02/cc10_n01.pdf (22 February 2018).

Hoppenstand, Gary (1983). 'Yellow Devil Doctors and Opium Dens: A Survey of the Yellow Peril Stereotypes in Mass Media Entertainment'. *The Popular Culture Reader*. Eds. Christopher D. Geist and Jack Nachbar. 3rd ed. Bowling Green: Ohio UP: 171–85.

Huckvale, David (2012). *Ancient Egypt in the Popular Imagination: Building a Fantasy in Film, Literature, Music and Art*. Jefferson, NC: McFarland.

Hughes, William (2000). *Beyond Dracula: Bram Stoker's Fiction and Its Cultural Context*. London: Macmillan.

Humphreys, Fred (1995). 'The Curse of the Mummy's Tomb'. *Dark Terrors* December: 30–5.

Hunt, Leon A. (2000). 'A (Sadistic) Night at the Opera: Notes on the Italian Horror Film'. *The Horror Reader*. Ed. Ken Gelder. London: Routledge: 324–35.

Hunt, Leon, Sharon Lockyer and Milly Williamson (2014). *Screening the Undead: Vampires and Zombies in Film and Television*. London: I.B. Tauris.

Hunter, Jack, Ed. (1996). *The Complete Hammer Films Story*. London: Creation.
Huss, Roy and T. J. Ross, Eds. (1972). *Focus on the Horror Film*. Englewood Cliffs, NJ: Prentice Hall.
Hutchings, Peter (1993). *Hammer and Beyond: The British Horror Film*. Manchester: Manchester UP.
Hutchings, Peter (1999). 'We're the Martians Now: British SF Invasion Fantasies of the 1950s and 1960s'. *British Science Fiction Cinema*. Ed. I. Q. Hunter. London: Routledge: 33–47.
Hutchings, Peter (2001). *Terence Fisher*. Manchester: Manchester UP.
Hutchings, Peter (2002). 'Scrolls of Life: Universal's 1940s Mummy Films'. *Exploiting Fear: The Art and Appeal of Horror on Film Conference*. U of Hull, Hull. 11–13 October.
Hutchings, Peter (2008). *Historical Dictionary of Horror Cinema*. Lanham, MD: Scarecrow.
Hutchinson, Tom and Roy Pickard (1983). *Horrors: A History of Horror Movies*. London: Hamlyn.
Hyams, Ronald (1990). *Empire and Sexuality: The British Experience*. Manchester: Manchester UP.
Illustrated Films Monthly (1914). March: 193–8.
Jacobs, Steven (2011). *Boris Karloff: More than a Monster: The Authorized Biography*. Sheffield: Tomahawk P.
Jancovich, Mark, Ed. (2002). *Horror: The Film Reader*. London: Routledge.
Jenkins, Alan (1974). *The Twenties*. London: Book Club.
Jensen, Paul M. (1974). *Boris Karloff and His Films*. New York: Barnes.
Jensen, Paul M. (1996). *The Men Who Made the Monsters*. New York: Twayne.
Johnson, Tom (1997). *Censored Screams: The British Ban on Hollywood Horror in the Thirties*. Jefferson, NC: McFarland.
Johnson, Tom and Deborah Del Vecchio (1996). *Hammer Films: An Exhaustive Filmography*. Jefferson, NC: McFarland.
Johnston, John J. (2013). 'Going Forth by Night'. *Unearthed*. Eds. John J. Johnston and Jared Shurin. London: Jurassic London: 1–34.
Johnston, John J. and Jared Shurin, Eds. (2013). *Unearthed*. London: Jurassic London.
Jones, Stephen (1999). *The Essential Monster Movie Guide*. London: Titan.
Joseph, M. K. (1971). 'Introduction'. *Frankenstein, or, the Modern Prometheus*. Mary W. Shelley. Ed. M. K. Joseph. London: Oxford UP: vii–xv.
Kalem Kalendar (1912a). 1 August: 12.
Kalem Kalendar (1912b). 15 November: 13.
Kawin, Bruce (1984). 'The Mummy's Pool'. *Planks of Reason: Essays on the Horror Film*. Ed. Barry Keith Grant. Metuchen, NJ: Scarecrow: 3–20.
King, Lucile (1930). 'Notes on Poe's Sources'. *Texas Studies in English* 10: 128–34.
King, Stephen (1993). *Danse Macabre*. London: Warner.
Kinsey, Wayne (2002). *Hammer Films: The Bray Studio Years*. London: Reynolds & Hearn.
Klemensen, Richard (1994). 'Hammer Films Unearth the Mummy'. *A Tribute to Hammer Films*. Spec. Issue of *Midnight Marquee* Summer: 74–87.
Klinger, Barbara (1984). '"Cinema/Ideology/Criticism" Revisited: The Progressive Text'. *Screen* 25.1: 30–44.
Kuhn, Annette (2002). *An Everyday Magic: Cinema and Cultural Memory*. London: I.B. Tauris.

Kurta, Jeff (2001). 'Unwrapping a Hammer Mummy'. *Castle of Frankenstein* Spring: 44–51.
Lane, Edward William (1836). *An Account of the Manners and Customs of the Modern Egyptians*. Reprinted. New York: Dover Publications, 1973.
Lant, Antonia (1997). 'The Curse of the Pharaoh, or How Cinema Contracted Egyptomania'. *Visions of the East: Orientalism in Film*. Eds. Matthew Bernstein and Gaylyn Studlar. New Brunswick, NJ: Rutgers UP: 69–98.
LeBorg, Reginald (1978). 'Lon Chaney Jr.: A Man Living in a Shadow'. *Close-Ups: The Movie Star Book*. Ed. Danny Peary. New York: Simon & Schuster: 336–9.
Leca, Ange-Pierre (1980). *The Cult of the Immortal: Mummies and the Ancient Egyptian Way of Death*. Trans. Louise Asmal. London: Souvenir.
Lee, Christopher (1977). *Tall, Dark and Gruesome*. London: W. H. Allen.
Lee, Walt (1973). *Reference Guide to Fantastic Films, Science Fiction, Fantasy and Horror*. Los Angels, CA: Chelsea-Lee.
Legassic, Cory (2014). '"The Perfect Neanderthal Man:" Rondo Hatton as the Creeper and the Cultural Economy of 1940s B-Films'. *Recovering 1940s Horror Cinema: Traces of a Lost Decade*. Eds. Mario DeGiglio-Bellemare, Charlie Ellbé, and Kristopher Woofter. Lanham: Lexington: Plymouth: 295–318.
Leggett, Paul (2002). *Terence Fisher: Horror Myth and Religion*. Jefferson, NC: McFarland.
Lhamon, Jr., W. T. (2003). *Jump Jim Crow: Lost Plays, Lyrics, and Street Prose of the First Atlantic Popular Culture*. Cambridge, MA: Harvard UP.
Lindsay, Cynthia (1975). *Dear Boris: The Life of William Henry Pratt a.k.a Boris Karloff*. New York: Knopf.
Lodge, Jack (1994). 'Fantasy Thirties Style'. *Hollywood: 60 Great Years*. Eds. Jack Lodge, John Russell Taylor, Adrian Turner, Douglas Jarvis, David Castell and Mark Kermode. London: Prion: 52–67.
Lombardi, Fred, Ed. (1994). *The Variety Book of Movie Lists*. London: Hamlyn.
Loudon, Jane (1827). *The Mummy!: A Tale of the Twenty-Second Century*. Reprinted. Introduction and Abridgement by Alan Rauch. Ann Arbor: U of Michigan P, 1994.
Loudon, J. W. (1847). 'A Short Account of the Life and Writings of John Claudius'. *Self-Instruction for Young Gardeners, Foresters, Bailiffs, Land-Stewards and Farmers*. J. C. Loudon. London: Longman, Brown, Green and Longmans: ix–li.
Luckhurst, Roger (2012). *The Mummy's Curse: The True History of a Dark Fantasy*. Oxford: Oxford UP.
Lucretius (1977). 'Folly of the Fear of Death'. *The Portable Roman Reader*. Ed. and trans. Basil Davenport. Harmondsworth: Penguin: 201–33.
Ludlam, Harry (1962). *A Biography of Bram Stoker: Creator of Dracula*. London: Fireside.
Luft, Herbert G. (1963). 'Karl Freund'. *Films in Review* 2.14: 93–108.
Lupton, Carter (2003). '"Mummymania" for the Masses – Is Egyptology Cursed by the Mummy's Curse?' *Consuming Ancient Egypt*. Eds. Sally MacDonald and Michael Rice. London: UCL P: 23–46.
Lupton, Carter (2015). 'The Mummy on Television'. *Mummies around the World: An Encyclopedia of Mummies in History, Religion, and Popular Culture*. Ed. Matt Cardin. Santa Barbara, CA: ABC-CLIO: 291–6.
MacCabe, Colin (1974). 'Realism and the Cinema: Notes on Some Brechtian Theses'. *Screen* 15.3: 7–27.

MacDonald, Sally and Michael Rice, Eds. (2003). *Consuming Ancient Egypt*. London: UCL P.
Mack, Robert L. Ed. and intro. (1992). *Oriental Tales*. Oxford: Oxford UP.
Madison, Arnold (1980). *Mummies in Fact and Fiction*. New York: Franklin Watts.
Malkmus, Lizbeth and Roy Armes (1991). *Arab & African Film Making*. London: Zed.
Mallory, Michael (2009). *Universal Studio's Monsters: A Legacy of Horror*. New York: Universe.
Manchel, Frank (1970). *Terrors of the Screen*. Englewood Cliffs, NJ: Prentice-Hall.
Mank, Gregory William (1986). 'Universal's "Golden Age:" Some Facts and Figures'. *Midnight Marquee* Fall: 11–4.
Mank, Gregory William (1999a). 'The Mummy Walks'. *Cinefantastique* 31.6: 32–9, 61.
Mank, Gregory William (1999b). *Women in Horror Films, 1940s*. Jefferson, NC: McFarland.
Mank, Gregory William, Ed. (2000). *MagicImage Filmbooks Presents 'The Mummy's Curse'*. Universal Filmscripts Ser. Classic Horror Films 11. Absecon, NJ: MagicImage.
Marchetti, Gina (1993). *Romance and the 'Yellow Peril:' Race, Sex, and Discursive Strategies in Hollywood Fiction*. Berkeley: U of California P.
Marra, Peter (2014). '"Strange Pleasure:" 1940s Proto-Slasher Cinema'. *Recovering 1940s Horror Cinema: Traces of a Lost Decade*. Eds. Mario DeGiglio-Bellemare, Charlie Ellbé and Kristopher Woofter. Lanham: Lexington: Plymouth: 27–45.
Marriott, James and Kim Newman (2010). *Horror! 333 Films to Scare You to Death*. London: Carlton.
Maxford, Howard (1996a). *The A-Z of Horror Films*. London: Batsford.
Maxford, Howard (1996b). *Hammer, House of Horror: Behind the Screams*. London: Batsford.
McCarthy (1932). 'The Mummy'. *Motion Picture Herald* 3 December. *Boris Karloff and His Films*. Ed. Paul M. Jensen. New York: Barnes: 68.
McCarty, John (1984). *Splatter Movies: Breaking the Last Taboo of the Screen*. New York: St. Martin's.
McCarty, John (2002). *The Pocket Essential Hammer Films*. Harpenden: Pocket Essentials.
McDonald, Liam T. (1992). 'The Horrors of Hammer: The House That Blood Built'. *Cut! Horror Writers on Horror Film*. Ed. Christopher Golden. New York: Berkley: 151–60.
McGeough, Kevin (2006). 'Heroes, Mummies, and Treasure: Near Eastern Archaeology in the Movies'. *Near Eastern Archaeology* 69.3–4: 174–85.
McKay, Sinclair (2007). *A Thing of Unspeakable Horror: The History of Hammer Films*. London: Aurum.
Mercer, Kobena and Isaac Julien (1988). 'Race, Sexual Politics and Black Masculinity: A Dossier'. *Male Order: Unwrapping Masculinity*. Ed. Rowena Chapman and Jonathan Rutherford. London: Lawrence & Wishart: 97–164.
Miller, David (2000). *The Peter Cushing Companion*. London: Reynolds & Hearn.
Miller, Mark A. (1995). *Christopher Lee and Peter Cushing and Horror Cinema: A Filmography of Their 22 Collaborations*. Jefferson, NC: McFarland.
Mitchell, Lisa (1994). 'Mummy Dearest'. *Cult Movies* 12: 33–5.
Moshenska, Gabriel (2014). 'Unrolling Egyptian Mummies in Nineteenth-Century Britain'. *British Journal for the History of Science* 47.3: 451–77.
Motion Picture Herald (1932). 108.10. 3 September: 43.
Motion Picture News (1916a). 13.1. 8 January: 104.

Motion Picture News (1916b). 14.2. 15 July: 234.
Motion Picture News (1918a). 17.17. 27 April: 2523.
Motion Picture News (1918b). 18.23. 7 December: 3430.
Motion Picture News (1923a). 27.16. 21 April: 1859.
Motion Picture News (1923b). 27.20. 19 May: 2405.
Motion Picture News (1923c). 27.22. 2 June: 2584.
Motion Picture News (1925). 32.13. 26 September: 1514.
Motion Picture News (1928). 37.9. 3 March: 754.
Motography (1914a). 11.7. 4 April: 217.
Motography (1914b). 12.19. 7 November: 16.
Motography (1914c). 12.20. 14 November: 2.
Motography (1914d). 12.21. 21 November: 717.
Motography (1915). 13.3. 16 January: 110.
Motography (1916). 16.2. 8 July: 109–10.
Motography (1918). 19.16. 20 April: 779.
The Moving Picture Weekly (1916). 3.7. 19 August: 37.
The Moving Picture Weekly (1919). 8.22. 19 July: 25.
The Moving Picture Weekly (1921). 13.10. 23 April: 28–9.
Moving Picture World (1908a). 2.10. 7 March: 193.
Moving Picture World (1908b). 3.11. 12 September: 201–2.
Moving Picture World (1908c). 3.13. 26 September: 243.
Moving Picture World (1911a). 8.10. 11 March: 546.
Moving Picture World (1911b). 9.10. 16 September: 820.
Moving Picture World (1911c). 10.8. 25 November: 658.
Moving Picture World (1912a). 14.3. 19 October: 251.
Moving Picture World (1912b). 14.7. 16 November: 620.
Moving Picture World (1912c). 14.13. 28 December: 1276.
Moving Picture World (1914a). 19.9. 28 February: 1154.
Moving Picture World (1914b). 21.3. 18 July: 468, 470.
Moving Picture World (1914c). 21.13. 26 September: 1830.
Moving Picture World (1914d). 22.6. 7 November: 789.
Moving Picture World (1914e). 22.9. 28 November: 1274.
Moving Picture World (1915a). 26.1. 2 October: 94.
Moving Picture World (1915b). 26.2. 9 October: 338.
Moving Picture World (1915c). 26.5. 30 October: 862.
Moving Picture World (1915d). 26.14. 25 December: 2425.
Moving Picture World (1916a). 27.7. 19 February: 1142.
Moving Picture World (1916b). 29.10. 2 September: 1559.
Moving Picture World (1917a) 32.4. 28 April: 678.
Moving Picture World (1917b). 32.8. 26 May: 1339.
Moving Picture World (1917c). 33.7. 18 August: 1114–15.
Moving Picture World (1918). 36.10. 8 June: 1450.
Moving Picture World (1926). 78.9. 27 February: 797.
Mullin, Donald (1987). *Victorian Plays: A Record of Significant Productions on the London Stage*. London: Greenwood.
Mulvey, Laura (1975). 'Visual Pleasure and Narrative Cinema'. *Screen* 16.3: 6–18.

Murphy, Robert, Ed. (1997). *The British Cinema Book*. London: BFI.

Musser, Charles (1991). 'Role Playing and Film Comedy'. *Unspeakable Images: Ethnicity and the American Cinema*. Ed. Lester D. Friedman. Chicago: U of Illinois P: 39–81.

Naha, Ed (1975). *Horrors: From Screen to Scream: An Encyclopedic Guide to the Greatest Horror and Fantasy Films of All Time*. New York: Avon.

Naremore, James (1995–6). American Film Noir: The History of an Idea'. *Film Quarterly* 49.2: 12–28.

Naylor, David (1981). *American Picture Palaces: The Architecture of Fantasy*. New York: Von Nostrand Reinhold.

Neale, Stephen (1980). *Genre*. London: BFI.

Newitz, Annalee (2006). *Pretend We're Dead: Capitalist Monsters in American Pop Culture*. New York: Duke UP.

Newman, Kim (1986). '*The Mummy* (1932)'. *The Penguin Encyclopedia of Horror and the Supernatural*. Ed. Jack Sullivan. New York: Viking: 294–5.

Newman, Kim (1988). *Nightmare Movies: A Critical Guide to Contemporary Horror Films*. New York: Harmony.

Newman, Kim, Ed. (1996). *The BFI Companion to Horror*. London: Cassell.

Newman, Kim (1999). *Millennium Movies: End of the World Cinema*. London: Titan.

Newman, Kim (2002). 'Bring Back the Cat'. *Science Fiction/Horror: A Sight and Sound Reader*. Ed. Kim Newman. London: BFI: 100–3.

Newsom, Ted (1999). 'The Mummy Walks Again'. *Cinefantastique* 31.6: 40–5.

The New York Clipper (1904). 52.23. 30 July: 522.

The New York Clipper (1905). 52.47. 14 January: 1108.

The New York Clipper (1914). 61.52. 7 February: 15.

The New York Clipper (1917). 65.9. 4 April: 9.

The Nickelodeon (1911). 5.4. 28 January: 115.

Nichols, Marcia D. (2015). 'Poe's "Some Words with a Mummy" and Blackface Anatomy'. *Poe Studies* 48: 2–16.

Nowell-Smith, Geoffrey, Ed. (1996). *The Oxford History of World Cinema*. Oxford: Oxford UP.

Odell, Colin and Michelle Le Blanc (2001). *The Pocket Essential Horror Films*. Harpenden: Pocket Essentials.

Parish, James Robert and Michael R. Pitts (1973). 'Christopher Lee'. *Cinefantastique* 1.3: 4–23.

Parkinson, David (2000). '*The Mummy*'. *The Greatest Horror Movies Ever: The Definitive Guide*. Spec. Issue of *Empire* October: 18–9.

Patterson, Lindsay, Ed. (1975). *Black Films and Film-makers: A Comprehensive Anthology from Stereotype to Superhero*. New York: Dodd Mead.

Paul, Robert W. (1903). *Animatograph Films*. Catalogue.

Pauwels, Louis and Jaques Bergier (1960). *Le Matin des Magiciens*. Paris: Gallimard.

Peary, Danny, Ed. (1978). *Close-Ups: The Movie Star Book*. New York: Simon & Schuster.

Peirse, Alison (2013). *After Dracula: The 1930s Horror Film*. London: I.B. Tauris.

Pendo, Stephen (1975). 'Universal's Golden Age of Horror 1931–1941'. *Films in Review* 3.26: 155–61.

The Photo-Play Journal (1917). 1.10. February: 7.

Pinedo, Isabel Cristina (1997). *Recreational Terror: Women and the Pleasures of Horror Film Viewing*. New York: State U of New York P.

Pirie, David (1973). *A Heritage of Horror: The English Gothic Cinema 1946-1972*. London: Gordon Fraser.
Pirie, David (1977). *The Vampire Cinema*. Leicester: Galley.
Pirie, David (1980). *Hammer: A Cinema Case Study*. London: BFI.
Pitts, Michael R. (1981). *Horror Film Stars*. Jefferson, NC: McFarland.
Poe, Edgar Allan (1845). 'Some Words With a Mummy'. *The Face of Tutankhamun*. Ed. Christopher Frayling. London: Faber, 1992: 159–70.
Pohle Jr., Robert R. and Douglas C. Hart (1983). *The Films of Christopher Lee*. Metuchen, NJ: Scarecrow.
Pollard, Luther (n.d). 'Business Letter to a West Coast Distributor'. *Pioneers of African-American Cinema*. Sean Axmaker, TCM.com, 17 February. http://www.tcm.com/this-month/article.html?isPreview=&id=1227368%7C1227540&name=Two-Knights-of-Vaudeville-Mercy-the-Mummy-Mumbled (3 August 2017).
Pollin, Burton R (1970). 'Poe's *Some Words with a Mummy* Reconsidered'. *Emerson Society Quarterly* 60: 60–7.
Pollock, Griselda (2007). 'Freud's Egypt: Mummies and M/others'. *Parallax* 13.2: 56–79.
Prawer, S. S. (1980). *Caligari's Children: The Film as Tale of Terror*. Oxford: Oxford UP.
The Princeton Alumni Weekly (1907). 7.21, March 2: 4.
Pronzini, Bill, Ed. (1980a). *Mummy! A Chrestomathy of Cryptology*. New York: Arbor House.
Pronzini, Bill, Ed. (1980b). *Tales of the Dead*. London: Book Club.
Pulliam, June (2015). 'Boris Karloff'. *Mummies around the World: An Encyclopedia of Mummies in History, Religion, and Popular Culture*. Ed. Matt Cardin. Santa Barbara, CA: ABC-CLIO: 195–7.
Putnam, Nina Wilcox (1932). 'Cagliostro'. *Cagliostro, The King of the Dead*. An Alternative History for Classic Film Monsters. Ed. Philip J. Riley. Albany, GA: BearManor Media, 2010: 15–26.
Rasmussen, Randy Loren (1998). *Children of the Night: The Six Archetypal Characters of Classic Horror Films*. Jefferson, NC: McFarland.
Rauch, Alan (1994). 'Introduction'. *The Mummy!: A Tale of the Twenty-Second Century*. Jane (Webb) Loudon. Reprinted. Introduction and Abridgement by Alan Rauch. Ann Arbor: U of Michigan P, 1994: ix–xxxiv.
Rebhorn, Matthew (2012). *Pioneer Performances: Staging the Frontier*. Oxon: Oxford UP.
Reddick, Lawrence (1944). 'Of Motion Pictures'. *Black Films and Film-makers: A Comprehensive Anthology from Stereotype to Superhero*. Ed. Lindsay Patterson. New York: Dodd Mead, 1975: 3–24.
Rice, Thomas Dartmouth (1835). *Virginia Mummy: A Farce in One Act. Jump Jim Crow: Lost Plays, Lyrics and Street Prose of the First Atlantic Popular Culture*. Ed. W. T. Lhamon. Jr. Cambridge, MA: Harvard UP, 2003: 159–77.
Richards, Jeffrey (2008). *Hollywood's Ancient Worlds*. London: Bloomsbury.
Rigby, Jonathan (1994). 'Canopic Jars, Razor Blades and "The Pyramid Inch."' *Hammer Horror* May: 19.
Rigby, Jonathan (2001). *Christopher Lee: The Authorised Screen History*. London: Reynolds & Hearn.
Rigby, Jonathan (2002). *English Gothic: A Century of Horror Cinema*. 2nd ed. London: Reynolds & Hearn.

Rigby, Jonathan (2017). *American Gothic: Six Decades of Classic Horror Cinema*. Cambridge: Signum.

Riley, Philip J., Ed. (1989). *MagicImage Filmbooks Presents 'The Mummy'*. Universal Filmscripts Ser. Classic Horror Films 7. 2nd ed. Absecon, NJ: MagicImage.

Riley, Philip J., Ed. (1990). *MagicImage Filmbooks Presents 'Dracula'*. Universal Filmscripts Ser. Classic Horror Films 13. Absecon, NJ: MagicImage.

Riley, Philip J., Ed. (2010). *Cagliostro, The King of the Dead*. An Alternative History for Classic Film Monsters. Albany, GA: BearManor Media.

Ringel, Harry (1975). 'Terence Fisher: Underlining'. *Cinefantastique* 3.4: 19–29.

Ringel, Harry (1976). 'Hammer Horror: The World of Terence Fisher'. *Graphic Violence on the Screen*. Ed. Thomas R. Atkins. New York: Monarch: 35–45.

Rohmer, Sax (1914). *The Romance of Sorcery*. London: Methuen.

Roman, Robert C. (1964). 'Boris Karloff'. *Films in Review* 7.15: 389–412.

Rosen, Philip (2001). *Change Mummified: Cinema, Historicity, Theory*. Minneapolis: U of Minnesota P.

Roth, Lane (1984). 'Film, Society and Ideas: *Nosferatu* and *Horror of Dracula*'. *Planks of Reason: Essays on the Horror Film*. Ed. Barry Keith Grant. Metuchen, NJ: Scarecrow: 245–54.

Sachs, Bruce and Russell Wall (1999). *Greasepaint and Gore: Hammer Monsters of Roy Ashton*. Sheffield: Tomahawk.

Said, Edward (1978). *Orientalism: Western Conceptions of the Orient*. Awd. 1995. London: Penguin.

Said, Edward (1983). 'Egyptian Rites.' *Village Voice* 28.35: 43–6.

San Francisco Dramatic Review (1900). 11.3. 24 March: 8.

Sangster, Jimmy (2001). *Inside Hammer: Behind the Scenes at the Legendary Film Studio*. London: Reynolds & Hearn.

Setoodeh, Ramin and Brent Lang (2017). 'Inside *The Mummy's* Troubles'. *Variety.com* 14 June. https://variety.com/2017/film/news/the-mummy-meltdown-tom-cruise-1202465742 (3 April 2017).

Schadia-Hall, Tim and Genny Morris (2003). 'Ancient Egypt on the Small Screen - From Fact to Faction in the UK'. *Consuming Ancient Egypt*. Eds. Sally MacDonald and Michael Rice. London: UCL P: 195–214.

Schatz, Thomas (1981). *Hollywood Genre: Formulas, Filmmaking and the Studio System*. New York: Random House.

Senn, Bryan (1992). *Golden Horrors: An Illustrated Critical Filmography of Terror Cinema, 1931-1939*. Jefferson, NC: McFarland.

Senn, Bryan and John Johnson (1992). *Fantastic Cinema Subject Guide: A Topical Index to 2500 Horror, Science Fiction, and Fantasy Films*. Jefferson, NC: McFarland.

Sevastakis, Michael (1993). *Songs of Love and Death: The Classical American Horror Film of the 1930s*. Westport, CT: Greenwood.

Shelley, Mary (1818). *Frankenstein: 1818 Text*. Oxford: Oxford UP, 1993.

Shohat, Ella (1991). 'Ethnicities-in-Relation: Toward a Multicultural Reading of American Cinema'. *Unspeakable Images: Ethnicity and the American Cinema*. Ed. Lester D. Friedman. Chicago: U of Illinois P: 215–50.

Shohat, Ella (1997). 'Gender and Culture of Empire: Toward a Feminist Ethnography of the Cinema'. *Visions of the East: Orientalism in Film*. Eds. Matthew Bernstein and Gaylyn Studlar. New Brunswick, NJ: Rutgers UP: 19–66.

Shurin, Jared, Ed. (2013). *The Book of the Dead*. London: Jurassic London.

Sibley, Raymond (1985). *The Mummy*. Ladybird Horror Classics. Loughborough: Ladybird.

Sight and Sound (1947). supp. January: 9.

Skal, David J. (1990). *Hollywood Gothic: The Tangled Web of Dracula from Novel to Stage to Screen*. New York: Norton.

Skal, David J. (1994). *The Monster Show: A Cultural History of Horror*. London: Plexus.

Skal, David J. (1996). *V Is for Vampire: The A-Z Guide to Everything Undead*. New York: Plume.

Smith, Don G. (1996). *Lon Chaney Jr.: Horror Film Star, 1906-1973*. Jefferson, NC: McFarland.

Smith, Gary A. (2000). *Uneasy Dreams: The Golden Age of British Horror Films, 1956-1976*. Jefferson, NC: McFarland.

Soister, John T. (1998). *Of Gods and Monsters: A Critical Guide to Universal Studios' Science Fiction, Horror and Mystery Films, 1929-1939*. Jefferson, NC: McFarland.

Soren, David (1977). *The Rise and Fall of the Horror Film: An Art Historical Approach to Fantasy Cinema*. Columbia, MO: Lucas Brothers.

Spadoni, Robert (2007). *Uncanny Bodies: The Coming of Sound Film and the Origins of the Horror Genre*. Berkeley, CA: U of California P.

Spencer, Kathleen L. (1992). 'Purity and Danger: *Dracula*, the Urban Gothic, and the Late Victorian Degeneracy Crisis'. *ELH* 59: 197–225.

Stacy, Jan and Ryder Syvertsen (1983). *The Great Book of Movie Monsters*. Chicago, IL: Contemporary.

Stanley, John (1981). *Creature Features Movie Guide, or An A to Z Encyclopedia to the Cinema of the Fantastic, or Is There a Mad Doctor in the House?* Pacifia, CA: Creatures at Large.

Steiger, Brad (1965a). *Master Movie Monsters*. New York: Merit.

Steiger, Brad (1965b). *Monsters, Maidens and Mayhem: A Pictorial History of Horror Film Monsters*. New York: Merit.

Stephens, John Richard, Ed. (2001). *Into the Mummy's Tomb*. New York: Berkley.

Stine, R. L. (1993). *The Curse of the Mummy's Tomb*. London: Hippo.

Stine, R. L. (1995). *Return of the Mummy*. London: Hippo.

Stine, R. L. (1998). *Diary of a Mad Mummy*. London: Hippo.

Stine, R. L. (1999). *The Mummy Walks*. London: Hippo.

Stoker, Bram. (1897). *Dracula*. London: Penguin, 1993.

Stoker, Bram (1903). *The Jewel of Seven Stars*. Oxford: Oxford UP, 1996.

Stoler, Ann (1989). 'Making Empire Respectable: The Politics of Race and Sexual Morality in Twentieth-Century Colonial Cultures'. *American Ethnologist* 16.4: 634–60.

Strickrodt, S. (1999). 'On Mummies, Balloons and Moving Houses: Jane (Webb) Loudon's "The Mummy! A Tale of the Twenty-Second Century" (1827)'. *Lost Worlds and Mad Elephants: Literature, Science and Technology 1700-1990*. Eds. E. Schenkel and S. Welz. Berlin: Galda and Wilch: 51–9.

Studlar, Gaylyn (1997). '"Out-Salomeing Salome:" Dance, the New Woman, and Fan Magazine Orientalism'. *Visions of the East: Orientalism in Film*. Eds. Matthew Bernstein and Gaylyn Studlar. New Brunswick, NJ: Rutgers UP: 99–129.

Sudendorf, Werner (1993). 'Expressionism and Film: The Testament of *Dr. Caligari*'. *Expressionism Reassessed*. Eds. Shulamith Behr, David Fanning and Douglas Jarman. Manchester: Manchester UP: 91–102.

Sugg, Richard (2011). *Mummies, Cannibals and Vampires: The History of Corpse Medicine from the Renaissance to the Victorians*. Oxford: Routledge.

Sugg, Richard (2015). 'Medicine and Mummies'. *Mummies around the World: An Encyclopedia of Mummies in History, Religion, and Popular Culture*. Ed. Matt Cardin. Santa Barbara, CA: ABC-CLIO: 225–30.

Sullivan, Jack, Ed. (1986). *The Penguin Encyclopedia of Horror and the Supernatural*. New York: Viking.

Sullivan, Timothy (1986). 'Karl Freund'. *The Penguin Encyclopedia of Horror and the Supernatural*. Ed. Jack Sullivan. New York: Viking: 164.

The Sun, [New York] (1907). 'Princeton Boys in Opera. The Mummy Monarch has a Real Plot and Unreal Girls'. April 7: 4.

Syder, Andrew and Dolores Tierney (2005). 'Importation/Mexploitation, or, How a Crime-Fighting, Vampire-Slaying Wrestler Almost Found Himself in an Italian Sword-and-Sandals Epic'. *Horror International*. Eds. Steven Jay Schneider and Tony Williams. Detroit, MI: Wayne State UP: 33–55.

Taves, Brian (1987). 'Universal's Horror Tradition'. *American Cinematographer* April: 36–48.

Taves, Brian (1993). *The Romance of Adventure: The Genre of Historical Adventure Movies*. Jackson: Mississippi UP.

Taylor, Al and Sue Roy (1979). *Making a Monster: The Creation of Screen Characters by the Great Make-up Artists*. New York: Crown.

Taylor, Alma (1925). 'The Land of Mystery'. *Pictures and the Picturegoer*. 9.49, January: 58.

Telotte, J. P. (1987). 'Through a Pumpkin's Eye: The Reflexive Nature of Horror'. *American Horrors: Essays on the Modern American Horror Film*. Ed. Gregory A. Waller. Urbana: U of Illinois P: 114–28.

Telotte, J. P. (2003). 'Doing Science in Machine Age Horror: *The Mummy's* Case'. *Science Fiction Studies* 30.2: 217–30.

Thomas, John (1972). '"Gobble, Gobble ... One of Us!"' *Focus on the Horror Film*. Eds. Roy Huss and T. J. Ross. Englewood Cliffs, NJ: Prentice Hall: 135–8.

Tophar Mumie, Die (1920). Pressbook [in German].

Towlson, Jon (2016). *The Turn to Gruesomeness in American Horror Films, 1931-1936*. Jefferson, NC: McFarland.

Trafton, Scott (2004). *Egypt Land: Race and Nineteenth-Century American Egyptomania*. Durham, NC: Duke UP.

Triman, Tom (2001). 'The Universal Mummies'. *Castle of Frankenstein* Spring: 11–21.

Tudor, Andrew (1986). 'Genre'. *Film Genre Reader*. Ed. Barry Keith Grant. Austin: U of Texas P: 3–10.

Tudor, Andrew (1989). *Monsters and Mad Scientists: A Cultural History of the Horror Movie*. Oxford: Basil Blackwell.

Twain, Mark (1869). *The Innocents Abroad: The New Pilgrim's Progress*. New York: Harper & Row.

Twitchell, James B. (1985). *Dreadful Pleasures: An Anatomy of Modern Horror*. New York: Oxford UP.

Tyldesley, Joyce (1999). *The Mummy: Unwrap the Ancient Secrets of the Mummies' Tombs*. London: Carlton.

Tyldesley, Joyce (2012). *Tutankhamen's Curse: The Developing History of an Egyptian King*. London: Profile.

Underwood, Peter (1972). *Horror Man: The Life of Boris Karloff*. London: Leslie Frewin.

The Universal Weekly (1915). 6.24, 12 June: 32.

The Universal Weekly (1929). 30.21, 28 December: 32.

Uricchio, William and Roberta E. Pearson (1993). *Reframing Culture: The Case of the Vitagraph Quality Films*. Princeton, NJ: Princeton UP.

Variety (1907). 9 March: 12.

Variety (1910). 23 April: 14.

Variety (1911). 14 January: 16.

Variety (1915). 27 August: 12.

Variety (1918). 27 September: 15.

Variety (1920). 2 January: 75.

Variety (1921). 8 July: 15.

Variety (1923a). 10 May: 16.

Variety (1923b). 1 November: 32.

Variety (1926). 20 January: 9.

Variety (1932). 13 December: 16.

Vieira, Mark A. (2003). *Hollywood Horror: From Gothic to Cosmic*. New York: Harry N. Abrams.

Walker, Alexander (1974). *Hollywood, England: The British Film Industry in the Sixties*. London: Joseph.

Walker, Alexander (1977). *Rudolph Valentino*. London: Sphere.

Waller, Gregory A., Ed. (1987). *American Horrors: Essays on the Modern American Horror Film*. Urbana: U of Illinois P.

Watz, Edward (2001). *Wheeler and Woolsey: The Vaudeville Comic Duo and Their Films, 1929-1937*. Jefferson, NC: McFarland.

We Put the World before You by Means of the Bioscope and Urban Films (1903). Catalogue. November. London: Charles Urban Trading Company.

Wearing, J. P. (2014). *The London Stage 1890-1899: A Calendar of Productions, Performers, and Personnel*. 2nd ed. Lanham, MD: Rowman and Littlefield.

Weaver, Tom (1988). *'B' Science Fiction and Horror Movie Makers*. Jefferson, NC: McFarland.

Weaver, Tom (1991). 'History of Horror'. *Fangoria* March: 6–11.

Weaver, Tom (1999). *John Carradine: The Films*. Jefferson, NC: McFarland.

Weaver, Tom and Michael Gingold (1999). 'Mummy Mania: Show Me the Mummy'. *Fangoria* May: 14–22, 66–7.

Weissman, Judith (1988). 'Women and Vampires: *Dracula* as a Victorian Novel'. *Dracula: The Vampire and the Critics*. Ed. Margaret L. Carter. Ann Arbor: UMI Research: 69–77.

Wells, Paul (2000). *The Horror Genre: From Beelzebub to 'Blair Witch'*. Short Cuts. London: Wallflower.

Welsh, Paul (1975). *The Spine Chillers: Lon Chaney Jr., Peter Cushing, Christopher Lee, Vincent Price*. Ilfracombe, Devon: Stockwell.

Willis, Donald C. (1997). *Horror and Science Fiction Films IV*. Metuchen, NJ: Scarecrow.

Winans, Delbert (1977). 'Zita Johann Interviewed: Revisiting the Pool of Time'. *Midnight Marquee* September: 38–9.

Wlaschin, Ken (2009). *Silent Mystery and Detective Movies: A Comprehensive Filmography*. Jefferson, NC: McFarland.

Wolf, Leonard (1989). *Horror: A Connoisseur's Guide to Literature and Film*. New York: Facts on File.

Wong, Eugene Franklin (1978). *On Visual Media Racism: Asians in the American Motion Pictures*. New York: Arno.

Wood, Gerald C. (1988). 'Horror Film'. *Handbook of American Film Genres*. Ed. Wes D. Gehring. New York: Greenwood: 211–28.

Wood, Robin (1984). 'An Introduction to the American Horror Film'. *Planks of Reason: Essays on the Horror Film*. Ed. Barry Keith Grant. Metuchen, NJ: Scarecrow: 164–200.

Wood, Robin (1986). *Hollywood from Vietnam to Reagan*. New York: Columbia UP.

Wright, Bruce Lanier (1995). *Nightwalkers: Gothic Horror Movies*. Dallas, TX: Taylor.

Wright, Gene (1987). *Horrorshows: The A-to-Z of Horror in Film, TV, Radio and Theatre*. Newton Abbot: David & Charles.

Young, Elizabeth (1996). 'Here Comes the Bride: Wedding Gender and Race in *Bride of Frankenstein*'. *The Dread of Difference: Gender and the Horror Film*. Ed. Barry Keith Grant. Austin: U of Texas P: 309–37.

Index

Abbott and Costello Meet Frankenstein (Barton, USA) 138
Abbott and Costello Meet the Mummy (Lamont, USA) 138
Abrams, J. J. 4
Account of the Manners and Customs of the Modern Egyptians, An (Lane) 45
Ace of Scotland Yard, The (Taylor, USA) 93 n.12
Adler, Gilbert 19 n.49
Adventure of the Egyptian Tomb, The (Christie) 52, 83
Adventures of Captain Marvel (English and Witney, USA) 5, 139 n.6
Adventures of P.C. 49, The (Grayson, UK) 145
Adventures of Shorty Hamilton (film series, USA) 72
After Three Thousand Years (Austin) 47
Agrama, Frank 19 n.37
Aida (stage play) 59 n.20
Akhnaton (Christie) 83
Alcott, Louisa May 47
Alf Layla wa-Layki (The Arabian Nights) 25
Alfredson, Tomas 10
Alkon, Paul K. 57 n.3
All Bound Round (d.u., USA) 67, 93 n.16
All New Adventures of Laurel and Hardy, The (Harmon and Cherry, South Africa/USA) 31 n.5
All-New Super Friends Hour: The Mummy of Nazca, The (Hanna and Barbera, USA) 19 n.55
Almereyda, Michael 17 n.5
Al-Mummia (The Night of Counting the Years a.k.a. *The Mummy*, Salam, Egypt) 17 n.10
Altman, Rick 28, 30, 122, 158
Amazing Stories: Mummy Daddy (Dear, USA) 19 n.51
American Mummy (Pinion, USA) 29

American Whig Review 45
Ames, Ramsay 133
Amis, Kingsley 112
A Múmia Közbeszól (The Mummy Interrupts, Gábor, Hungary) 18 n.13
Ancestors' Blood, The. See *Das Blut der Ahnen*
Ancient Allan, The (Haggard) 52
Ancient Egypt in the Popular Imagination (Huckvale) 90
Ancient Evil: Scream of the Mummy (DeCoteau, USA) 17 n.3
And He Came Straight Home (d.u., USA) 72
Andrews, Nigel 122, 129, 137
Annals of the New York Stage (Odell) 37
Arab (Ingram, USA) 70
Arabian Love (Storm, USA) 70
Arabian Nights, The. See *Alf Layla wa-Layki*
Arab world 25–6
Arata, Stephen D. 48, 156
Arbuthnot, John 53
Archbold, Rick 35
archetypes, in horror studies 9
Archie's Weird Mysteries: Curse of the Mummy (Gassin, USA) 19 n.39
Asher, Jack 144
Ashton, Roy 149
Aured, Carlos 18 n.17
Austin, Jane 47
Avenging Hand, The (a.k.a. *The Wraith of the Tomb,* Calvert, UK) 80, 86
Awakening, The (Newell, UK) 4, 13, 29, 51, 58 n.17, 159
Aylmer, Felix 145
Aylott, David 78
Aztec Mummy, The. See *La Momia Azteca*

Back to Earth (stage play) 55
Bacon, Lloyd 65
Baker, George D. 76

Balderston, John L.   53, 98, 99, 101, 107, 109, 117 nn.2–3
Bales, Paul   159
Ball, Alan   123
Band, Albert   10
Band, Charles   19 nn.29, 35, 29
Bara, Theda   92 n.7
Barbera, Joseph   19 n.55
Barbour, Alan G.   7
Barnes, Alan   162 n.1
Barnum, P. T.   37, 158
Bartlett, Charles   77
Barton, Charles T.   138
Basilisk, The (Hepworth, UK)   92 n.4
Bass, Jules   18 n.23
Battle Beneath the Earth (Tully, UK)   155
Bat Whispers, The (West, USA)   65
Bava, Mario   9
Bazin, André   63
Beaudine, William   67, 76
Beaumont, Harry   67
Beaver, Harold   42, 57 n.5, 59 n.19
Beeman, Greg   31 n.5
Beetle, The (Butler, UK)   80
Beetle, The (Marsh)   48, 80
Beggs, Lee   66
Bella Donna (Fitzmaurice, USA)   70
Bellows, Walter C.   75
Belphégor: Le Fantôme du Louvre (Belphegor, Phantom of the Louvre, Salomé, France)   19 n.47
Belphegor, Phantom of the Louvre. See *Belphégor: Le Fantôme du Louvre*
Belzoni, Giovanni   35, 36, 44
Benshoff, Harry M.   11, 114
Berenstein, Rhona J.   26, 104, 105, 106, 110, 113
Bergier, Jaques   58 n.16
Bernard, James   144
Bernard, William Bayle   53
Besson, Luc   18 n.11, 29
Bey, Turhan   126
Bhalla, Alok   157 n.4
Bierman, Robert   9
Bioscope (trade magazine)   66, 71, 74
Bitter Tea of General Yen, The (Capra, USA)   113, 117
Blackton, James Stuart   62
Blackwood, Algernon   58 n.16
Blacula (Crain, USA)   9

Blake, Edmund   53
Bloch, Robert   22 n.85
Blood from the Mummy's Tomb (Holt and Carreras, UK)   8, 9, 51, 143, 159
Bloodsucking Pharaohs in Pittsburgh (Tschetter, USA)   29
Bluebeard (Ulmer, USA)   22 n.85
Bluebeard's 8th Wife (Wood, USA)   92
Bodin, Jean   43
Boese, Carl Heinz   82
Boot, Andy   146
Booth, Walter   57 n.9, 64
Boothby, Guy   13
Borutski, Jessica   19 n.32
Boughedir, Ferid   153
Bourgeois, Gérard   75
Boutella, Sofia   4
Bowers, Robert Hood   55
Brabin, Charles   80
Bradbury, Robert N.   138 n.5
Bradley, Doug   5
Brady's Beasts: How to Impress a Girl with Your Mummy (Deyriès, Canada/France)   19 n.53
Brahm, John   9, 22 n.85
Brahmin's Miracle, The. See *Le Miracle du Brahmane*
Bram Stoker's Burial of the Rats (Golden, USA)   57 n.1
Bram Stoker's Dracula (Coppola, USA)   4, 57 n.1, 160
Bram Stoker's Legend of the Mummy (Obrow, USA)   31 n.5, 57 n.1, 159, 160
Bram Stoker's Shadow Builder (Dixon, USA)   57 n.1
Branagh, Kenneth   4
Bride of Frankenstein, The (Whale, USA)   14, 44, 121
Bride of the Nile (stage play)   55
Brides of Dracula, The (Fisher, UK)   157 n.2
Bridges, Alan   155
Bridges, Meilee D.   51
Brier, Bob   21 n.66, 119
Broadway to Tokio (stage play)   55
Broken Blossoms (Griffith, USA)   70
Brontë, Emily   112
Brood of the Witch Queen, The (Rohmer)   52, 79
Browne, Bothwell   55

Browning, Tod 4, 5, 31 n.4, 65, 70, 131
Brunas, Michael 100, 112, 119, 121, 124–5, 129, 130, 131, 158
Brunswick, Dor 21 n.66
Bubba-ho-tep (Coscarelli, USA) 19 n.43
Budge, Wallis 37
Buffy the Vampire Slayer: Inca Mummy Girl (Pressman, USA) 18 n.19
Bunker Bean (Killy and Hamilton, USA) 67
Bunnicula: Mumkey Business (Borutski, USA) 19 n.32
Burghclere, Lady 85
Burke, John 58 n.17
Burton, Tim 19 n.31
Bustamante, Adolfo Fernández 18 n.16
Butler, Alexander 80
Butler, Ivan 3
Byron, George Gordon 44

Cabanne, Christy 4, 5
Cabinet of Dr. Caligari, The. See *Das Cabinet des Dr Caligari*
Cahn, Edward L. 17 n.4
Calvert, Charles 66, 80
Campbell, Dirk 10
Caño, Manuel 17 n.6
Capper, Richard 55
Capra, Frank 113, 135
Captain Clegg (Scott, UK) 157 n.2
Capulina Against the Mummies. See *Capulina Contra las Momias*
Capulina Contra las Momias (*Capulina Against the Mummies*, Zacharias, Mexico) 18 n.16
Capulina Contra los Monstruos (*Capulina vs. the Monsters*, Morayta, Mexico) 18 n.16
Capulina vs. the Monsters. See *Capulina Contra los Monstruos*
Cardona, René 18 n.16
Cardoso, Ivan 17 n.8
Carle, Richard 55
Carnarvon, Lord 84, 85, 86, 88, 89, 90
Carnival of Souls (Harvey, USA) 136
Carpenter, John 127
Carradine, John 133
Carreras, James 149
Carreras, Michael 8, 58 n.17
Carrie (De Palma, USA) 136
Carroll, Noël 10, 11, 33, 104

Carter, Howard 35, 47, 58 n.13, 83–90, 93 n.14, 97–8, 99
Castle of Frankenstein (magazine) 3
Castle of the Monsters, The. See *El Castillo de los Monstruos*
Castle of the Mummies of Guanajuato, The. See *El Castillo de las Momias de Guanajuato*
Castro, Joe 159
Cat Creature, The (Harrington, USA) 22 n.85
Cat Creeps, The (Julian and Willard, USA) 65
Cat People (Tourneur, USA) 7, 124, 131
Cawelti, John George 28, 30
Centurions: The Mummy's Curse (d.u., USA) 19 n.36
Ceram, C.W. 93 n.14
Chabelo and Pepito vs. the Monsters. See *Chabelo y Pepito Contra los Monstruos*
Chabelo y Pepito Contra los Monstruos (*Chabelo and Pepito vs. the Monsters*, Estrada, Mexico) 18 n.16
Champollion, Jean-Francois 35, 44
Chaney, Lon, Jr. 5, 6, 10, 120, 123, 126, 128–31, 138, 147
Chaney, Lon, Sr. 129
Chaudhuri, Napur 31 n.2
Cheat, The (DeMille, USA) 70
Cherry, John 31 n.5
Chesebro, Geo 65
Chetwynd-Hayes, R. 58 n.17
Christie, Agatha 52, 66, 68, 74, 83
Christine, Virginia 130
Clarens, Carlos 3, 100, 114, 120, 124
Cleopatra (Edwards, USA) 92 n.7
Cleopatra (Haggard) 52
Cléopâtre (Méliès, France) 55, 64
Clue of the Scarab, The (d.u., USA) 68
Coe, Peter 130
Cohen, Joel 19 n.42
Cohen, Rob 17 n.7
Coleby, A. E. 66
Collins, Max Allan 58 n.17
Colloquium of the Seven About Secrets of the Sublime (Bodin) 43
Come Rubammo la Bomba Atomica (*How We Stole the Atomic Bomb*, Fulci, Italy) 19 n.25

Cook, Thomas   35
Cooper, Ian   158
Cooper, Merian C.   11
Coppola, Francis Ford   4
Corelli, Marie   90
Cornhill Magazine, The   49
Coscarelli, Don   19 n.43
Count of Monte Cristo, The (Dumas)   85
Cowie, Susan D.   22 n.82, 60, 90, 120, 157 n.3
Crain, William   9
Crane, Jonathan Lake   1
Craven, Wes   31 n.5
Creed, Barbara   101
Creeps, The (Band, USA)   19 n.29
Cronos (del Toro, Mexico)   10
Cruise, Tom   4
Curiel, Federico   18 n.16
Curse of the Aztec Mummy, The. See *La Maldición de la Momia Azteca*
curse of the Mummy   79, 83, 86, 90, 93 n.13, 98, 99
Curse of Frankenstein, The (Fisher, UK)   4, 44, 144, 145, 149, 152
Curse of the Cat People, The (Fritsch and Wise, USA)   124
Curse of the Faceless Man (Cahn, USA)   17 n.4
Curse of the Mummy's Tomb, The (Carreras, UK)   58 n.17, 143, 158
Curse of the Werewolf, The (Fisher, UK)   144, 157 n.2
Curtis, Allen   72, 77
Curtiz, Michael   31 n.4, 70, 155
Cushing, Peter   144, 145, 147, 152

Dadoun, Roger   11, 116
Daffin, Alfred   145
Daily Express (newspaper)   86
Daily Mail (newspaper)   86, 145
Daley, Ed   56
Daly, Nicholas   58 n.15
Dancer of the Nile, The (Earle, USA)   91
Daniels, Les   8, 15–16
Dante, Joe   130
Darkest Americans (stage play)   56
Das Blut der Ahnen (*The Ancestors' Blood*, Gerhardt, Germany)   81
Das Cabinet des Dr Caligari (*The Cabinet of Dr. Caligari*, Wiene, Germany)   12, 134

Das Geheimnis der Mumie (*The Mystery of the Mummy*, Janson, Germany)   82
Das Rätsel der Sphinx (*The Riddle of the Sphinx*, Gärtner, Germany)   82
Das Zeichen des Malay (*The Sign of the Malay*, Boese, Germany)   81–2
David, Rosalie   35
Davis, Richard   29, 38 n.1
Dawley, Searle J.   64, 78
Dawn of the Mummy (Agrama, Egypt/Italy/USA)   19 n.37, 29
Day, Jasmine   12, 13, 22 nn.81–2, 29, 119
Day, London D.   55
Day, Robert   156
Day of the Mummy (Tabor, USA/Venezuela)   29
Deane, Bradley   51
Deane, Hamilton   53, 117 n.2
Dear, William   19 n.51
Death of Dracula, The. See *Drakula Halála*
Death Rides the Range (Newfield, USA)   139 n.5
'Debris of Majesty, The' (Haggard)   93 n.15
DeCoteau, David   17 n.3
Dekker, Fred   29
Del Ruth, Roy   19 n.44, 119
del Toro, Guillermo   10
Demicheli, Tulio   17 n.1
DeMille, Cecil B.   61, 70, 93 n.18, 155
Den Levande Mumien (*The Living Mummy*, Magnussen, Sweden)   18 n.18, 68, 69
Denon, Dominique Vivant   35, 42
De Palma, Brian   136
Der Golem (*The Golem*, Galeen and Wegener, Germany)   80
Der Golem, Wie Er in die Welt Kam (*The Golem, How He Came into the World*, Boese and Wegener, Germany)   5
Der Letzte Mann (*The Last Laugh*, *The Last Man*, Murnau, Germany)   5
Derry, Charles   11
Der Schädel der Pharaonentochter (*The Skull of the Pharaoh's Daughter*, Tollen, Germany)   82
Der Student von Prag (*The Student of Prague*, Wegener and Rye, Germany)   80
Description of Egypt (Institut d'Égypte)   35
Desroches-Noblecourt, Christiane   86

Detective Lloyd (Macrae, UK/USA)   126
Devil Story. See *Il Était une Fois le Diable*
Deyriès, Gilles   19 n.53
Dick, Bernard F.   124
Dick Barton: Special Agent (Goulding, UK)   145
Diddled! (Calvert, UK)   66, 73
Die Augen der Maske (*The Eyes of the Mask*, Gerhardt, Germany)   81
Die Augen der Mumie Ma (a.k.a. *Die Mumie Ma*, *The Eyes of the Mummy Ma*, a.k.a. *The Eyes of the Mummy*, Lubitsch, Germany)   81, 82
Die Jagd nach dem Tod (*The Hunt for Death*, Gerhardt, Germany)   82
Die Tophar Mumie (*The Tophar Mummy*, Guter, Germany)   81, 82
Dillard, R. H. W.   2, 32
Dinesen, Robert   17 n.9, 80
Disraeli, Benjamin   48
Dixon, Jamie   57 n.1
Dixon, Wheeler Winston   137
Dixson, Harry L.   56
Dobson, Eleanor   13, 47
Dr. Jekyll and Mr Hyde (Henderson, USA)   64
Dr. Jekyll and Mr. Hyde (Mamoulian, USA)   31 n.4
Dr. No (Young, UK)   155
Doctor Who: Mummy on the Orient Express (Wilmshurst, UK)   20 n.58
Doctor Who: Pyramids of Mars (Russell, UK)   19 n.24
Don Juan (Byron)   44
Down Through the Ages (Olcott, USA)   73
Doyle, Arthur Conan   8, 48, 49, 58 nn.12, 16, 86, 90, 98, 158
Dracula   33, 116, 160
    as sexual aggressor   11
Dracula (Browning, USA)   4, 5, 10, 53, 65, 97, 98, 101, 102, 106, 107, 108, 116, 119, 131, 145
Dracula (Fisher, UK)   4, 144, 149, 155, 156
Dracula (Stoker)   11, 48, 53, 156
Dracula's Daughter (Hillyer, USA)   132
Dracula's Dog (Band, USA)   10
Drake, Douglas   25, 131
Drakula Halála (*The Death of Dracula*, Lajthay, Hungary)   64
Dream of a Painting, The (Curtis, USA)   72

Dream of a Rarebit Fiend (Porter, USA)   93 n.9
Dream of the Rarebit Fiend series of cartoons (McCay)   93 n.9
Dumas, Alexandre   85
Dungeonmaster, The (Band, USA)   29
Dupont, Ewald André   6
Durstine, R. S.   55
Dust of Egypt, The (Baker, USA)   76, 77
Dyson, Jeremy   1, 101, 102, 125

Eagleton, Terry   16
Earle, William P. S.   91
Eason, Reeves, B.   139 n.6
Edelson, Edward   137
Edison, Thomas   65
Edwards, J. Gordon   92 n.7
Egypt   26, 31 n.1, 34, 92 n.2, 114
    ancient   61–2
    ancient, rediscovery of   42–3
    and cinema   61–3
    and early horror   78–80
Egyptian, The (Curtiz, USA)   155
Egyptian Coquette, An (Holland)   51
Egyptian Mummy, The (Beggs, USA)   66
Egyptian Mummy, The (burlesque show)   55
Egyptian Mummy, The (d.u., USA)   66
Egyptian Mystery, The (Dawley, USA)   78
Egyptian Princess, The (Bellows, USA)   75
Egyptology   35
Egyptomania   36
Eisenstein, Sergei   62
El Castillo de las Momias de Guanajuato (*The Castle of the Mummies of Guanajuato*, Novaro, Mexico)   18 n.16
El Castillo de los Monstruos (*The Castle of the Monsters*, Soler, Mexico)   18 n.16
Elixir of Life (Curtis, USA)   77
El Latigo Contra Las Momias Asesinas (*The Whip vs. The Killer Mummies*, Vázquez, Mexico)   19 n.26
El Robo de las Momias de Guanajuato (*Robbery of the Mummies of Guanajuato*, Novaro, Mexico)   18 n.16
Elsaesser, Thomas   104
Emmerich, Roland   29
Enchanted Mummy, The (stage play)   56

Endeavour: Cartouche (Wilson, UK) 18 n.22
English, John 5
English Opera House (London) 52
Englund, Robert 5
Enright, Ray 138 n.3
Escarabajos Asesinos (*Scarab,* Jaffe, Spain) 18 n.17, 29
Estrada, José 18 n.16
Eternal, The (Almereyda, Ireland/USA) 17 n.5, 31 n.5
Evans, Walter 15
Everett, Henrietta 51
Everson, William K. 5, 120, 124, 130, 131
Evil Dead, The (Raimi, USA) 136
Evil of Frankenstein, The (Francis, UK) 157 n.2
Evil Unleashed (Castro, USA) 159
Exhibitors Herald (trade magazine) 81
Explorer, The (stage play) 56
expressionistic visual style 100
Extraordinary Adventures of Adèle Blanc-Sec, The. See *Les Aventures Extraordinaires d'Adèle Blanc-Sec*
Eyes of the Mask, The. See *Die Augen der Maske*
Eyes of the Mummy, The. See *Die Augen der Mumie Ma*
Eyes of the Mummy, The (Bloch) 22 n.85
Eyles, Allen 145

Face of Fu Manchu, The (Sharp, Germany/UK) 155
Face of the Screaming Werewolf (Solares, Mexico/USA) 9
Fade to Black (Zimmerman, USA) 18 n.21, 29
Famous Monsters of Filmland (magazine) 3
Fear of The Mummy. See *Yami Ni Hikaru*
Fenton, Louise 6
Feramisco, Thomas M. 21 n.78, 139 n.8
Feuer, Jane 28
Fifth Element, The (Besson, France/USA) 29, 30
Fischer, Dennis 6, 138 n.2
Fisher, Terence 3, 4, 144, 145, 147, 148, 149, 157 n.2
Fitzmaurice, George 70
Flaubert, Gustave 70
Flint, David 7
Florescu, Radu 53

Florey, Robert 99
Foran, Dick 138 n.5
Ford, Francis 79
Forshaw, Barry 151, 158
Forster, E. M. 26
For the Love of Tut (Lyons, USA) 90
Foster, John 19 n.44
Four Feathers, The (Mason) 48
Foy, Bryan 65
Francis I of France 34
Francis, Freddie 157 n.2
Francis, Kevin 158
Frankenstein (Dawley, USA) 64, 65
Frankenstein (Shelley) 43, 52
Frankenstein (Whale, USA) 4, 10, 15, 41, 44, 53, 98, 119
Frankenstein: An Adventure in the Macabre (stage play) 53
Frankenstein's Monster 1, 3, 9, 10, 13–14, 32, 52, 60, 104, 121, 128
Frankenstein Meets the Wolf Man (Neill, USA) 1, 7, 120, 135
Frankenstein Sings (a.k.a. *Monster Mash: The Movie,* Cohen and Sokolow, USA) 19 n.42
Frankenstein vs. The Mummy (Leone, USA) 29
Frankenweenie (Burton, USA) 19 n.31
Franklin, Chester M. 70
Frayling, Christopher 47, 57 n.9, 84, 88, 89, 116
Freaks (Browning, USA) 31 n.4
Freeland, Cynthia A. 101
Freeman, Richard 22 n.81, 93 n.17
Fregonese, Hugo 17 n.1
Freund, Karl 3, 4, 5, 6, 83, 99, 100, 101, 102, 114, 120, 137
Friday the 13th series 15
Friday the Thirteenth Part 2 (Miner, USA) 128
Friedland, Anatol 55
Friedman, Seymour 145
Fritsch, Gunther V 124
Fritt et Plock Detectives (*Two Clever Detectives*, d.u., France) 67
Fritze, Ronald H. 98
Fulci, Lucio 19 n.25
Furneaux, Yvonne 145

Gábor, Oláh 18 n.13
Gaines, Jane 109

Galeen, Henrik   80
Ganja & Hess (Gunn, USA)   9
Garris, Mick   10
Gärtner, Adolf   82
Gasnier, Louis J.   74
Gassin, Louis   19 n.39
Gato, Enrique   17 n.2
Gautier, Théophile   46, 47, 57 n.8, 71, 80, 86
Gay, John   53
gaze, aesthetics and significance of   107–9
Gelder, Ken   11
genre, notion of   28–30
Gerhardt, Karl   81, 82
Ghostbusters: Mummy Dearest (Schmidt, USA)   19 n.28
Ghost of Frankenstein, The (Kenton, USA)   122, 135
Ghoul, The (Hunter, UK)   118 n.4, 119
Gifford, Dennis   139 n.6
Gilling, John   143
Gliddon, George Robins   36, 42, 45
Glover, David   58 nn.15–16
Gloves of Ptames, The (a.k.a. *Mysterious Gloves*, Aylott, UK)   78
Glut, Donald F.   3, 100, 137, 139 n.7
Glynn, Basil   138 n.1
Golden, Dan   57 n.1
Goldwyn Picture Company   89
Golem, The. See *Der Golem*
Golem, How He Came into the World, The. See *Der Golem, Wie Er in die Welt Kam*
Goodwins, Leslie   4
Gordon, Charles   48
Gorilla, The (Foy, USA)   65
Gottlich, Michael   29
Goulding, Alfred J.   145
Grayson, Godfrey   145
Green, Peter   33
Greenberg, Harvey Roy   113
Green Eyes of Bast, The (Rohmer)   52
Green Hell (Whale, USA)   124
Green Venus, The (stage play)   55
Griffith, D. W.   70, 93 n.8
Guest, Val   145
Guiol, Fred   119
Gulliver's Travels (Swift)   32
Gung Ho! (Ray Enright, USA)   138 n.3
Gunn, Bill   9
Günther, Carl   82

Guran, Paula   11
Guter, Johannes   81

Haggard, H. Rider   25, 31 n.3, 52, 57 n.8, 64, 71, 87, 93 n.15, 101, 102, 156
Haining, Peter   100
Halliwell, Leslie   22 n.81, 100, 116, 125, 126
Halloween (Carpenter, USA)   127, 128
Halloween series   15
Halloweentown (Dunham, USA)   19 n.45
Halperin, Victor   6
Hamilton, William   67
Hammer Horror Omnibus, The (Burke)   58 n.17
Hammer Film Productions   3, 9, 13, 30, 50
Hands of the Ripper, The (Sasdy, UK)   157 n.2
Hangover Square (Brahm, USA)   22 n.85
Hanna, William   19 n.55
Hanson, Babe   127, 128
Haram Alek (Ismail Yassin Meets Frankenstein, Karama, Egypt)   17 n.10
Harmon, Larry   31 n.5
Harrington, Curtis   104
Harris, Harry   19 n.57
Harrison, John   31 n.5
Harrison, Louis   55
Harvey, Herk   136
Haunted Curiosity Shop, The (Paul's Animatograph Films, UK)   57 n.9, 64
Hawks, Howard   155
Headless Horseman, The (Venturini, USA)   65
Hearn, Marcus   162 n.1
Hélene-Huet, Marie   10
Hellraiser series   5
Henderson, Lucius   64
Hepburn, Katherine   107
Hepworth, Cecil M.   92 n.4
Herodotus   33
Hessler, Gordon   19 n.24
Hickman, Howard   84
Hickox, Anthony   29
Hickox, Douglas   19 n.35
Hidden Valley (Bradbury, USA)   138 n.5
hieroglyphic cinema   62
Highlander (Sommers, UK/USA)   4
Hill, John   155
Hiller, Arthur   10

Hillyer, Lambert 132
Hirschhorn, Clive 126–7, 157 n.2
His Egyptian Affinity (Christie, USA) 74, 93 n.16
His Majesty, Bunker Bean (Taylor, USA) 67
His Majesty, Bunker Bean (Beaumont, USA) 67
Hitchcock, Alfred 22 n.85
Hobart, George V. 55
Holden, Lansing C. 135
Holland, Clive 51
Holston, Kim R. 1, 9, 123
Holt, Seth 8
Hooper, Tobe 10
Hopkins, Lisa 57 n.4
Hoppenstand, Gary 116
horror, carriers of 8–9
Horror Film, The (Butler) 3
Hough, John 157 n.2
House of Dracula (Kenton, USA) 1, 120, 122, 132
House of Frankenstein (Kenton, USA) 135
House of Terror. See *La Casa del Terror*
Howard, Shemp 119
How We Stole the Atomic Bomb. See *Come Rubammo la Bomba Atomica*
Huckvale, David 7, 90, 125
Hughes, William 51, 58 n.16
Hull, Henry 114, 123
Hunger, The (Scot, UK/USA) 29
Hunt, Leon 124, 161
Hunt for Death, The. See *Die Jagd nach dem Tod*
Hunter, T. Hayes 118 n.4
Huntley, Fred W. 75
Hutchings, Peter 7, 10, 11, 14, 22 n.81, 135, 143, 146, 151, 155, 161
Hutchinson, Tom 28, 29
Hyams, Ronald 31 n.2

I Am Legend (Matheson) 148
I Bought a Vampire Motorcycle (Campbell, UK) 10
If I Were Young Again (d.u., USA) 76
Il Était une Fois le Diable (*Devil Story*, Launois, France) 29
Illustrated Films Monthly (magazine) 93 n.11
Illustrated History of the Horror Film, An (Clarens) 3, 124

Il Mostro di Frakestein (*The Monster of Frankenstein*, Testa, Italy) 64
Image Maker, The (Moore, USA) 74
imperial striptease 51
In Ancient Days. See *La Momie*
Ingram, Rex 70
Interview with the Vampire (Jordan, USA) 123
Intolerance (Griffith, USA) 70, 110, 134
Invasion (Bridges, UK) 155
Iras, a Mystery (Everett) 51
Island of Dr Moreau, The (Wells) 48
Island of Lost Souls (Kenton, USA) 31 n.4
Isle of the Dead (Robson, USA) 124
Ismail Yassin Meets Frankenstein. See *Haram Alek*
I Walked With a Zombie (Tourneur, USA) 7

Jaffe, Steven-Charles 18 n.17
Jancovich, Mark 6
Jannings, Emil 82
Janson, Victor 82
Jay, Griffin 125
Jensen, Paul M. 41
Jenson, Babe. See Hanson, Babe
Jewel of Seven Stars, The (Stoker) 50, 51–2, 54, 58 n.17, 79, 80, 159
Johann, Zita 105, 107, 110
Johnson, John 6, 17 n.1, 120
Johnson, Noble 115
Johnson, Tom 22 n.82, 60, 90, 120, 157 n.3
Johnston, John J. 31 n.3
Jordan, Neil 123
Jungle Book, The (Sommers, USA) 4

Kaiser-Titz, Erich 82
Karama, Issa 17 n.10
Karloff, Boris 5, 6, 9, 25, 50, 105, 118 n.4, 119, 125, 131, 137, 145, 147
Kawin, Bruce 15, 22 n.81, 111, 133, 134, 135
Kearsley, Seth 19 n.52
Kellino, W. P. 72
Kennedy, Tom 19 n.35
Kenton, Erle C. 1, 31 n.4, 122, 135
Kid Millions (Ruth and Pogany, USA) 19 n.44, 119
Killy, Edward 67
King, Burton L. 70
King, Lucille 57 n.7

King, Stephen 8
King Kong (Schoedsack and Cooper, USA) 11, 106, 113, 115, 131
King Tut-Ankh -Amen's Eighth Wife (a.k.a. *The Mystery of King Tut-Ankh-Amen's Eighth Wife*, d.u. USA) 90, 91
Kiss Meets the Phantom of the Park (Hessler, USA) 19 n.24
Kiss of the Vampire (Sharp, UK) 157 n.2
Klinger, Barbara 16
Knickerbocker, The (magazine) 58 n.11
Knox, Elyse 130
Kosleck, Martin 130
Kramer, John 5
Kuhn, Annette 22 n.84
Kung Fu Mummy, The (Morgan, USA) 19 n.34
Kurtzman, Alex 4

La Cabeza Viviente (*The Living Head*, Urueta, Mexico) 18 n.16
La Casa del Terror (*House of Terror*, Solares, Mexico) 18 n.16
La Colonne de Feu (*The Pillar of Fire*, Méliès, France) 64
Laemmle Jr., Carl 5, 10, 103
Lajthay, Károly 64
Lalor, Frank 55
La Maldición de la Momia Azteca (*The Curse of the Aztec Mummy*, Portillo, Mexico) 18 n.16
La Mansion de las Siete Momias (*The Mansion of the Seven Mummies*, Lanuza, Mexico) 18 n.16
La Momia Azteca (*The Aztec Mummy*, Lopez, Mexico) 18 n.16
La Momia Contra el Robot Humano (*The Robot vs. the Aztec Mummy*, Portillo, Mexico) 18 n.16
La Momia Nacional (*The National Mummy*, Larraz, Spain) 18 n.17, 29
La Momie (*The Mummy*, d.u., France, 1908) 68
La Momie (*The Mummy, In Ancient Days*, d.u., France, 1911) 71
La Momie (*The Mummy*, Méliès, France) 64
La Momie du Roi (*The Mummy of the King Ramses*, Bourgeois, France) 75
Lamont, Charles 138
Land of the Pharaohs (Hawks, USA) 155

Lane, Edward William 45, 70
Lang, Fritz 6
Lant, Antonia 61–2, 89, 92 n.2
Lanuza, Rafael 18 n.16
Larraz, José Ramón 18 n.17
Larriva, Rudy 19 n.30
Las Aventuras de Tadeo Jones (*Tad, the Lost Explorer*, Gato, Spain) 17 n.2
Las Luchadoras Contra la Momia (*Rock 'n' Roll Wrestling Women vs. the Aztec Mummy/Wrestling Women vs. the Aztec Mummy*, Cardona, Mexico) 18 n.16
Las Momias de Guanajuato (*The Mummies of Guanajuato*, Curiel, Mexico) 18 n.16
Las Momias de San Ángel (*The Mummies of San Ángel*, Martínez, Mexico) 18 n.16
Last Laugh, The/Last Man, The. See *Der Letzte Mann*
Last Man, The (Shelley) 43
Låt den Rätte Komma In (*Let the Right One In*, Alfredson, Sweden) 10
La Venganza de la Momia (*The Mummy's Revenge*, Aured, Spain) 18 n.17
La Vie de Moïse (*The Life of Moses*, d.u., France) 62
Lawrence, G. W 31 n.5
Lawrence, Quentin 157 n.2
Le Blanc, Michelle 32
LeBorg, Reginald 1, 3, 4, 130, 134
Leca, Ange-Pierre 87, 93 n.13
Lee, Christopher 5, 13, 124, 144, 145, 147, 148, 149, 150, 152
Lee, Edgar 51
Lee, Rowland V. 119, 138 n.3
Legion of the Dead (Bales, USA) 159
Le Miracle du Brahmane (*The Brahmin's Miracle*, Chomón, France) 72
Le Monstre (*The Monster*, Méliès, France) 64
Leone, Damien 29
Leopard Man, The (Tourneur, USA) 22 n.85
Le Palais des Milles et une Nuits (*The Palace of the Arabian Nights*, Méliès, France) 70
Le Pied de Momie (*The Mummy's Foot* or *Princess Hermonthis*) (Gautier) 46, 47, 80

Le Roman de la Momie (*The Romance of the Mummy*, Capellani, France) 71, 97
Le Roman de la Momie (*The Romance of the Mummy*) (Gautier) 46–7, 86
Le Saint, Edward J. 74
Les Aventures Extraordinaires d'Adèle Blanc-Sec (*The Extraordinary Adventures of Adèle Blanc-Sec*, Besson, France) 18 n.11
Let the Right One In. See *Låt den Rätte Komma In*
Letter from a Revived Mummy 57 n.7
Levinson, Barry 29
Levy, Shawn 56
Lewton, Val 7, 124
Lifeforce (Hooper, USA) 10
Life of Moses, The (1906), *The*. See *La Vie de Moïse*
Life of Moses, The (Blackton, USA, 1909–10) 62
Life Without a Soul (Smiley, USA) 64
Lindsay, Vachel 62
Living Head, The. See *La Cabeza Viviente*
Living Mummy, The. See *Den Levande Mumien*
Living Mummy, The (Pratt) 52
Lockyer, Sharon 161
Lodge, Jack 103
Lodger, The (Brahm, USA) 22 n.85
Logan, John 14
London after Midnight (Browning, USA) 65
Lopez, Rafael 18 n.16
L'Oracle de Delphes (*The Oracle of Delphi*, Méliès, France) 64
Lord, Del 119
Lord John's Journal (Le Saint, USA) 74
Lorre, Peter 114
Los Monstruos del Terror (*The Monsters of Terror*, Demicheli and Fregonese, Italy/Germany/Spain) 17 n.1
Lost Horizon (Capra, USA) 135
Lost in a Pyramid, or the Mummy's Curse (Alcott) 47
Lot No. 249 (Doyle) 48, 49, 50, 57 n.10, 59 n.17
Lubin, Arthur 120
Lubitsch, Ernst 3, 80–1
Luckhurst, Roger 7, 92 n.2, 93 n.13
Lucretius 32

Ludlam, Harry 58 n.15
Lugosi, Bela 5, 101, 114
Lupton, Carter 20 n.59, 21 n.66, 58 n.12, 159–60
Lure of Egypt, The (Hickman, USA) 84
Lyons, Eddie 90, 93 n.16

MacCabe, Colin 108
McCarty, John 65
McCay, Winsor 93 n.9
McCutcheon, Wallace 71
McDonald, J. Farrell 73
McFadden, Bob 21 n.66
McGeough, Kevin 139 n.5
McKay, John 31 n.5
MacKenzie, Donald 74
McManus, John 1
McManus, Patrick 29
MacMunn, George Fletcher 26–7
MacRae, Henry 65, 126
Made for Love (Sloane, USA) 72, 90, 91
Madison, Arnold 28, 137
Mad Love (Freund, USA) 114
Mad Monster Party (Bass, USA) 18 n.23
Magic Mummy, The (Foster, USA) 19 n.44
Magnussen, Fritz 18 n.18
Maid and the Mummy, The (stage play) 55
Maltby, Tim 19 n.50
Mamoulian, Rouben 31 n.4
Manchel, Frank 97
Man from Egypt, The (Semon, USA) 78
Man in the Iron Mask, The (Sommers, UK/USA) 4
Mank, Gregory William 126
Mannequin (Gottlich, USA) 29
Manners, David 101
Mansion of the Seven Mummies, The. See *La Mansion de las Siete Momias*
Marchetti, Gina 113, 116
Mariette, Auguste 35, 37
Marra, Peter 22 n.85
Marriott, James 7, 101, 145
Marsh, Richard 48, 80
Martin (Romero, USA) 9
Martin, Richard 57 n.10
Martínez, Arturo 18 n.16
Mary Shelley's Frankenstein (Branagh, USA) 4, 57 n.1
Mason, A. E. W. 48
Maspero, Gaston 35, 37

Matheson, Richard   148
Maxford, Howard   146
Medici, Catherine de   34
Melford, George   70
Méliès, Georges   3, 55, 64, 70
Men of Sherwood Forest (Guest, UK)   145
Mercy, the Mummy Mumbled (Phillips, USA)   28, 69
Metropolis (Lang, Germany)   6, 99
MGM   31 n.4
Milton The Monster: Crumby Mummy (Seeger, USA)   19 n.33
Miner, Steve   128
Missing Mummy, The (Beaudine, USA)   67
Mitchell, Bruce   65, 66
Mitchell, Lisa   111
Modern Sphinx, A (Bartlett, USA)   77
Monster, The. See *Le Monstre*
Monster High (Poe, USA)   19 n.48, 29
Monster Mash: The Movie. See *Frankenstein Sings*
Monster of Frankenstein, The. See *Il Mostro di Frakestein*
monsters   104, 121, 123
 analogy with adolescent experience   15
 as meaning machines   10
 as metaphor resistant   15
Monsters and Mad Scientists (Tudor)   60
Monster Show, The (Skal)   3
Monsters of Terror, The. See *Los Monstruos del Terror*
Monster Squad, The (Dekker, USA)   29
Moore, Eugene   74
Moran, Peggy   138 n.4
Morayta, Miguel   18 n.16
Morgan, Randy   19 n.34
Morgan, Sidney   90
Morning Star (Haggard)   52
Morris, Genny   21 n.64
Motion Picture Herald (trade magazine)   105
Mulcahy, Russell   4
Muertos de Risa (Bustamante, Mexico)   18 n.16
Mulvey, Laura   109
Mumiens Halsbånd (*The Mummy's Necklace/The Fatal Necklace*, Dinesen, Denmark)   17 n.9, 80
Mummies Alive!: Dog Bites Mummy (Kearsley, USA)   19 n.52

Mummies in Fact and Fiction (Madison)   137
Mummies of Guanajuato, The. See *Las Momias de Guanajuato*
Mummies of San Ángel, The. See *Las Momias de San Ángel*
mummification   33, 63
Mummy
 ambiguous origins of   8
 in America   131–3
 cartoons featuring   20 n.60
 curse of   84–92
 demise and rise of   137–8
 distinctiveness of   14
 diversity of   2
 first horror movies of   80–4
 first on-screen   63–4
 Hammer's resurrection of   143–57
 as inferior concept   7
 innovation in 1940s films of   122–4
 literary life of   43–6
 as medicine   34
 as memento   34–6
 monstrous, of literature   47–50
 Oriental, as Western projection   25–8
 as Other   10
 as popular subject for comics   20 n.62
 pop videos featuring   21 n.65
 as public attraction   36–8
 records about   21 n.66
 reinvention of   124–6
 as repetitious monster   3
 romance and   46–7
 as romantic character   69–77
 sexuality of   12–13
 in silent comedies   64–9
 television appearance of   20 n.59
 in the theatre   52–6
 video games featuring   21 n.64
Mummy, The. See *Al-Mummia*; *La Momie*
Mummy, The (d.u., USA, Thanhouser)   71, 72, 73
Mummy, The (Fisher, UK)   4, 13, 50, 138, 143–7, 158, 160
 aftermath of Suez   152–7
Mummy, The (Freund, USA)   3, 4, 5–6, 8, 13, 15, 22 n.84, 25, 26, 27, 50, 51, 83, 92, 97–9, 119, 125, 126, 131, 133, 137, 145
 delicate horror of   102–5

dichotomized damsel in 106–11
as Gothic romance 111–14
and Nubian 114–17
Mummy, The (Kurtzman, USA) 4, 15, 159, 160, 161
Mummy, The (Sommers, USA) 4, 9, 13, 15, 22 n.87, 31 n.5, 47, 51, 58 n.17, 159, 160, 161
Mummy, The (stage play) 55
Mummy, The (Taurog, USA) 90
Mummy, The! A Tale of the Twenty-Second Century (Webb) 43–5
Mummy, The: The Animated Series (Houchins, USA) 160
Mummy, The: Tomb of the Dragon Emperor (Cohen, USA) 17 n.7, 58 n.17, 160
Mummy, The; or, The Liquor of Life! (stage play) 53
Mummy's Boys (Guiol, USA) 119
Mummy's Curse, The (Goodwins, USA) 1, 51, 119, 129, 133, 135–6, 137, 138 n.3, 139 n.7, 146
Mummy's Dungeon, The (Lawrence, USA) 31 n.5
Mummy's Foot, or Princess Hermonthis, The. See *Le Pied de Momie*
Mummy's Ghost, The (LeBorg, USA) 1, 15, 51, 119, 125, 130, 133–5, 136, 146
Mummy's Hand, The (Cabanne, USA) 5, 6, 15, 25, 119, 120, 123, 124–6, 127, 134, 138 nn.4–5, 146, 147, 150
Mummy Interrupts, The. See *A Múmia Közbeszól*
Mummy Nanny, The (Vinciguerra, France/Germany) 19 n.46
Mummy's Necklace, The/Fatal Necklace, The. See *Mumiens Halsbånd*
Mummy of the King Ramses, The. See *La Momie du Roi*
Mummy's Revenge, The. See *La Venganza de la Momia*
Mummy's Shroud, The (Gilling, UK) 143, 159
Mummy's Soul, The (anonymous) 58 n.11
Mummy Theme Park, The (Passeri, Italy) 18 n.13
Mummy's Tomb, The (Young, USA) 12, 15, 119, 125, 126–8, 131, 132, 133, 134, 138, 146

Mummy and the Cowpunchers, The (d.u., USA) 67, 68
Mummy Complex 63
Mummy Girl, The (stage play) 55
Mummy in Fact, Fiction and Film, The (Cowie and Johnson) 90
Mummy Lives, The (O'Hara, USA) 31 n.5
Mummy Love (Perez, USA) 90
Mummy-makers of Egypt, The (stage play) 55
Mummy Monarch, The (stage play) 55
Mummy or Ramses the Damned, The (Rice) 29
Mummy Resurrected, The (McManus, USA) 29, 159
Mummy Returns, The (Sommers, USA) 51, 58 n.17, 160
Murders in the Rue Morgue (Florey, USA) 99, 114, 134
Murnau, F. W. 5, 11, 64, 121
Murphy, Eddie 31 n.5
My Mummy's Arms (Staub, USA) 119
Mysterious Gloves. See *Gloves of Ptames, The*
Mystery and Imagination: Curse of the Mummy (Verney, UK) 51
Mystery Magazine 118 n.5
Mystery of King Tut-Ankh-Amen's Eighth Wife, The. See *King Tut-Ankh-Amen's Eighth Wife*
Mystery of the Mummy, The. See *Das Geheimnis der Mumie*
Mystery of the Wax Museum, The (Curtiz, USA) 31 n.4, 131

Naremore, James 29
National Mummy, The. See *La Momia Nacional*
Naylor, David 92 n.3
Necklace of Rameses, The (Brabin, USA) 80, 86
Negri, Pola 81
Neil, Roy William 1
Nevin, Paul 56
Newell, Mike 3, 4
Newfield, Fred 68
Newfield, Sam 139 n.5
Newman, Kim 1, 7, 8, 27, 57 n.9, 70, 83, 101, 114, 145
Newsom, Ted 147, 154

New Woman   106–7
New York Evening Mirror
    (newspaper)   57 n.7
New York Morning Post, The
    (newspaper)   86
New York Times, The (newspaper)   41, 86, 88
New York World, The (newspaper)   99
New York World Telegram (newspaper)   1
Nichols, Marcia D.   59 n.19
Night at the Museum (Levy, USA)   56
Nightmare (Francis, UK)   157 n.2
Nightmare before Christmas, The (Selick, USA)   18 n.20
Nightmare on Elm Street series   5
Night of Counting the Years, The. See *Al-Mummia.*
Night of Magic, A (Wynne, UK)   19 n.56
Night of the Living Dead (Romero, USA)   15
Nightwing (Hiller, USA)   10
Noah's Ark (Curtiz, USA)   70
Nosferatu: A Symphony of Horror. See *Nosferatu, eine Symphonie des Grauens*
Nosferatu, eine Symphonie des Grauens (*Nosferatu: A Symphony of Horror*, Murnau, Germany)   11, 64, 121
Novaro, Tito   18 n.16
Now Watch the Professor! (d.u., USA)   68

Obrow, Jeffrey   31 n.5
Odell, Colin   32, 37
O'Hara, Gerry   31 n.5
Oh Mummy. See *Tut! Tut! King*
Oh! You Mummy (d.u., USA)   67
Oh, Johnny, How You Can Love (Lamont, USA)   138 n.4
Olcott, Sidney   73
On the Nature of Things (Lucretius)   32
Ontology of the Photographic Image, The (Bazin)   63
Oracle of Delphi, The. See *L'Oracle de Delphes*
Orient   25–8, 113, 114
Orientalism (Said)   45, 70
O Segredo da Múmia (*The Secret of the Mummy*, Cardoso, Brazil)   17 n.8, 29
Ott, Matthew   55
Out Again In Again (Beaudine, USA)   76

Ozymandias (Shelley)   42

Palace of the Arabian Nights, The. See *Le Palais des Milles et une Nuits*
Paramount Pictures   31 n.4
Paranoiac (Francis, UK)   157 n.2
Parker, Eddie   128–9, 130, 138
Parkinson, David   1, 100
Pasha, Sa'id   37
Passage to India, A (Forster)   26
Passeri, Alvaro   18 n.13
Pastell, George   145
Pauwels, Louis   58 n.16
Peake, Richard Brinsley   52
Peirse, Alison   22 n.81, 129
Penicher, Louis   43
Penny Dreadful (Logan, UK/USA)   14
Pepper, Bob   130
Perez, Marcel   90
Perils of Pauline, The (Gasnier and MacKenzie, USA)   74, 75
Perils of Pauline, The (Taylor, USA)   119
Perils of Pork Pie, The (Kellino, UK)   72
Perry, Pauline   55
Perry, Scott   31 n.5
Pettigrew, Thomas Joseph   36
Petrified (Band, USA)   19 n.35
Phantom, The (Eason, USA)   139 n.6
Phantom of the Opera, The (Fisher, UK)   157 n.2
Phantom of the Opera (Lubin, USA)   120, 144
Pharaoh's Daughter (Lee)   51
Pharos the Egyptian (Boothby)   13
Phillips, Bertram   90
Phillips, R. G.   28
Phipps, William   130
Phoenix, The (Hickox, USA)   19 n.35, 29
Pichel, Irving   135
Pickard, Roy   28, 29
Picture of Dorian Gray, The (Wilde)   48
Pierce, Jack   50, 128, 129, 145
Pillar of Fire, The. See *La Colonne de Feu*
Pinedo, Isabel Cristina   11, 132
Pirie, David   60, 130, 131, 143
Pitts, Michael   130, 145
Planet of the Vampires (Bava, Italy)   9
Plastic Man: Plastic Mummy Meets Disco Mummy (Larriva, USA)   19 n.30
Pleasance, Donald   127

PM (newspaper)   1
Poe, Edgar Allan   8, 45, 46, 47, 57 nn.5–7, 59 n.19
Poe, Rudiger   19 n.48
Pogany, Willy   19 n.44
Polidori, John   52
Pollin, Burton R.   37, 53
Pollock, Griselda   13, 22 n.81, 161
Pope, Alexander   53
Porter, Edwin S.   93 n.9
Portillo, Rafael   18 n.16
Pratt, Ambrose   52
Pratt, Theodore   56
Prawer, S. S.   10, 15, 41, 100, 131
Presley, Elvis   2
Pressman, Ellen S.   18 n.19
Princess in the Vase, The (McCutcheon, USA)   71, 72, 73
Production Code of the Motion Picture Producers and Directors of America   103
Professor's Mummy, The (stage play)   56
Psycho (Hitchcock, USA)   22 n.85
Puppet Master (Schmoeller, USA)   29
Putnam, Nina Wilcox   98, 101, 111, 118 n.5, 138 n.2

Quatermass Xperiment, The (Guest, UK)   145
Queen of the Dawn (Haggard)   52

Raimi, Sam   136
Rarin' to Go (burlesque show)   56
Rasmussen, Randy Loren   9
Ray, Fred Olen   29
Rebhorn, Matthew   54
Reddick, Lawrence   114
Reed, Arthur   55
Reed, Langford   61
reincarnation   73–4, 75, 133, 154, 160
Remo, Andrew   93 n.17
Revenge of the Mummy: The Ride, The   22 n.87
Revolt of the Mummies, The (stage play)   56
Rice, Anne   29
Rice, Thomas Dartmouth   54
Richards, Jeffrey   36
Richter, Ellen   82
Riddle of the Sphinx, The. See *Das Rätsel der Sphinx*

Rigby, Jonathan   7, 12, 118 n.4, 119, 159
Riley, Philip J.   65, 118 n.5
Ringel, Harry   146
Ring of Love, The (d.u., USA)   78
Ring of Thoth, The (Doyle)   48, 49, 50, 98, 158
   radio adaptation of   57 n.10
RKO   7, 117 n.3, 124, 138 n.1
Robbery of the Mummies of Guanajuato. See *El Robo de las Momias de Guanajuato*
Robbing Cleopatra's Tomb. See *Cléopâtre*
Robinson, Bernard   144
Robonic Stooges, The: I Want My Mummy (d.u., USA)   19 n.54
Robot vs. the Aztec Mummy, The. See *La Momia Contra el Robot Humano*
Robson, Mark   124
Rock 'n' Roll Wrestling Women vs. the Aztec Mummy/Wrestling Women vs. the Aztec Mummy. See *Las Luchadoras Contra la Momia*
Rohmer, Sax   52, 58 n.16, 79, 83, 86, 92 n.5
Romance of the Indian Frontiers, The (MacMunn)   27
Romance of the Mummy, The. See *Le Roman de la Momie* (Capellani)
Romance of the Mummy, The. See *Le Roman de la Momie* (Gautier)
Romero, George, A.   9, 15
Rosen, Philip   63
Rosetta Stone   35, 42
Roth, Lane   149
Rupert, Julian   65
Russell, Al   74
Russell, Paddy   19 n.24
Ruth, Roy Del   65
Rye, Stellan   80

Said, Edward   26, 31 n.1, 34, 45, 70
Saint's Return, The (Friedman, UK)   145
Salam, Shadi Abdel   17 n.10
Salem's Lot (Hooper, USA)   10
Salomé, Jean-Paul   19 n.47
Salter, Hans   7, 126
Sangster, Jimmy   144, 145, 146
Santo and Blue Demon vs. the Monsters. See *Santo y Blue Demon vs. los Monstruos*

Santo and the Vengeance of the Mummy.
    See *Santo en la Vengenza de la Momia*
Santo en la Vengenza de la Momia (*Santo and the Vengeance of the Mummy*, Cardona, Mexico)   18 n.16
Santo y Blue Demon vs. los Monstruos (*Santo and Blue Demon vs. the Monsters*, Solares, Mexico)   18 n.16
Sasdy, Peter   157 n.2
Saw series   5
Schadia-Hall, Tim   21 n.64
Scarab. See *Escarabajos Asesinos*
Schatz, Thomas   8, 28
Schayer, Richard   98, 118 n.5
Schmidt, Ernie   19 n.28
Schmoeller, David   29
Schoedsack, Ernest B.   11
Scott, Tony   29
Scott, Peter Graham   157 n.2
Screening the Undead (Hunt, Lockyer and Williamson)   3
Searle, Francis   145
Secret of Blood Island, The (Lawrence, UK)   157 n.2
Secret of Sebek, The (Bloch)   22 n.85
Secret of the Mummy, The. See *O Segredo da Múmia*
Seeger, Hal   19 n.33
Selick, Henry   18 n.20
Semon, Lawrence   78
Senn, Brian   6, 17 n.1, 120
Sevastakis, Michael   101
Severed Scarabs, The. See *Undying Flame, The*
Shadow of Egypt, The (Morgan, UK)   90
Shanghai Express (Sternberg, USA)   113
Sharp, Don   155, 157 n.2
She (Day, UK)   156
She (Haggard)   57 n.8, 64, 101–2, 156
She (Holden and Pichel, USA)   135
Sheik, The (Melford, USA)   70
Shelley, Mary   43, 44, 52, 53
Shelley, Percy Bysshe   42
She Who Sleeps (Rohmer)   52
Shock!   144
Shohat, Ella   61
Short Stories of Conan Doyle, The (Martin, UK)   57 n.10

Shorty Unearths a Tartar (d.u., USA)   72
Sibley, Raymond   58 n.17
Sight and Sound (magazine)   81
Sign of the Malay, The. See *Das Zeichen des Malay*
Silent Mystery, The (Ford, USA)   79, 126
Silver Bottle, The (stage play)   55
Singer, Bryan   29
Sins of Séverac Bablon, The (Rohmer)   52, 79
Siodmak, Robert   7, 22 n.85
Skal, David J.   3, 9, 59 n.18, 103, 104
Skull of the Pharaoh's Daughter, The. See *Der Schädel der Pharaonentochter*
Slave Trading in a Harem. See *Vente d'Esclaves au Harem*
Sleepwalkers (Garris, USA)   10
Slim and the Mummy (d.u., USA)   67
Sloane, Paul   72
'Smarter Set' company   55
Smiley, Joseph W.   64
Smith and the Pharaohs (Haggard)   25, 52
Sokolow, Alec   19 n.42
Solares, Gilberto Martínez   18 n.16
Soler, Julián   18 n.16
Some Words with a Mummy (Poe)   45, 59 n.19
Sommers, Stephen   4, 159
Song of Love (Franklin, USA)   70
Son of Dracula (Siodmak, USA)   7, 120, 123, 131, 135
Son of Frankenstein (Lee, USA)   119, 121, 124
Soren, David   11
Spadoni, Robert   93 n.18
Spencer, Kathleen L.   48
Spiral Staircase, The (Siodmak, USA)   22 n.85
Stargate (Emmerich, USA)   29, 30
Stark Mad (Bacon, USA)   65
Star Trek (Abrams, USA)   4
Staub, Ralph   119
Stedman, Albert   55
Sternberg, Josef von   113
Stevenson, Robert Louis   48, 85
Stine, R. L.   59 n.17
Stoker, Bram   8, 11, 48, 50–1, 53, 57 n.1, 58 nn.13, 15–17, 79, 156, 159
Storm, Jerome   70

Strange Case of Dr. Jekyll and Mr. Hyde, The (Stevenson) 48
Strickrodt, S. 57 n.3
Strobels, Margaret 31 n.2
Student of Prague, The. See *Der Student von Prag*
Studlar, Gaylyn 71
Stumar, Charles 99
Sullivan, Timothy 6
Swift, Jonathan 32
Syder, Andrew 162

Tabor, Johnny 29
Tad, the Lost Explorer. See *Las Aventuras de Tadeo Jones*
Talbot, Lawrence 5
Tale of the Mummy (a.k.a *Talos the Mummy*, Mulcahy, UK/USA) 4, 31 n.5, 160
Tales from the Crypt Presents: Bordello of Blood (Adler, USA) 19 n.49
Tales From the Darkside: The Movie (Harrison, USA) 31 n.5, 57 n.10
Tales of Secret Egypt (Rohmer) 52, 83
Talos the Mummy. See *Tale of the Mummy*
Tamura, Masakura 18 n.15
Taurog, Norman 90
Taves, Brian 28
Taylor, Ray 93 n.12, 119
Taylor, William D. 67
Teenage Cat Girls in Heat (Perry, USA) 31 n.5
Telotte, J. P. 9, 22 n.81
Temptation of Joseph, The (Reed, UK) 61
Ten Commandments, The (DeMille, USA) 61, 70, 155
Terror, The (Ruth, USA) 65
Testa, Eugenio 64
Three Hours After Marriage (stage play) 53
Through the Centuries (Huntley, USA) 75
Tierney, Dolores 162
Times, The (newspaper) 86
Time Walker (Kennedy, USA) 19 n.35, 29
Tollen, Otz 82
Tom and Jerry Tales: Tomb It May Concern (Maltby, USA) 19 n.50
Tomb, The (Ray, USA) 29, 159
Too Much Elixir of Life (Mitchell, USA) 66
Tophar Mummy, The. See *Die Tophar Mumie*
Tourneur, Jacques 7, 22 n.85

Tourneur, Maurice 74, 92 n.4
Tower of London (Lee, USA) 138 n.3
Towlson, Jon 128
'Trade in the Dead, The' (Haggard) 93 n.15
Traité des Embaumements Selon les Anciens et les Modernes (*Treatise on Embalming According to the Ancient and Modern Ways*) (Penicher) 43
Transylvania 6-5000 (De Luca, Rudy, USA/Yugoslavia) 29
Travels in Lower and Upper Egypt (Denon) 35, 42
Treasure Island (Stevenson) 85
Treatise on Embalming According to the Ancient and Modern Ways. See *Traité des Embaumements Selon les Anciens et les Modernes*
Trilby (Tourneur, USA) 92 n.4
Triman, Tom 100
True Blood (Ball, USA) 123
Tschetter, Dean 29
Tsuburaya, Hajime 19 n.41
Tudor, Andrew 9, 10, 30, 60, 92 n.1, 100, 123, 133
Tully, Montgomery 155
Tut! Tut! King (a.k.a *Oh Mummy*, Watson, USA) 91–2
Tutankhamun's tomb 47, 49, 79, 83–4, 93 n.15
  Tutmania and 84–92
Tutt, T. Homer 55
Tut-Tut and His Terrible Tomb (Phillips, UK) 90
Twain, Mark 37
Twilight Zone, The (Brahm, USA) 9
Twins of Evil (Hough, UK) 157 n.2
Twitchell, James B. 8, 14, 15, 121, 122, 131, 158
Two Clever Detectives. See *Fritt et Plock Detectives*
Tyldesley, Joyce 14, 35, 84, 85, 87, 88
Tyler, Tom 5, 6, 125, 139 n.6, 147

Ulmer, Edgar G. 22 n.85
Ultraman: Cry of the Mummy (Tsuburaya, Japan) 19 n.41
Under the Crescent (King, USA) 70
Under Wraps (Beeman, USA) 31 n.5
Undying Flame, The (a.k.a. *The Severed Scarabs*, Tourneur, USA) 74, 97

Universal studios   1, 3, 7, 10, 30, 100, 103, 121, 122, 123, 124, 130, 144, 150
Urueta, Chano   18 n.16

Valerius (Shelley)   43
Vamp (Wenk, USA)   29
vampire   9, 10, 11–12, 52, 60, 101, 132, 149, 157 n.4
Vampire's Kiss (Bierman, USA)   9
Vampire in Brooklyn (Wes Craven, USA)   31 n.5
Vampyr (Dreyer, France/Germany)   121
Vampyre, The (Polidori)   52
van Dyke, H. J.   55
Van Sloan, Edward   101
Variety (Dupont, Germany)   6
Vázquez, Ángel Rodríguez   19 n.26
Vengeance of Egypt, The (d.u., France)   79
Vengeance of Nitocris, The (Williams)   58 n.14
Vente d'Esclaves au Harem (*Slave Trading in a Harem*, Méliès, France)   70
Venturini, Edward D.   65
Verney, Guy   51
Vinciguerra, Luc   19 n.46
Virginia Mummy, The (stage play)   54–5, 65, 69
Virgin of Stamboul, The (Browning, USA)   70
Voodoo Black Exorcist. See *Vudú Sangriento*
Voyage to the Bottom of the Sea: The Mummy (Harris, USA)   19 n.57
Vudú Sangriento (*Voodoo Black Exorcist*, Caño, Spain)   17 n.6

Waggner, George   120
Walker, Alexander   155
Walker, Stuart   114
Wanted – A Mummy (Coleby, UK)   66, 73
Warner Bros.   31 n.4
Warren, Jerry   9
Watch George (Newfield, USA)   68
Watson, William   91
Waxwork (Hickox, USA)   29
Weaver, Tom   120, 122, 123
Webb, Jane   43–4, 45, 46, 53, 57 nn.2–3, 57 n.7
Wegener, Paul   80
Weird Tales (magazine)   41
Weissman, Judith   116

Wells, H. G.   48
Wells, Paul   104
Wenk, Richard   29
werewolf   9, 10, 33, 60
Werewolf, The (MacRae, USA)   65
Werewolf of London (Walker, USA)   114, 123
West, Roland   65
Wet and Dry (McKay, UK)   31 n.5
We Want Our Mummy (Lord, USA)   119
Whale, James   4, 5, 14, 15, 124
Whebling, Peggy   53
When Soul Meets Soul (McDonald, USA)   73
When the Mummy Cried for Help (Christie, USA)   66–7, 93 n.16
Whip vs. The Killer Mummies, The. See *El Latigo Contra Las Momias Asesinas*
Whispering Smith Hits London (Searle, UK)
White Horseman, The (Russell, USA)   74
'White Privilege and Looking Relations' (Gaines)   109
White Zombie (Halperin, USA)   6, 10, 114
Whitney, Salem Tutt   55
Wiene, Robert   12
Wilde, Oscar   48
Willard, John   65
Williams, Tennessee   58 n.14
Williamson, Milly   161
Wilmshurst, Paul   20 n.58
Wilson, Andy   18 n.22
Winchester, Tom   1, 9, 123
Winters, Jack de   56
Wise, Robert   124
With the Mummies' Help (Christie, USA)   68
Witney, William   5
Wolf, Leonard   101
Wolfblood: A Tale of the Forest (Mitchell and Chesebro, USA)   65
Wolf Man, The (Waggner, USA)   120, 123, 128, 129
Wood, Gerald C.   6
Wood, Robin   3, 27, 104, 131
Wood, Sam   92
Woolf, Edgar Allan   55
Wraith of the Tomb, The. See *Avenging Hand, The*
Wright, Bruce Lanier   156
Wright, Gene   2, 105

Wuthering Heights (Brontë)   112
Wynne, Herbert   19 n.56

X-Men Apocalypse (Singer, USA)   29, 30

Yami Ni Hikaru Me (Fear of The Mummy,
    Tamura, Japan)   18 n.15
Yellow Girl, The (Haggard)   52
Young, Elizabeth   115

Young, Harold   4, 15, 119, 125
Young, Terence   155
*Young Sherlock Holmes and the Pyramid of
    Fear* (Levinson, UK/USA)   29

Zacharlas, Alfredo   18 n.16
Zimmerman, Vernon   18 n.21
zombie   6, 33, 34, 60
Zucco, George   124, 125

www.ingramcontent.com/pod-product-compliance
Lightning Source LLC
Chambersburg PA
CBHW052043300426
44117CB00012B/1948